How the Mac Works

Millennium Edition

How the Mac Works

Millennium Edition

John Rizzo and K. Daniel Clark

A division of Macmillan Computer Publishing, USA
201 W. 103rd Street
Indianapolis, IN 46290

How the Mac Works, Millennium Edition

Copyright © 2000 by Que®

Associate Publisher	Greg Wiegand
Executive Editor	Beth Millett
Acquisitions Editor	Heather Banner Kane
Development Editors	Sarah Robbins & Nicholas J. Goetz
Managing Editor	Thomas F. Hayes
Project Editor	Karen S. Shields
Copy Editor	Megan Wade
Indexer	Kelly Castell
Proofreader	Maribeth Echard
Technical Editor	Terry Rawlings
Illustrator	K. Daniel Clark
Team Coordinator	Julie Otto
Book Designers	Dan Armstrong & Anne Jones
Production	Mike Poor & Trina Wurst

International Standard Book Number: 0-7897-2428-6

Library of Congress Catalog Card Number: 00-101759

Printed in the United States of America

First Printing: October, 2000

02 01 00   4 3 2 1

Trademarks

Warning and Disclaimer

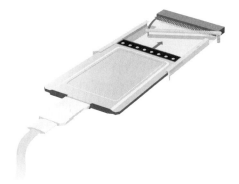

For my wife, Christine, who takes the time out of her own work to help support me with mine.

—John Rizzo

For my family. They graciously give me the tools, the talent, and the freedom to do my best.

—K. Daniel Clark

Introduction   xi

Part 1: Inside the Mac   1

Chapter 1
Inside the iMac   4

Chapter 2
Inside the Power Mac   8

Chapter 3
Inside the PowerBook and iBook   12

Part 2: Mac OS   16

Chapter 4
How Startup Works   20

Chapter 5
How the Mac OS Works   26

Chapter 6
How the Finder Works   36

Part 3: Processor and Memory   44

Chapter 7
Binary Numbers and Transistors   48

Chapter 8
How the Processor Works   52

Chapter 9
How RAM Works   60

Chapter 10
How Virtual Memory Works   68

Chapter 11
How a Cache Works   72

Chapter 12
How a RAM Disk Works   78

Part 4: Disk Storage   82

Chapter 13
How a Floppy-Disk Drive Works   86

Chapter 14
How a Hard-Disk Drive Works   90

Chapter 15
How Optical and Zip Storage Works   96

Part 5: Getting Information In and Out   104

Chapter 16
How USB Works   108

Chapter 17
How FireWire Works   112

Chapter 18
How the Keyboard, Mouse, and
Trackpad Work   116

Chapter 19
How SCSI Works   122

Chapter 20
How Expansion Slots Work   126

Chapter 21
How Multimedia Works   136

"Go a

head."

Part 6: Display 148

Chapter 22
How QuickDraw Works 152

Chapter 23
How Aqua Works 160

Chapter 24
How a CRT Display Works 164

Chapter 25
How Flat-Panel Displays Work 168

Part 7: Networks and the Internet 174

Chapter 26
How Mac OS Networks 178

Chapter 27
How Networks Work 182

Chapter 28
How Wireless Networks Work 192

Chapter 29
How Internet Connections Work 196

Part 8: Printing and Publishing 204

Chapter 30
How Printers Work 208

Chapter 31
How PostScript Works 214

Chapter 32
How Print Publishing Works 218

Chapter 33
How Web Publishing Works 226

Index 232

Foreword

MANY people view computers as no more than a useful tool. In the same way that a microwave oven helps them defrost or reheat food, a computer helps them write reports or create a presentation. They neither think about nor care about how a computer actually works, any more than they think about how it is that a microwave oven performs its magic. And in both cases, if the device should ever fail to work as expected, it will be up to someone else to fix it.

Simply by the fact that you have picked up this book, I am betting that the previous paragraph does not describe you. Instead, you are someone who is intrigued by the prospect of discovering more about your Mac and gaining the power that comes with this knowledge. Congratulations. You came to the right place. *How the Mac Works, Millennium Edition* takes you on a guided tour of the inner workings of your computer.

How the Mac Works is not a book of tips and hints. It has a different goal: to give you a deeper level of understanding of what's behind all the tips and hints that other books talk about. It accomplishes this without resorting to the jargon that is too often understood only by people who already know what is being explained. Instead, it relies on clear, easy-to-follow prose and gorgeously rendered 3D illustrations.

Learning about how computers work is a bit like peeling away the layers of an onion. A deeper level of understanding is always waiting to be revealed at the next layer. *How the Mac Works, Millennium Edition* takes you several layers deeper than you might have previously gone. For example, if you have ever gotten an "out of memory" error, you might know several things to do that can fix it. You might know to quit unnecessary open applications, increase the amount of virtual memory, or (if the problem occurs often enough) buy and install more RAM. But do you know what RAM really is? Or exactly what happens when a program is "loaded into RAM" when it is launched? Or how virtual memory can trick the Mac into thinking it has more memory than it really does? This is the sort of knowledge that *How the Mac Works, Millennium Edition* gives you.

Do you know why SCSI-2 is faster than ordinary SCSI? Or what happens when you format a disk? Or how putting your finger on a trackpad gets the mouse cursor to move? Again, *How the Mac Works, Millennium Edition* gives you the inside scoop.

As a long-time Mac troubleshooter, I assure you that this is exactly the type of knowledge that is invaluable when trying to solve problems that elude the quick fixes you might have already learned. Beyond this practical value, *How the Mac Works, Millennium Edition* offers another benefit. When studying nature, some people find wonder and beauty in what cannot be explained. They revel in the mystery of it all. Others find that the true beauty is in understanding what *can* be explained, from the intricacies of the genetic code to the mechanisms of natural selection. Computer users follow a similar dichotomy. If you count yourself in the latter group, then start reading *How the Mac Works, Millennium Edition* and discover the sense of wonder behind the Mac that you use every day.

Ted Landau

Ted Landau is the author of *Sad Macs, Bombs, and Other Disasters* and runs the MacFixIt.com Web site.

Tell Us What You Think!

AS the reader of this book, *you* are our most important critic and commentator. We value your opinion and want to know what we're doing right, what we could do better, what areas you'd like to see us publish in, and any other words of wisdom you're willing to pass our way.

As an associate publisher for Que, I welcome your comments. You can fax, email, or write me directly to let me know what you did or didn't like about this book—as well as what we can do to make our books stronger.

Please note that I cannot help you with technical problems related to the topic of this book, and that due to the high volume of mail I receive, I might not be able to reply to every message.

When you write, please be sure to include this book's title and author as well as your name and phone or fax number. I will carefully review your comments and share them with the author and editors who worked on the book.

Fax: 317-581-4666

Email: consumer@mcp.com

Mail: Greg Wiegand
            Que
            201 West 103rd Street
            Indianapolis, IN 46290 USA

Introduction

EVER wonder what happens when you pull down a menu? Insert a CD-ROM disc? Move a mouse? Ever wonder what makes a Mac so easy to use? The answers lie behind the screen, inside the microchips, and among the bits and bytes we call software and data.

This book will take you inside the Mac's hardware (the complex system of circuits and electrical and mechanical subsystems) and the Mac's software (the instructions that tell the hardware what to do). The hardware and software described in this *Millennium Edition* of *How the Mac Works* are similar in some ways to the technology of the original Macintosh of 1984, but most of it has changed. The earlier generations of Mac described in two previous editions of this book were slower and less powerful, but they were also designed for different users.

When I wrote and Daniel Clark illustrated the first edition of *How Macs Work* in 1993, desktop publishing was the Mac's *big deal*. The Internet was a mere curiosity used by half a million scientists and geeks—the first Web browsers for the Mac and Windows had yet to be released. When we created the second edition three years later, *multimedia* was the hot technology—but only on CD-ROM discs. The Internet, which had grown to 10 million computers, was still largely text and simple pictures. By the time we published the third edition, the Internet had 300 million users. The most popular Macs—iMacs and iBooks—have *Internet* in their names as well as their design. More people now buy Macs to get online than to do desktop publishing, and most people take multimedia for granted, both online and off.

What hasn't changed is the basic philosophy of Macintosh design. It's a philosophy of integrated systems, automatic configuration, and quality in the hardware and the user experience. It's about not having to be a computer expert to perform multiple tasks. The Mac user interface is not something slapped on top of the system, but is an integral part of the system itself.

We tried to follow this philosophy throughout the book, which has its own Mac-like "user interface" with a consistent graphical language. For instance, you'll see the same images represent the same functions throughout the book. The same is true with the text. I've tried to integrate concepts of software and hardware that are often presented in two different technical languages. With Macs, you cannot separate the two.

You might want to start with the first three chapters in Part 1, "Inside the Mac," where you'll find descriptions of the major components of today's Macs. Each of these components is described in more detail in another chapter. From the first three chapters, you can jump to an area that interests you or forge straight ahead. If you read this book linearly, you'll first find the core Mac processes, and gradually move out toward the functions and peripherals outside the Mac case. We end, appropriately, with the desktop publishing that created this book and the Web processes that everyone uses.

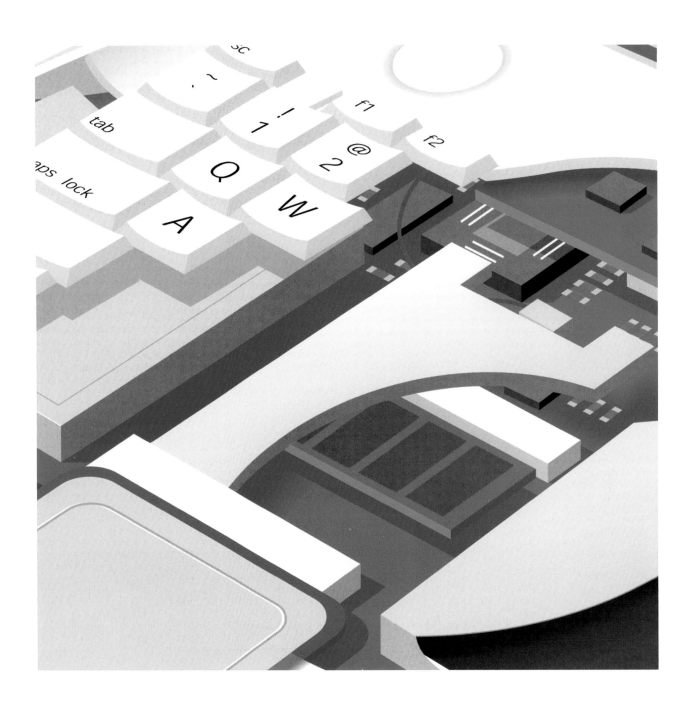

P A R T

INSIDE THE MAC

Chapter 1: Inside the iMac

4

Chapter 2: Inside the Power Mac

8

Chapter 3: Inside the PowerBook and iBook

12

MACS come in different shapes and sizes, from the small, flat, portable PowerBook and iBook, to the egg-shaped iMac, to the long, tall Power Mac. These shapes are geared toward different types of users. Yet, they are all Macs—what appears onscreen is the same. Inside each model are the same basic components operating in a similar manner. Just what are these components and what do they do?

Looking inside a Mac doesn't tell you what creates the icons and menus of the Mac. The mysterious jumble of cables, metal, and plastic doesn't give much of a clue as to what is occurring inside the microscopic, electronic circuits and macroscopic, mechanical subsystems.

Of course, you don't *need* to know what is going on inside to use a Mac. Since the original 128K Macintosh, the system has been designed to enable you to do everything you need to with the keyboard, mouse, and exterior ports. Unless you are upgrading or repairing a Mac, there is little reason to open one up. There are no switches to set, and most internal hardware can be reconfigured through software with the click of a mouse. Plug in, turn on, and tune in.

Still, knowing what goes on inside can help when you want to troubleshoot a problem or upgrade software and hardware. Or, you might just want to know. In this section, Part 1, we'll start with the basic hardware components—most of which are common to all Macs, even though they might take different forms in different models. In the rest of the book, we'll go into more detail about these and other components, as well as describe the software.

The most important part of every Mac is the *logic board*, which contains the thinking parts of any personal computer. The name comes from the fact that it consists of digital circuitry, which operates on the mathematical principle called Boolean *logic*. (In the first Macs, another board called the *analog board* contained the analog power circuitry that powered the logic board and other components.) The logic board's digital circuitry includes the processor, random-access memory (RAM), and some operating system code built into a microchip called *read-only memory (ROM)*.

The processor is the commander of the logic board and of the Mac. Some of today's Macs use the PowerPC G3 processor, whereas others are run by the faster PowerPC G4. No processor, however, can hold all the software code and data it needs to run a computer. That's where RAM comes in. The Mac's RAM acts as a high-speed storage bin for the processor, temporarily holding code and data.

The Mac logic board also contains controller chips that create and use sound and graphics and communicate with other subsystems, such as the hard disk and input/output ports. Other controller chips communicate with peripheral devices, such as printers and scanners, and with other computers through networks and the Internet. Still other controller chips run the logic board's expansion slots, which enable you to plug in new circuitry that adds functionality to your Mac.

Other types of cards also plug into the logic board and can be removed as well. These include the RAM modules, internal modems, and in some Macs, the processor itself. Because cards that plug into the logic board are often called *daughter cards*, you'll often see the logic board referred to as the *motherboard*. We'll use this term when we talk about connecting things inside the Mac.

The logic board/motherboard also connects the user to every other part of the Mac. You tell the Mac what to do using the keyboard and mouse. The Mac tells you what it is doing with the video display and speakers. Inside the Mac, a *hard-disk drive* stores your work and software for safekeeping when your Mac is turned off and for quick access when it's turned on. A *CD-ROM or DVD drive* reads multimedia data from encoded optical discs, plays your favorite audio CDs, and in the case of DVD, plays movie discs as well.

These and other components introduced in the next three chapters are common to all Mac models, large and small. Yet, components also exist that are unique to specific Mac models. For instance, PowerBooks and iBooks have batteries that enable you to use them while traveling. Only the iMac has a specially designed sound system for home entertainment. In addition, PowerBooks have a small expansion slot for adding portable functionality, whereas Power Macs have large expansion slots for upgrading and adding new functionality.

Regardless of shape or cost, all Macs can run the same software and have a high degree of compatibility with each other. The role of software is just as important as the hardware, but we'll start with hardware in this section. In the next three chapters, we'll take a look at the hardware in the four different types of Macs. We'll start the inside-the-Mac tour with the unique Apple model that most closely resembles the ancestral 128K Mac—the iMac.

CHAPTER

1

Inside the iMac

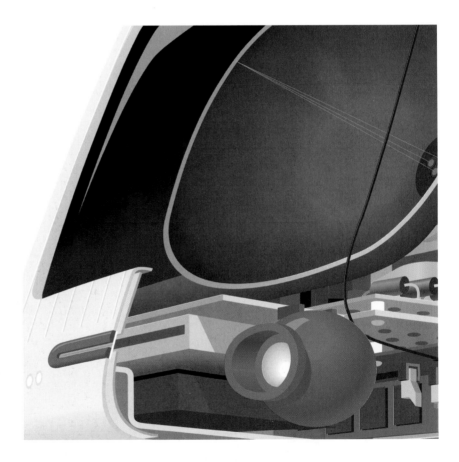

SINCE its introduction in 1998, the iMac has become the flagship of the Macintosh line as well as one of the most successful and influential personal computers ever. Its compact curves, bright colors, and translucent surface has earned the iMac design awards and spurred a new phase in consumer product design. Today, personal CD and tape players, cameras, office equipment, and even cars bare the unmistakable influence of the iMac.

One of the basic features of the iMac is the convenience of its all-in-one design. There's no assembly required, it doesn't require a nest of cables, and it leaves room on your desk for other things. Yet, the all-in-one concept isn't new at all, but is the same revolutionary feature used by the very first Macintosh 14 years earlier. Other all-in-one Macs have existed in the intervening years, but none with the style or functionality of the iMac.

Inside the style is plenty of substance. Although it lacks some features of the Power Mac, such as expansion slots and faster PowerPC processors, the iMac has never been a cheap version of the Macintosh. The iMac has always sported a high-quality 15" color display, 2D/3D graphics acceleration with graphics memory, 100MB/sec Ethernet, and a built-in modem. The iMac was the first Mac to eliminate the archaic floppy disk drive. It was also the first Mac to sport the versatile Universal Serial Bus (USB) port for connecting keyboard and mouse, scanners, printers, Zip drives, and, if you really want one, a floppy drive.

Since 1998, the iMac has become not only faster, but smaller, quieter, better sounding, more expandable, and more of a home entertainment center. Unlike just about every personal computer ever made, the iMac now has no fan. It is cooled by *convection*, the natural movement of hot air, making it a very quiet machine for bedroom or library. The high-tech speakers sound much better than their small size would indicate. And starting in late 1999, every iMac includes a trayless, slot-loading compact disc drive that smoothly pulls in discs—just like CD players in cars.

The iMac DVs introduced DVD drives for playing movies and Apple's iMovie software for editing your own home movies. Just plug in your digital camera to one of the FireWire ports. Or use FireWire to add one or more external hard drives.

Part of the iMac design concept is to highlight what's inside, not to hide it behind gray plastic. The gray "tinted windshield" of the iMac DV Special Edition provides an exceptionally clear view of what's in the top two-thirds of the iMac. However, the bottom third remains tantalizingly obscured by the translucent plastics and interior metal walls. Now, by turning the page, you can get a look into the heart of the iMac, and at what makes it tick.

iMac

Video display tube
The iMac's internal 15-inch video tube is similar to those found in separate display monitors. The tube is the main reason you can't pop open an iMac: The tube is dangerous to you, carrying high voltages even when unplugged. You are also dangerous to it— the tube is fragile. You can plug in an external display monitor on some models via a graphics port on the back.

CD-ROM/DVD-ROM drive
In the DV models, this drive plays DVD movies and data discs as well as CD-ROMs and audio CDs. The *slot loading* drives of recent iMacs don't have a tray. Inserting a disc about halfway in pushes two tabs aside, triggering a mechanism that grips the disc by both edges without touching the surface.

Hard-disk drive
The hard-disk drive stores software applications and data used by the processors, as well as Mac OS. You can plug in additional storage devices via the FireWire port on more recent models.

Built-in stereo speakers
These two tiny speakers are part of the iMac's Odyssey sound system specially designed by Harman-Kardon. Odyssey includes the speaker itself, a housing that enables air to move freely about, and a dedicated audio amplifier on the logic board. The result is a system that produces sound from 100 hertz to 20,000 hertz and an eight-octave range—both higher and lower than most computer speakers. Odyssey's electronics alter the speaker characteristics when you plug in Harman-Kardon's iSub subwoofer.

RAM
RAM holds temporary data and software code for the processor. Through an access door in the back, you can add memory in the form of memory modules called *SDRAM*.

Handle
Like the very first Macintosh, the handle makes it easy to tote the iMac around. The holes around it are part of the cooling system.

Convection cooling without a fan
Heated air escapes through the holes around the handle at top. This draws in cool air through holes in the iMac's bottom side, cooling the logic board and drives. A metal mesh on top of the logic board enables hot air to rise through it while acting as a shield from the electro-magnetic field generated by the video tube. An aluminum plate on top of that keeps heat generated by the video tube from harming the logic board below. This plate has holes in it, as does the circuit board holding the power supply, which enables hot air below to rise and escape through the top.

MAC FACT

The first Macs had the signatures of the original Macintosh design team embossed on the inside of the casing.

Power supply
The power supply converts AC power from a wall receptacle and delivers AC and DC power of varying voltages to all the electronic parts inside the iMac, as well as to the keyboard and mouse outside.

Logic board
The logic board contains most of the iMac's digital circuitry, including processor, RAM, ROM, and video memory, and the circuitry for graphics acceleration, communications, and sound.

Processor
The brains of the iMac, the *processor* performs all the calculations your software asks it to do. The processor is the actual *computer* inside a computer. The iMac uses a PowerPC G3 processor.

Input/Output ports
A set of ports connects the logic board to the world outside, including the keyboard and mouse (USB ports), external hard disks and video cameras (FireWire ports), networks (Ethernet port), and audio devices (sound in/out). A telephone port connects a phone line to the internal modem.

ROM
The read-only memory contains permanent code used to start up the iMac, among other things.

AirPort card slot
Connects the iMac to other Macs with AirPort cards, or to a wired network or the Internet via an AirPort Base Station.

AirPort Antenna
Like all new Macs, the iMac has a built-in antenna for wireless networking.

CHAPTER
2

Inside the
Power Mac

POWER MACS are aimed at power users. They are the Macintosh models with the fastest processors and graphics systems, the biggest hard drive and RAM capacities, and the most data storage and expansion options. Just about everything in a Power Mac easily can be upgraded by the user.

The first Power Macintoshes appeared in 1994, 10 years after the first Mac. The only thing the 6100, 7100, and 8100 had in common was that they were the first to use the PowerPC processor. In other respects, these were three different computers with three different motherboards (also called *logic boards*, since they contain most of the digital circuitry). This made it all but impossible for a user to upgrade from one model to another.

Starting with the Power Macintosh 7500 and 8500, you could upgrade the processor, but you still could not get the advantages of the higher-end model. Worse yet, the multiple motherboard strategy was expensive and contributed to Apple's financial problems in the mid-1990s.

This changed in 1997 with the platinum-colored Power Macintosh G3—a single Power Mac model and motherboard with different options for processor speed, RAM, and other attributes. (An exception occurred for a few months in 1999, when two Power Mac G4 motherboards sold.) The single-motherboard strategy worked for Apple's bottom line. Contrary to popular belief, it was the Power Mac G3 that began Apple's return to profitability, nearly a year before the launch of the iMac.

By the summer of 2000, after several years of success, Apple decided to add a second logic board. The result was the Power Mac G4 cube, a low-end Power Mac squeezed into an 8-inch cube. The G4 Cube doesn't have all the features or expandability of the standard Power Mac, but it is one quarter of the size.

Today's Power Macs combine the latest electronic innovations with features of past Macs. For instance, the easily accessible case is a combination of an architecture that goes back to the Power Macintosh 8600 with the exterior design sense and style of the iMac. The iMac also contributed the multipurpose USB port, which replaced several slower ports used in older Macs. In addition, the iBook contributed AirPort wireless networking. The speedy FireWire port first appeared in the blue-and-white Power Mac G3.

It's easy to see for yourself what's inside a standard Power Mac—it invites you to open it. There are no screws to remove or covers to tug on. You lift the handle and the hinged door swings down to expose the interior. The logic board sits on the door itself. You can even open up a Power Mac while it is running, which is a handy feature for troubleshooting.

The standard Power Mac G4 can run three different hard drives: IDE ATA, SCSI, and FireWire. IDE ATA is the type of drive interface found in iMacs, PowerBooks, and iBooks. SCSI offers improved speed and the ability to use up to seven drives on one port. Macs no longer have built SCSI (small computer system interface) ports on the logic board, but optional SCSI cards in the Power Mac enable both internal and external SCSI hard drives.

The Power Mac G4 is the only Mac with an *interior* FireWire port as well as external ports. FireWire offers small size, portability, and hot swappability.

Power Mac G4

Handles
Another iMac-inspired feature.

DVD-ROM or DVD-RAM drive
DVD-RAM can write as well as read data. DVD-ROM can only read data. The tray holds both round media (CD-ROM, CD audio, and DVD movie discs) and rectangular media (DVD data cartridges). The drive connects to the other electronics via an IDE ATA bus interface.

ZIP drive
Standard on most configurations. You also can put something else in this space, such as a CD-RW drive.

Power supply
The 208-watt power supply provides enough power to run storage devices in the storage bays, as well as expansion cards in the PCI slots.

Hard drive
The four-wire connector delivers power. The wide ribbon cable transfers data between the processor and RAM on the logic board and SCSI or ATA drives. A FireWire drive communicates via a small, round FireWire cable connected to the internal FireWire port.

Expansion bays for storage
Three expansion bays can support up to three internal hard drives. This can be two ATA drives; or, with a SCSI card, three SCSI drives; or a combination of SCSI, ATA, and FireWire drives.

AirPort slot
For wireless networking. The antenna connected to the AirPort Card runs up the front left corner of the Power Mac.

Modem card
Connects to the exterior telephone line port via a single, black cable.

Door lock
If you pull out the tab and insert a padlock, the lock inserts metal tabs through the door handle's mechanism, preventing access to the interior.

MAC FACT

The Power Mac G4 was the first Macintosh to be officially called *Power Mac*. The official name of its predecessors, from the 6100 to the "blue and white" G3, was *Power Macintosh*.

PCI expansion slots
The slots enable you to add functionality, such as interfaces to special equipment and boards for audio processing and video special effects. The optional SCSI card sits in a PCI slot. It moves data 64 bits at one time.

Optional SCSI card

AGP slot and graphics card
AGP is a slot designed specifically for fast 2-D and 3-D graphics. It can move peak data four times faster than a PCI slot. The card in the slot contains a graphics processor and its own RAM. (Some G4s sold in 1999 have a fourth PCI slot instead of an AGP slot.)

Input/Output ports
The G4 has a set of external ports similar to the iMac DV, including USB, FireWire, Ethernet port, sound in and out, and a telephone port that connects a phone line to the internal modem.

Internal FireWire port
Enables you to install internal FireWire drives. FireWire drives get both data and power through the FireWire cable. FireWire and Ethernet are run by a single controller chip.

RAM Four DIMM slots can hold to 1.5 gigabytes of memory. That's over 12,000 times the amount of RAM in the original Mac.

Door
The metal door is hinged along its entire length.

Processor
The G4 processor lies underneath an aluminum heat sink, which keeps it cool by absorbing heat. (The G4 doesn't need its own fan—it is smaller and generates less heat than Pentium processors in PCs.) The heat sink is held on by two straps that you can pull off. Remove the heat sink, and you'll see the G4 processor sitting on a small card with some electronics. You can upgrade the processor to a faster model by removing the three screws.

CHAPTER

3

Inside the PowerBook and iBook

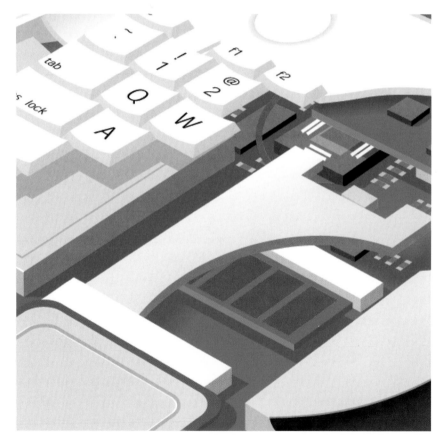

IMAGINE squeezing a Mac—with its monitor, storage drives, electronics, keyboard, and mouse—into a package that folds like a notebook to fit in a briefcase. Now add a battery or two. This is the recipe for the PowerBook and the iBook, the notebook versions of the professional users' Power Mac and the consumer iMac.

Inside the PowerBook and iBook, almost every square centimeter is filled with specially adapted components. The storage drives inside PowerBooks and iBooks are physically smaller than those found in desktop Macs. This conserves not only space and weight, but battery power as well. To extend battery life, processors used in notebook Macs are slower than those used in their desktop counterparts. The PowerPC G3 processor is low-powered enough to be used in the PowerBook and iBook without having to alter it. The G4 processor is not. But it won't be too long before a low-powered version of the G4 finds its way into a PowerBook.

The 6.1-pound PowerBook G3 squeezes in 10 ports (including FireWire), the same as found in the Power Mac. It also sports an expansion slot and a DVD drive and has more RAM and a bigger hard drive than the iBook.

The iBook was created with some of the design guidelines of the iMac and costs significantly less than the PowerBook. Still, a high-quality display and graphics acceleration make iBook a good gaming machine. And there is more to the iBook design than just looks. The polycarbonate body and thick, rubberized coating acts as a shock absorber against the bumps and knocks it might get from dorm-room living. The rounded corners enable you to carry the iBook in a backpack comfortably.

This kind of innovation goes back to the first PowerBooks, which introduced features that have since become standard on most PC notebook computers today. These were the first notebooks with a keyboard that sits back toward the display, providing room to maneuver your arms in tight places as well as a place to rest your wrists while typing. At a time when cursor controllers where a clip-on afterthought on PC notebook computers, the first PowerBooks integrated a trackball in a central position. They also introduced the capability to instantly connect external devices such as mice, keyboards, hard disks, and monitors.

Since then, PowerBooks and iBooks have continued to innovate and now include built-in antennae for wireless networking. Today's notebooks are also smaller and lighter, have bigger displays, and can run longer on a battery.

The longer battery life is due to new battery technology as well as special power conservation software and hardware inside the computer. For instance, a technique called *processor cycling* slows down the processor from hundreds of megahertz to about three megahertz while you stare at the wall thinking about what to write next. Press a key and the processor comes back up to full speed again.

PowerBook G3

Built-in microphone

Built-in modem

AirPort antenna
With an AirPort card installed, the built-in antenna enables the PowerBook to communicate with other Macs or PCs—even through walls.

Display
The active matrix liquid crystal display measures 14.1 inches, bigger than the screen in the original desktop Macintosh.

Built-in speakers

Hard-disk drive
The Ultra ATA hard drive in PowerBooks is typically under half an inch thick, weighs 5 ounces or less, and contains disks less than 2.5 inches in diameter.

Keyboard
Moving two tabs between the F4-F5 and F8-F9 keys releases the full-sized yet ultra-thin keyboard, which you can lift off to reveal the RAM and AirPort card slots.

PC Card slot
This slot can accept credit card–sized expansion cards, either the PC Card Type I or Type II (16-bit) or CardBus (32-bit). (PC Cards are sometimes called *PCMCIA* cards.) These cards can be memory devices, such as a flash memory card for transferring photos from digital cameras or backing up your hard drive. They also can be device interface cards, as well as other things.

AirPort card slot
This wireless networking card communicates with the built-in antenna and the logic board to connect the PowerBook on an 11Mbps wireless network—faster than standard Ethernet.

Logic board
PowerBooks have the smallest and lightest logic board of all the Macs. This logic board contains a PowerPC G3 processor, video RAM, and graphics acceleration hardware, among other things.

RAM
You can add up to 512MB (half a gigabyte) in two SO-DIMM slots.

Battery
The lithium-ion battery can last up to 5 hours. By adding a second battery in the right bay, you can get up to 10 hours of battery power.

Trackpad
The trackpad can detect when your finger is touching it. Similar to a mouse, the trackpad is sensitive to the speed with which you move your finger. A slow movement advances the cursor a short distance, and a rapid movement advances the cursor a greater distance. You also can set the trackpad to perform a mouse click when you tap it.

Removable DVD drive/ expansion bay
You can run DVD data and movie discs as well as CD-ROMs. This drive is also *hot swappable*. That means it can be removed and replaced with another drive without shutting down or restarting the PowerBook. You can replace the DVD drive with a Zip drive, a second hard drive, a floppy drive, or other devices.

iBook

AirPort antenna
If you look through the iBook's lid with a light behind it, you can see the wireless networking antenna through the translucent plastic.

Display
The active matrix liquid crystal display measures 12.1 inches, still bigger than the screen in the original desktop Macintosh.

iBook

Built-in speaker

Keyboard
Basically the same, ultra-thin keyboard used in the PowerBook, which lifts off by moving two tabs between the F4-F5 and F8-F9 keys. Underneath are the AirPort card and RAM slots.

Hard-disk drive
The hard drive in iBooks is typically under half an inch thick, weighs 5 ounces or less, and contains disks less than 2.5 inches in diameter.

Built-in modem

Fold-out handle

Logic board
This logic board contains a PowerPC G3 processor, video RAM, and graphics acceleration hardware, among other things.

RAM
You can add up to 320MB in the RAM slot.

CD-ROM drive
The drive mechanism, including the laser that reads the data on CDs, is contained right in the tray.

Battery
The lithium-ion battery can last up to 6 hours—longer than the PowerBook battery.

AirPort card slot
iBook was the first Mac with a slot for a wireless networking card. The whole slot lifts off to reveal the RAM slot.

Trackpad
The industrial look of the iBook's metal trackpad is due to the lack of a textured coating used in the PowerBook trackpads. The trackpad in both machines is functionally identical.

Mac Fact

Apple's first attempt at a battery-powered Mac, the Macintosh Portable, had a battery life of almost 12 hours, but weighed in at 17 pounds. It wasn't what users wanted, and Apple sold fewer than 100,000 units. 1991's 7-pound PowerBook, with a 3-hour battery life, was an instant success and became the best-selling notebook computer at the time: Apple sold $1 billion worth during the product's first year alone.

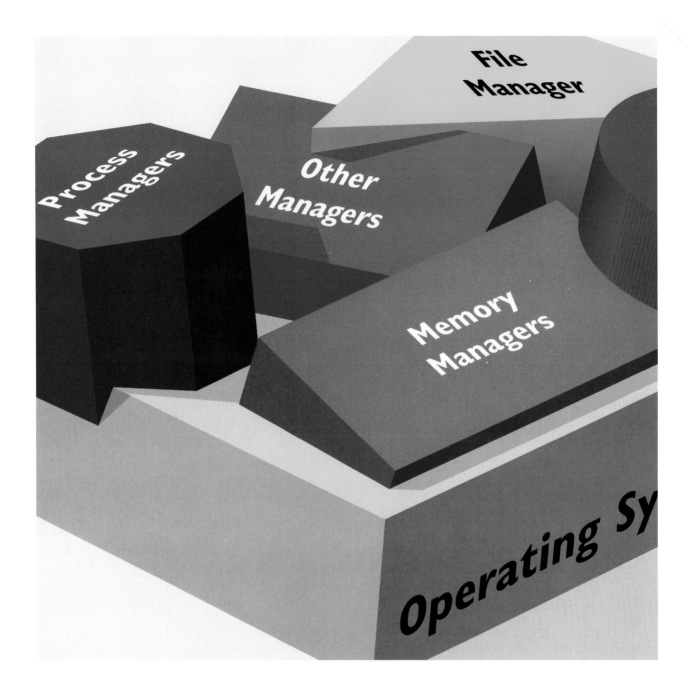

P A R T

2

MAC OS

Chapter 4: How Startup Works

20

Chapter 5: How the Mac OS Works

26

Chapter 6: How the Finder Works

36

TEN years after the first Macintosh, Apple created the product name Mac OS. Before 1994, the software that made the Mac a Mac had no proper name and had gone by various incomplete names: the Mac operating system, the Mac system software, System 7, the System folder, and the Mac ROM (random access memory). Mac OS encompasses all these things.

Mac OS comes preinstalled on your iMac, iBook, Power Mac, and PowerBook. It's what makes the Mac run. It starts up the Mac, displays graphic images onscreen, and produces sound. It opens and saves files to your hard disk, sends and receives data over a modem, and communicates with other computers on networks. Mac OS also creates the graphical interface for your word processor, Web browser, and other programs.

Mac OS is not a single piece of software, but a collection of software routines. In Mac OS 9 and earlier, this includes the System file, the Mac OS ROM file, and the hundreds of files in the System folder. Mac OS X is something altogether different. First, let's look at Mac OS 9.

Before the iMac, much of the operating system was permanently stored in a set of integrated circuit chips called the Apple ROM, short for *read only memory*. In the early days, this prevented other companies from building computers that ran Macintosh software—you couldn't run Mac software without the OS code in the Mac ROM, which only Apple had.

The problem with read-only memory is that you can't change anything in it. To fix bugs or add enhancements, Apple had to add software patches to the System file. This was difficult to program and an inefficient way to run software.

Beginning with the iMac, Apple moved most of the operating system code out of the ROM chip and into a file called Mac OS ROM, which sits in the System folder. Apple can upgrade this file just like any other file in the System folder. Today's Macs still store a little permanent operating system code in a much smaller ROM chip. This code is needed to start up the Mac before any file has loaded into RAM from the hard disk.

The Mac OS ROM file, now part of Mac OS 9, consists of procedures and functions called *managers* in a collection called the *Macintosh Toolbox*. The system file also contains some Toolbox managers. Every application uses Toolbox managers to create windows, menus, and dialog boxes, as well as communicate with printers and other devices you connect to the Mac. The Toolbox is one of the reasons all Mac programs look and work the same way.

One of the jobs of the Toolbox is to manage the Mac OS resources in the System folder, such as fonts, icons, and sounds. The System file contains thousands of resources used by your applications. Application files themselves also contain their own resources, such as menus and tool palettes.

Another important file in the System folder is the Finder, an application that creates the familiar Mac desktop—the most visible part of Mac OS. Through the Finder, you launch applications and control which files go onto your hard disk.

Other important parts of Mac OS 9 and earlier are Control Panels, where you record settings and turn features on and off, and extension files, which implement specific features in Mac OS.

Mac OS X (pronounced *ten*, as in the Roman numeral) is a different story. It doesn't have a System file, a Mac OS ROM file, or control panels. That's because Mac OS X is not actually a new version of Mac OS, but is a new and different operating system altogether.

Mac OS X was the first time that Apple completely rewrote Mac OS from the ground up. Apple started with a UNIX-based foundation, which gives Mac OS X improved performance through a more efficient structure and more dependability through an improved method of using memory. Memory is now managed by the Mach kernel, the core of Mac OS X that enforces *memory protection*, which prevents systemwide crashes. If an application crashes, you don't have to restart the whole Mac.

The Mach kernel is a central taskmaster, something Mac OS did not have before. It schedules work for the processor, ensuring all your software is sharing the processor's time in the most effective manner. This is called *pre-emptive multitasking*.

Mac OS X also changes the way Macs draw images onscreen. To draw three-dimensional graphics, OS X uses OpenGL, a technology used in high-end UNIX workstations. Mac OS X also contains a new two-dimensional image technology called Quartz. Based on the PostScript language long used in professional printing, Quartz displays two-dimensional graphics more quickly than before and enables the Aqua interface of Mac OS X. Aqua gives you more feedback than before, with buttons that gently pulsate, transparent menus, and animated windows that morph into icons. The Mac OS X Finder offers several new ways to maneuver through folders in search of your files.

Mac OS X also maintains backward-compatibility with older Mac software. You can run your old applications alongside brand-new software. However, only the newer Mac OS X-native applications get the new features of OS X.

Despite the radical differences between Mac OS X and Mac OS 9 and earlier, the new version keeps the basic philosophy that every version of Mac OS has ever had. For one, you never have to tell your Mac when you add new hardware, such as a new hard disk, expansion card, or monitor—Mac OS recognizes new hardware and knows how to communicate with it. You also never have to interact directly with the basic operating system code, such as the routines that deal with input/output and file management, as you must with other operating systems. Most of Mac OS is invisible. What you don't see not only won't hurt you, but can help a great deal.

CHAPTER
4

How Startup Works

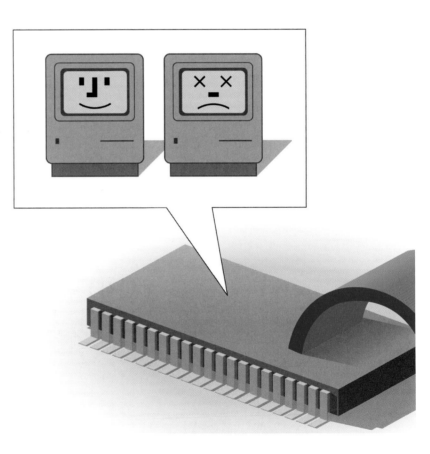

ONE of the busiest times for the Mac is during the first few moments after you turn it on. Within microseconds after you press the keyboard's power key, a tiny electric signal begins a flurry of activity that involves most of the Mac's components. Then, the Mac begins to methodically create the software structures and procedures of its functioning universe.

The creation of the Mac's universe during startup begins with a sort of big bang—a flash of energy that triggers an expanding chain of events. And similar to the big bang studied by physicists, the key events that determine the rules by which the system will operate occur in the first few moments. By the time you start to see something happen onscreen, the Mac has already checked itself out and established its operating environment.

Because everything in RAM is erased when you turn off a Mac, much of the startup procedure involves loading routines and information into RAM, so that the processor can access them when needed. The program necessary to run the startup procedure is loaded from a read-only memory (ROM) chip. The Mac then searches for a storage drive with a System folder. When it finds one, the Macintosh operating system is loaded into memory from the hard disk or other storage device. Then, the system extension files, which add functionality to the operating system, are loaded from the System folder.

The startup procedure described in this chapter is based on the procedure from Mac OS versions 9.x, with some of the differences of Mac OS X pointed out. Startup with Mac OS X is similar to Macs running older versions because much of the action occurs before the operating systems even loads.

Startup is sometimes referred to as the *boot* procedure, or *booting up*. This is old programmers' lingo that refers to the fact that a computer has to pick itself up by its own bootstraps, in a manner of speaking.

1 When you press the power button on the keyboard, it sends a signal to the power control circuitry on the logic board to detect a power-button press and turn on the power.

2 When the ROM chip receives power, a little program called Start Manager loads from the ROM to begin the startup sequence. It first tests the Mac hardware. The processors runs routines that send simple signals to various parts of the Mac, including expansion slots, disk drive controllers, and input/output ports. The last test is a check of all the installed RAM. (During a restart, only a portion of RAM is tested.)

Power Control Circuitry

ROM

Processor

RAM

Hard Disk

Ports

Expansion Slots

3 If a hardware problem is found, such as a bad RAM chip, the Mac displays a "Sad Mac" icon and plays the failed startup sound, a musical arpeggio, and startup halts. If no hardware problems are found, the Mac displays a "Happy Mac" icon and plays the successful startup sound (a musical chord). The icons and sounds are stored in ROM.

ROM

Processor

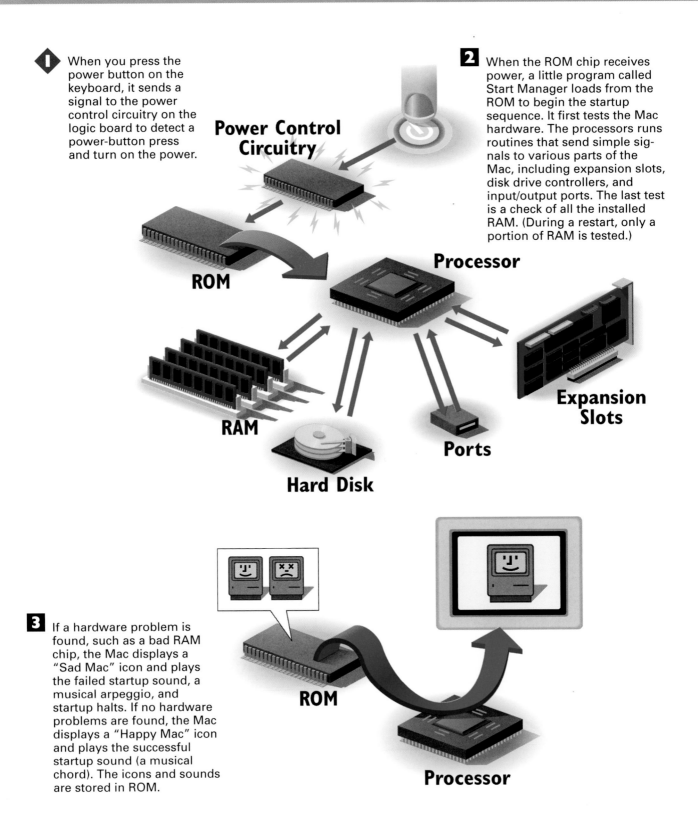

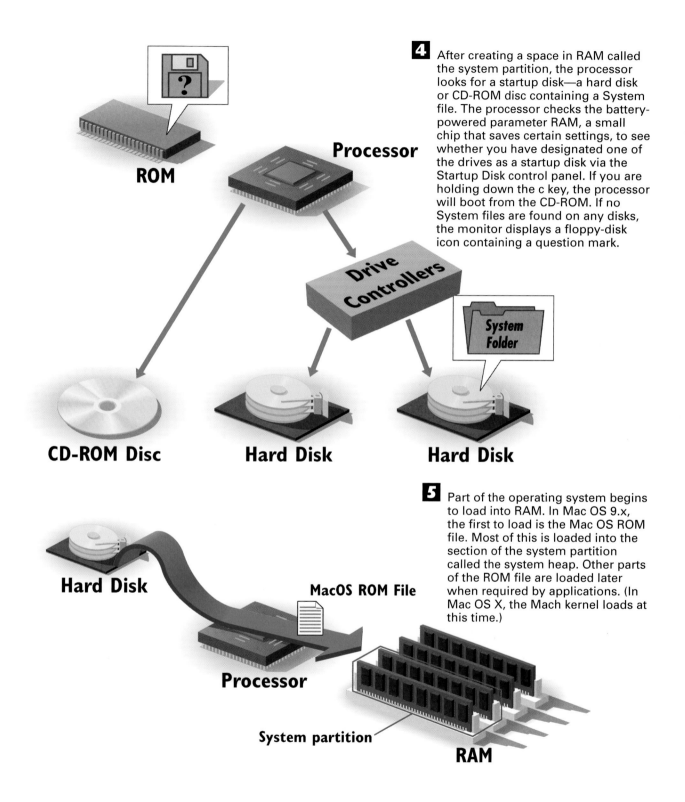

4 After creating a space in RAM called the system partition, the processor looks for a startup disk—a hard disk or CD-ROM disc containing a System file. The processor checks the battery-powered parameter RAM, a small chip that saves certain settings, to see whether you have designated one of the drives as a startup disk via the Startup Disk control panel. If you are holding down the c key, the processor will boot from the CD-ROM. If no System files are found on any disks, the monitor displays a floppy-disk icon containing a question mark.

ROM

Processor

Drive Controllers

System Folder

CD-ROM Disc

Hard Disk

Hard Disk

5 Part of the operating system begins to load into RAM. In Mac OS 9.x, the first to load is the Mac OS ROM file. Most of this is loaded into the section of the system partition called the system heap. Other parts of the ROM file are loaded later when required by applications. (In Mac OS X, the Mach kernel loads at this time.)

Hard Disk

MacOS ROM File

Processor

System partition

RAM

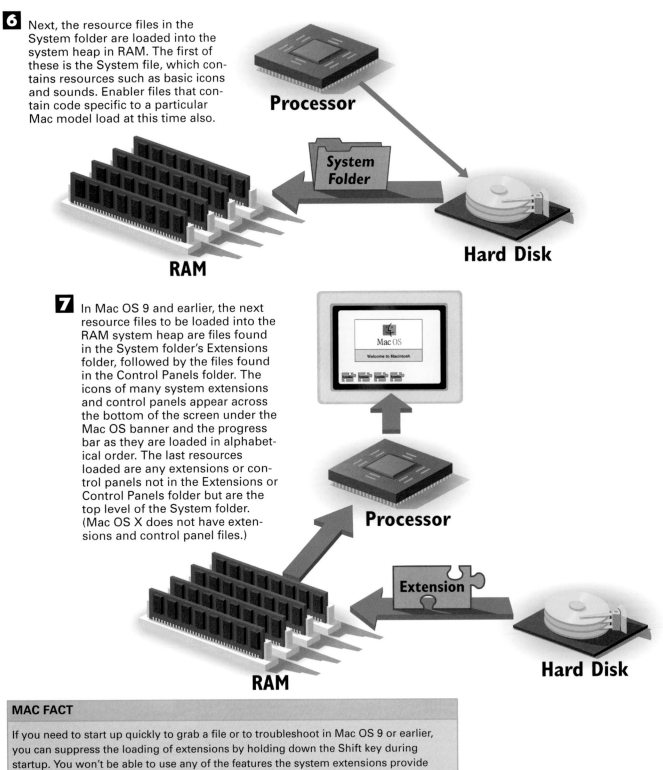

6 Next, the resource files in the System folder are loaded into the system heap in RAM. The first of these is the System file, which contains resources such as basic icons and sounds. Enabler files that contain code specific to a particular Mac model load at this time also.

Processor

System Folder

Hard Disk

RAM

7 In Mac OS 9 and earlier, the next resource files to be loaded into the RAM system heap are files found in the System folder's Extensions folder, followed by the files found in the Control Panels folder. The icons of many system extensions and control panels appear across the bottom of the screen under the Mac OS banner and the progress bar as they are loaded in alphabetical order. The last resources loaded are any extensions or control panels not in the Extensions or Control Panels folder but are the top level of the System folder. (Mac OS X does not have extensions and control panel files.)

Processor

Extension

Hard Disk

RAM

MAC FACT

If you need to start up quickly to grab a file or to troubleshoot in Mac OS 9 or earlier, you can suppress the loading of extensions by holding down the Shift key during startup. You won't be able to use any of the features the system extensions provide until you restart, but you will get to the Finder's desktop more quickly.

8 The Finder application is loaded into RAM and launched. The Mac desktop, with its icons for disks and the Trash, appears onscreen. The Finder opens folders you left open before shutting down.

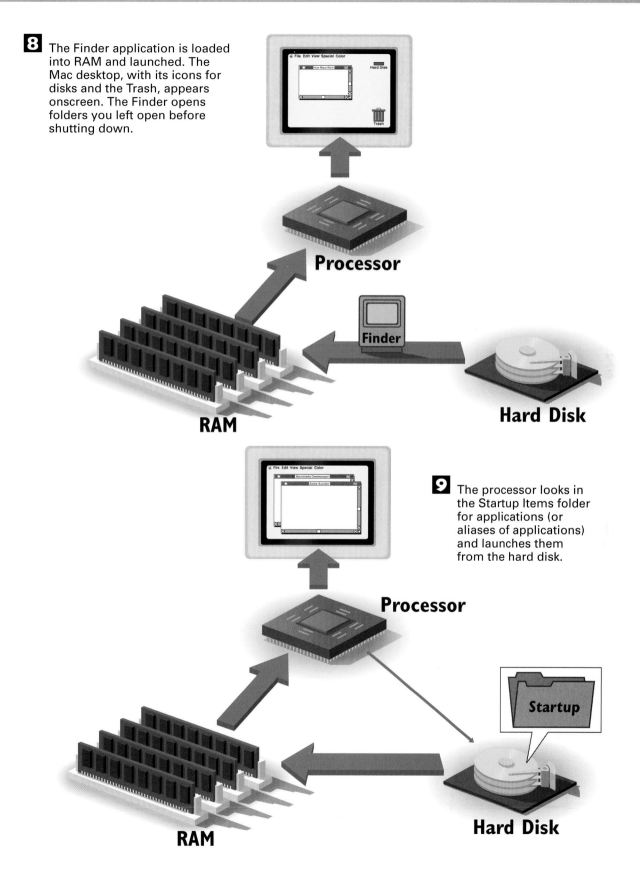

9 The processor looks in the Startup Items folder for applications (or aliases of applications) and launches them from the hard disk.

Processor

RAM

Finder

Hard Disk

Startup

CHAPTER 5

How the Mac OS Works

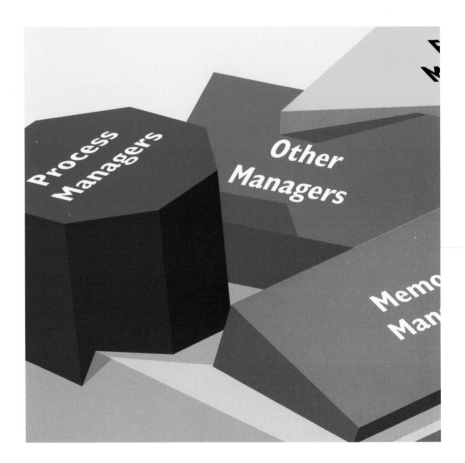

SYSTEM *software* is everything in the System folder—at least that's a basic definition in Mac OS 9. Closer inspection reveals some holes: Applications can add their own items to the System folder, and older Macs included operating system code in a ROM chip on the logic board. With Mac OS X, the basic definition weakens further. So, let's look at system software another way.

Think of system software as groups of managers and their supporting resources. *Managers* are groups of operating system code that perform a specific function. Software applications use the managers to create windows, menus, dialog boxes, and sound; to move data to and from hard disks and communications ports; and to create the Mac interface. For example, QuickDraw, the graphics manager, draws the text and graphics you see onscreen. (In Mac OS X, the main graphics manager is called Quartz.) Because every application uses the same set of managers to create the interface, most Mac applications work the same way.

The *system resources* are items that are shared by all applications, including the Finder. These can be interface elements, such as sounds, menus, dialog boxes, scrollbars, icons, and cursors. In Mac OS 9 and earlier, many resources are found in the System file.

Applications have their own resources, such as menu titles and menu items used by all documents of that application. So do document files, which contain information such as the location of the document window on screen. System, application, and document resources, which are stored on disk, are all managed by the Resource Manager. You replace many of your Mac's resources every time you upgrade your system or application software.

Although most of the OS 9 System file is taken up by resources, the system also contains some managers. Apple began adding managers to the System file with System 7. An example is the Apple Event Manager, which enables applications to exchange data and to control each other.

A third class of system software is *system extensions*, which are files that reside in the Extensions folder inside the System folder. Examples of Apple system extensions include QuickTime for the display of video and the Speech Manager, which enables your Mac to talk to you. Applications also can add their own extensions.

Mac OS X also has managers and resources, but it organizes them in a new way. It also mixes some of the old Mac technology, such as QuickTime and AppleScript, with standard UNIX technology and some brand-new Mac software. A major addition is the Mach kernel, a commander-in-chief that manages the Mac's resources.

The Mach kernel adds a feature called *pre-emptive multitasking*, which prevents any application from hogging the processor. Pre-emptive multitasking enables you to simultaneously copy a file, send email, render a complex graphics file, and type in a word processing program without the Mac *hanging*, or momentarily freezing.

The earlier versions of Mac OS don't have a boss—the applications are all supposed to cooperate together. When they don't, the Mac slows down or crashes.

The Mac OS ROM File

2 If the application is old software that is not PowerPC native, the 68LC040 emulation software is called. Some software is only partially native, so it causes the computer to switch modes on-the-fly.

1 When you issue a command in an application in Mac OS 9 and earlier, the application can make calls to the Macintosh Toolbox in the Mac OS ROM file, which in turn triggers a chain of events. (Mac OS X contains code similar to the toolbox code, but it is not collected together in a file.)

3 A series of Toolbox routines called managers are enacted. This drawing depicts some of the main managers, but the Toolbox contains many others. The Menu Manager handles how a menu works when the user pulls it down and selects a command, whereas the Window Manager keeps track of multiple windows open on the desktop. The Resource Manager enables the application to read and write system resources, such as the fonts, which reside on the startup disk.

4 A Set of graphics routines called QuickDraw displays the cursor and draws the menu on screen while erasing the part of the screen behind the menu. QuickDraw is also responsible for drawing the text, graphics, windows, and everything onscreen. (Mac OS X includes QuickDraw, as well as other graphics software called Quartz.)

9 When you quit an application after you save your file, the Process Manager terminates the application, removing it from RAM. The Process Manager launches an application when a user double-clicks its icon. It is the job of this manager to share the Mac's processor among multiple open applications in Mac OS 7, 8, and 9.

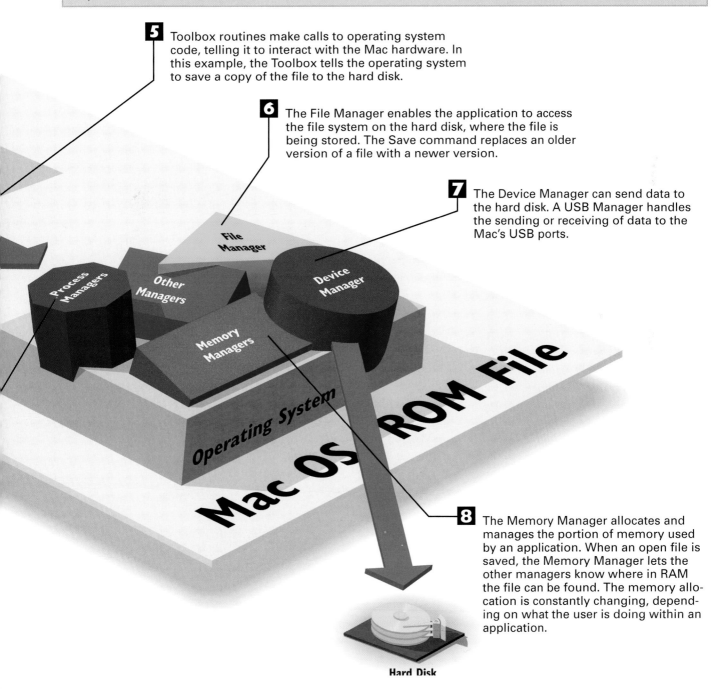

5 Toolbox routines make calls to operating system code, telling it to interact with the Mac hardware. In this example, the Toolbox tells the operating system to save a copy of the file to the hard disk.

6 The File Manager enables the application to access the file system on the hard disk, where the file is being stored. The Save command replaces an older version of a file with a newer version.

7 The Device Manager can send data to the hard disk. A USB Manager handles the sending or receiving of data to the Mac's USB ports.

8 The Memory Manager allocates and manages the portion of memory used by an application. When an open file is saved, the Memory Manager lets the other managers know where in RAM the file can be found. The memory allocation is constantly changing, depending on what the user is doing within an application.

Process Managers

Other Managers

File Manager

Device Manager

Memory Managers

Operating System

Mac OS ROM File

Hard Disk

The System File and Resources in OS 9 and Earlier

I At startup, the operating system opens the System file, making the system resources available to applications. This process is completely invisible to the user.

System Resources

System Folder

System
ALRT   snd   ICON
DLOG   MENU   card

System   Finder   Apple Menu Items   Fonts

Preferences   Control Panels   Extensions   Startup Items

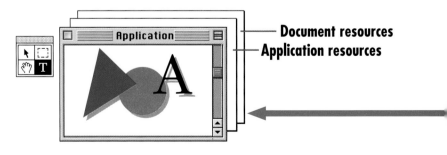

Process Managers   Other Managers   File Manager   Device Manager

Memory Managers

Operating System

2 Applications can have their own proprietary resources, which are shared by documents within the application. Individual data files also can have resources, such as preferences. When a document opens, the application looks in the System folder's Preferences folder and reads a preference file for settings saved by the user, such as default fonts and margins.

Application

Document resources
Application resources

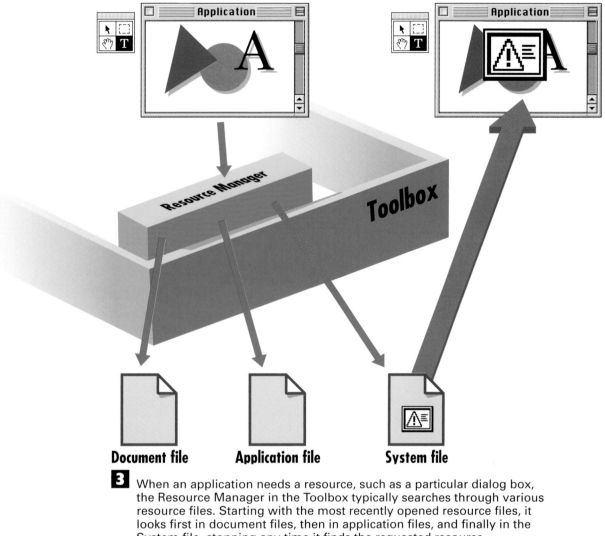

Document file   **Application file**   **System file**

3 When an application needs a resource, such as a particular dialog box, the Resource Manager in the Toolbox typically searches through various resource files. Starting with the most recently opened resource files, it looks first in document files, then in application files, and finally in the System file, stopping any time it finds the requested resource. Applications also can bypass the Resource Manager and specify particular resources for certain uses.

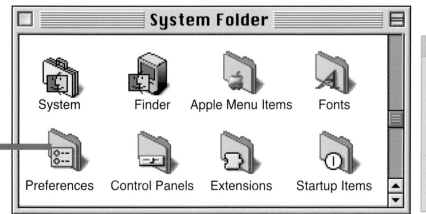

MAC FACT

Several hundred different *types* of resources are contained in the Mac OS 9 System file. Mac OS 8.5 introduced a second file called System Resources, which also contains resources. When you first start up a brand-new Mac, you might find this file in the trash. It's okay to empty the trash—that operating system looked at the type of hardware you have and created a new file in its place. However, you should not place the System Resources file in the trash yourself.

Extension Files in Mac OS 7.x, 8.x, and 9.x

Apple and application programmers can add new features by adding extensions files—software modules that contain the equivalent of new Toolbox managers, routines, or resources. An extension often enables a specific function, such as playing QuickTime movies. Extension files reside in the Extensions folder inside the System folder.

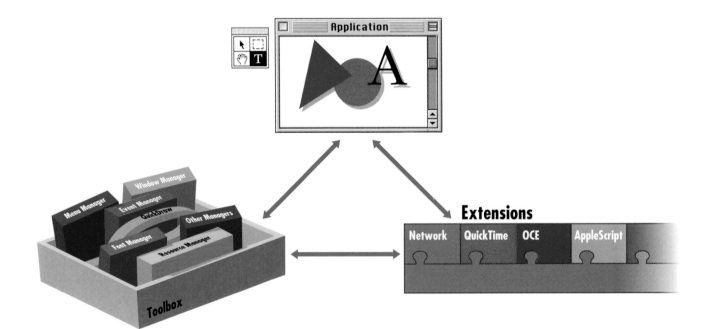

MAC FACT

System features sometimes start out as add-on extensions, are later included as a built-in part of the system software, and then finally become an actual Toolbox routine. 32-bit color QuickDraw, which enabled Macs to display in full color, started out as an extension and was later included in the Mac ROM starting with the Mac IIci.

1 At startup, the operating system looks inside the extension files. If a file identifies itself with a file type of INIT, the operating system loads the file into RAM and executes the code routines inside. In some ways, Mac extensions play the same role as lines of text in the AUTOEXEC.BAT file in DOS and Windows, where commands run pieces of code at boot time. For instance, the DOS MSCDEX command and the Mac's Apple CD-ROM extension both enable the computer to access a CD-ROM drive connected to the machine.

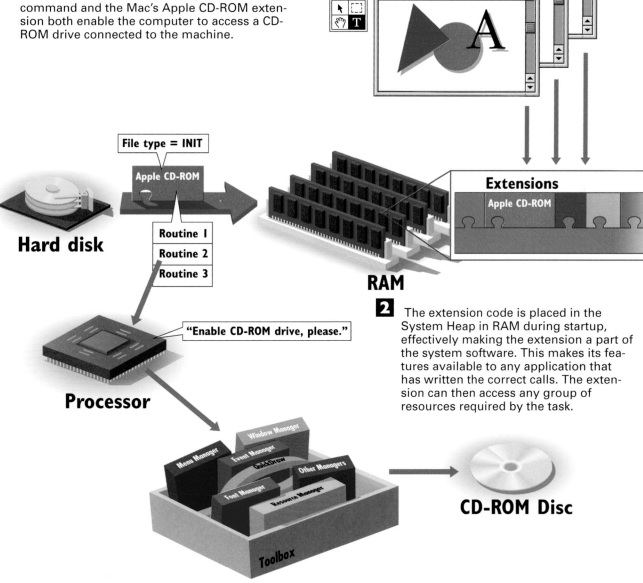

Application

File type = INIT

Apple CD-ROM

Hard disk

Routine 1
Routine 2
Routine 3

Extensions

Apple CD-ROM

RAM

2 The extension code is placed in the System Heap in RAM during startup, effectively making the extension a part of the system software. This makes its features available to any application that has written the correct calls. The extension can then access any group of resources required by the task.

"Enable CD-ROM drive, please."

Processor

Window Manager
Menu Manager
Event Manager
QuickDraw
Font Manager
Other Managers
Resource Manager

Toolbox

CD-ROM Disc

Mac OS X: Mac OS Reinvented

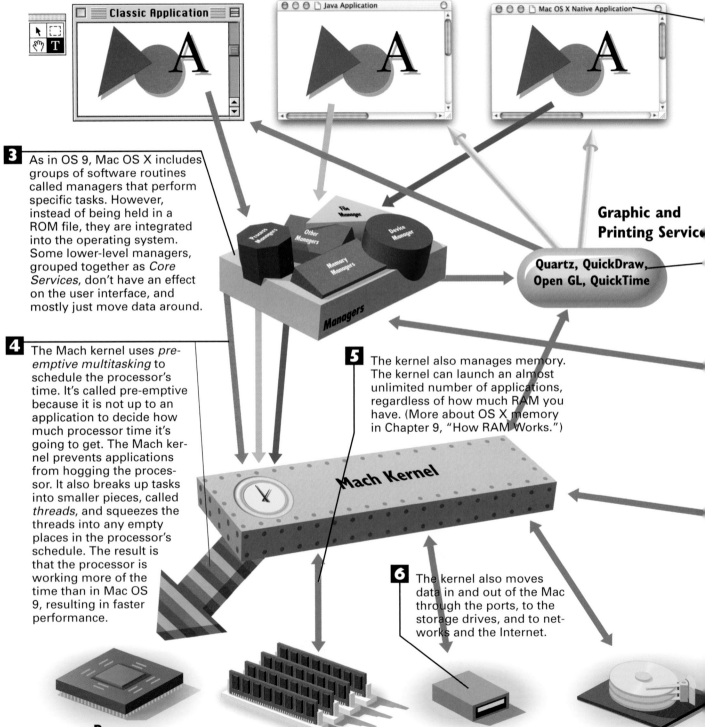

Classic Application

Java Application

Mac OS X Native Application

3 As in OS 9, Mac OS X includes groups of software routines called managers that perform specific tasks. However, instead of being held in a ROM file, they are integrated into the operating system. Some lower-level managers, grouped together as *Core Services*, don't have an effect on the user interface, and mostly just move data around.

Graphic and Printing Service

File Manager

Other Managers

Process Managers

Device Manager

Memory Managers

Managers

Quartz, QuickDraw, Open GL, QuickTime

4 The Mach kernel uses *pre-emptive multitasking* to schedule the processor's time. It's called pre-emptive because it is not up to an application to decide how much processor time it's going to get. The Mach kernel prevents applications from hogging the processor. It also breaks up tasks into smaller pieces, called *threads*, and squeezes the threads into any empty places in the processor's schedule. The result is that the processor is working more of the time than in Mac OS 9, resulting in faster performance.

5 The kernel also manages memory. The kernel can launch an almost unlimited number of applications, regardless of how much RAM you have. (More about OS X memory in Chapter 9, "How RAM Works.")

Mach Kernel

6 The kernel also moves data in and out of the Mac through the ports, to the storage drives, and to networks and the Internet.

Processor

1 Mac OS X can run several different types of applications all at the same time. OS X-native and Java applications will use the Aqua interface. *Classic* applications—older software written for OS 9 and earlier—retains the Mac OS 9 look and feel.

2 A new graphics technology called Quartz is responsible for drawing the Aqua look and feel. Quartz is a fast graphics engine for 2-D environments. (Older applications can use the older QuickDraw code.) Another set of routines called OpenGL draws 3-D images used in games and other places. Built-in QuickTime enables you to play movies right from preview windows in dialog boxes.

7 A custom version of BSD (Berkeley Standard Distribution) UNIX operating system works closely with the kernel in enabling network communications and the support of file systems on storage devices (including UNIX File System [UFS]). While the kernel is scheduling and moving the 1s and 0s in and out of the Mac, BSD supplies the interpretation of network standards, such as TCP/IP for the Internet. BSD also provides the basic user IDs when you log on to Mac OS X. Additionally, programmers can use BSD to enable UNIX programs to run on Mac OS X.

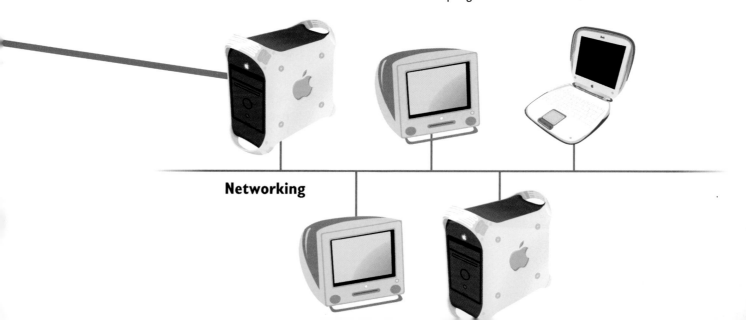

Networking

CHAPTER
6

How the Finder Works

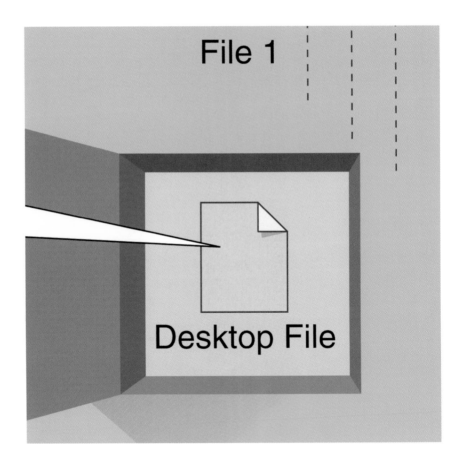

SHOW someone a picture of the Finder and ask them what it is. The most likely response is "a Mac." That's because the Finder is the most familiar thing about the Mac. You're "in" the Finder when the Mac first starts up. You use the Finder when you're opening folders and files. You also use the Finder to copy, move, rename, and delete files and folders, as well as to make aliases.

The Finder is not the Mac operating system: Mac OS launches the Finder at startup. The Finder is actually a software application, similar to a word processor or Web browser. However, unlike a word processor, you can't quit out of the Finder—it's always running.

The Finder's job is to depict application and data files as icons or as text lists in various windows. It does this through the use of invisible databases, called the *Desktop files*, stored on each of your drives. In these files, the Finder keeps track of the thousands of files on your hard disk and other storage media. It lists the location of each file, what type of icon they should use, and other data about the files. When you open a folder, the Finder consults these Desktop files to properly display the files and folders inside.

When you double-click a file's icon, the Finder initiates the *launch* of an application. This is the process of locating the application on a disk, loading it into RAM, and opening the application window on the desktop. The Finder also enables you to access files by clicking their *aliases*—small pointer files linked to a file. Double-clicking an alias opens the file to which it is linked without having to open any folders.

Mac OS 9 and OS X use the term Finder differently. From the first Mac's Finder 1.0 to Finder 9, the Finder includes everything you see when the Mac finishes starting up. It includes the desktop, windows, menus, and Trash and hard drive icons. When you want to go back to the desktop from another application, you switch to the Finder.

The Mac OS X calls everything you see the *Desktop*, not the Finder. The Finder in OS X is a window where you see files and folders, browse through them, and manipulate them. The Mac OS X Finder is part of the Desktop, instead of the other way around in earlier versions.

Similar to the Mac OS 9 Finder, the Mac OS X Desktop uses a database of files and folder information kept in an invisible Desktop file. However, instead a file for every disk or volume, Mac OS X has a Desktop file for every user. Various users logging on to the same Mac will see only the files that they or an administrator have installed.

The OS X Desktop has many of the same features as the OS 9 Finder as well as new features, such as a new column view. It also enables you to browse through your folders in a single window. However, you still have the option of multiple open windows if you want.

Opening a File in the OS 9 Finder

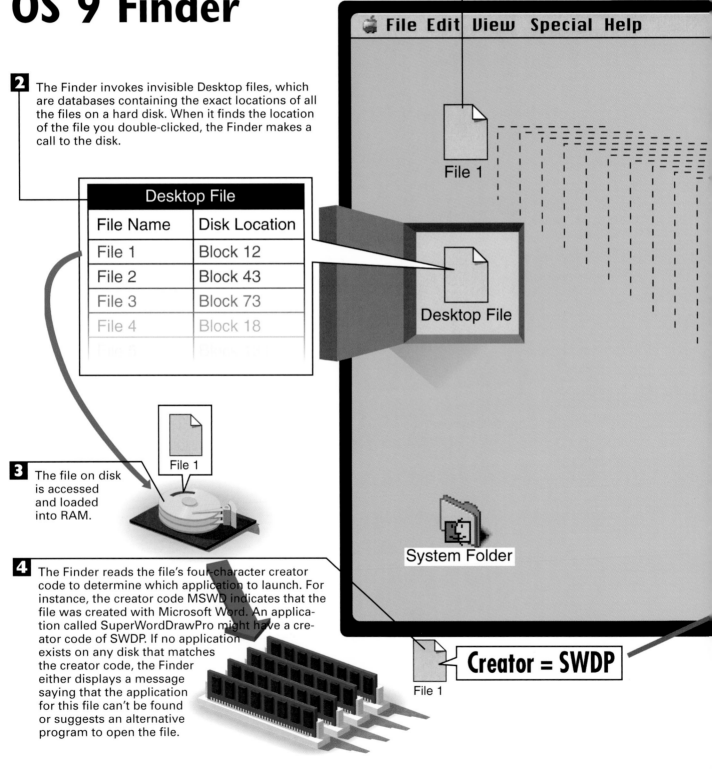

1 Double-clicking a data file starts the sequence of events that will launch the application and open the file.

2 The Finder invokes invisible Desktop files, which are databases containing the exact locations of all the files on a hard disk. When it finds the location of the file you double-clicked, the Finder makes a call to the disk.

Desktop File

File Name	Disk Location
File 1	Block 12
File 2	Block 43
File 3	Block 73
File 4	Block 18

File 1

Desktop File

3 The file on disk is accessed and loaded into RAM.

System Folder

4 The Finder reads the file's four-character creator code to determine which application to launch. For instance, the creator code MSWD indicates that the file was created with Microsoft Word. An application called SuperWordDrawPro might have a creator code of SWDP. If no application exists on any disk that matches the creator code, the Finder either displays a message saying that the application for this file can't be found or suggests an alternative program to open the file.

File 1

Creator = SWDP

File Edit View Special Help

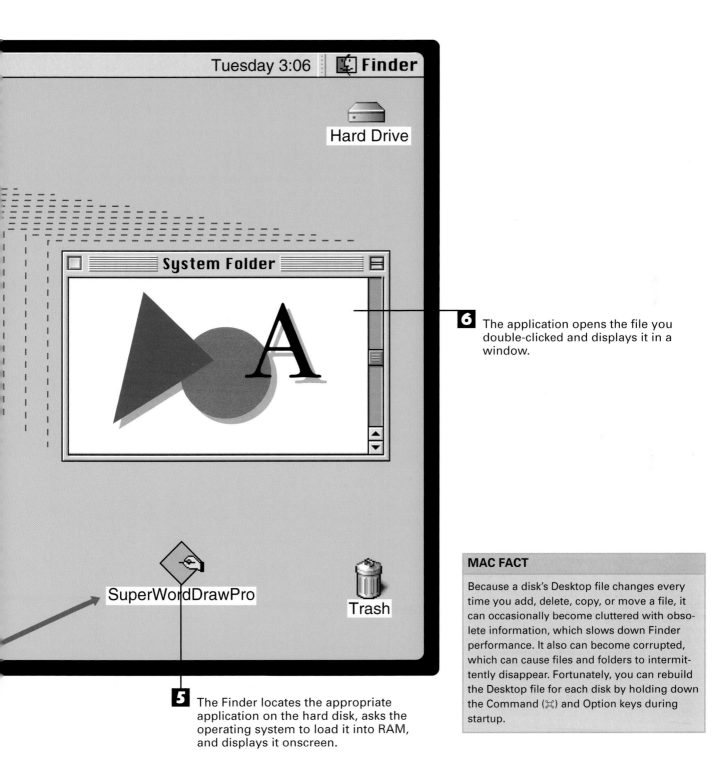

Tuesday 3:06   Finder

Hard Drive

System Folder

6 The application opens the file you double-clicked and displays it in a window.

SuperWordDrawPro

Trash

5 The Finder locates the appropriate application on the hard disk, asks the operating system to load it into RAM, and displays it onscreen.

MAC FACT

Because a disk's Desktop file changes every time you add, delete, copy, or move a file, it can occasionally become cluttered with obsolete information, which slows down Finder performance. It also can become corrupted, which can cause files and folders to intermittently disappear. Fortunately, you can rebuild the Desktop file for each disk by holding down the Command (⌘) and Option keys during startup.

Creating and Running an Alias

The Mac OS 9 and Mac OS X both offer aliases as a shortcut to your files. They share some similarities, such as both use the Alias Manager in the same way.

1 When you select a file or folder and choose Make Alias from the Finder's File menu, the Finder creates a small alias file. This acts as a pointer to the original file.

2 When the Finder creates the alias file, it asks the Alias Manager in Mac OS to create an *alias record*—an invisible piece of data that documents the name and location of the original file. You can move the alias into any folder or copy it to another disk, and the alias record will go with it. However, because the alias record describes the location of the original file, moving the original file effectively "breaks" the alias.

3 When you double-click an alias, the Finder sends the alias record to the Alias Manager.

4 The Alias Manager reads the alias record to find the location of the original file. The Finder then opens the original using the normal Finder process (depicted on the previous page). If the original file resides on a CD-ROM or Zip cartridge, the Finder asks you to insert the disk.

File Edit View Special Help   Tuesday 3:06   Finder

New Folder   ⌘N
Open   ⌘O
Print   ⌘P
Move To Trash   ⌘⌫
Close Window   ⌘W

Get Info   ▶
Label   ▶
Duplicate   ⌘D
Make Alias   ⌘M
Add To Favorites
Put Away   ⌘Y
Encrypt

Find...   ⌘F
Search Internet...⌘H
Show Original   ⌘R

Page Setup...
Print Window...

Hard Drive

Folder A

File 1

Folder B

Folder 1

File 2

Folder C

Folder D

Alias Record

File 2 Alias

Alias Record

Alias Manager

Trash

Deleting a File

1 To delete a file, you drag it and drop it in the Trash icon, which is actually a special folder. Before you empty the Trash, the files inside are still completely intact, but designated to be discarded. If an application calls for a file that happens to be in the Trash, the Finder sends a screen message asking you to remove it from the Trash. You can drag a file out of the Trash at any time before you invoke the Empty Trash command.

2 When you select Empty Trash from the Special menu, the Finder deletes the file's entry from the Desktop file, and the file's icon disappears from the Trash. Although the Finder can no longer locate the file, it still exists on the disk and can be recovered with file recovery software. However, the file is no longer protected from being overwritten, and it might be partially or totally erased from the disk the next time you save a file.

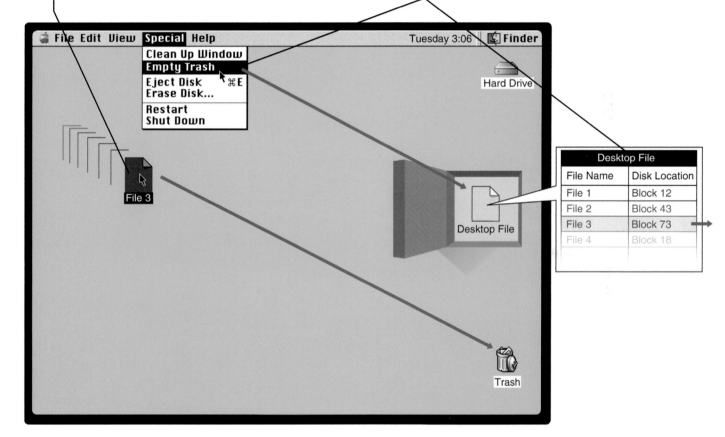

MAC FACT

Since System 7, the Finder has permitted multiple application windows to be open at the same time. System 6 allowed multiple application windows to be open at the same time only when you used a special program called MultiFinder. Prior to MultiFinder, you had to quit an application before you could go to the Finder or to another application. The first attempt at letting you open multiple applications was a program called the Switcher, but it could display only one application at a time. To switch from one application to another, you pressed an arrow, and the current application slid off the side of the screen while the new application slid in to replace it.

Mac OS X Desktop Finder

1 Unlike previous Mac OSs, drive icons in Mac OS X can appear in a window—a Finder window—as well as on the Desktop. The Finder is the part of the OS X Desktop application that interacts with the operating system's file system. You also can drag icons for internal and external drives to the Desktop.

2 The Network icon replaces the Chooser and the Network Browser of OS 9 and earlier.

3 Icons for drives and files look more realistic than in OS 9 because the OS X Desktop permits icons up to 128×128 pixels in size and in full 32-bit photographic color. In OS 9, the maximum size for icons is 32×32 pixels.

4 When you double-click a drive icon, the OS X Finder consults an invisible Desktop file to see which folders and files are in the Drive. Unlike OS 9 and earlier, which have a Desktop file for every drive, OS X has a Desktop file for every user. The Finder picks the Desktop file for the user who is logged in. The User's Desktop file contains information on all the drives the user has accessed, including network volumes.

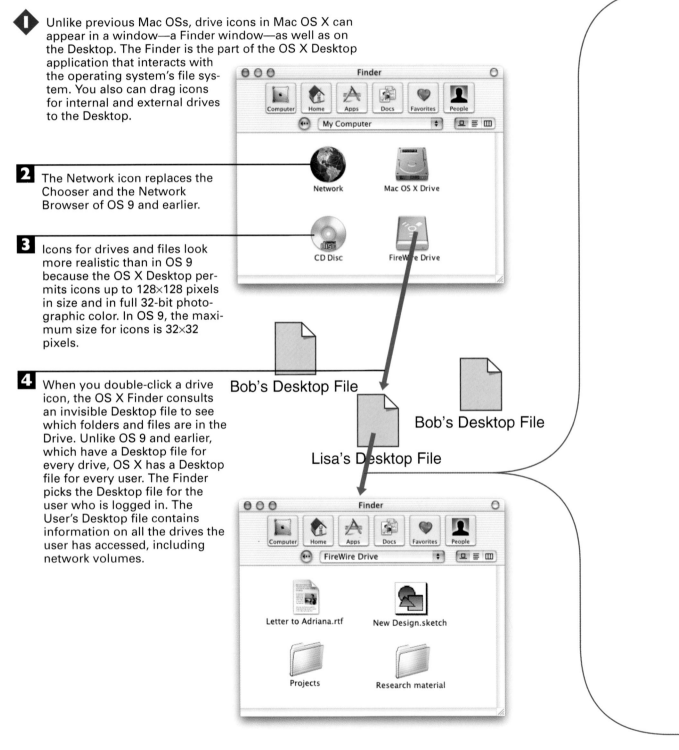

Bob's Desktop File

Bob's Desktop File

Lisa's Desktop File

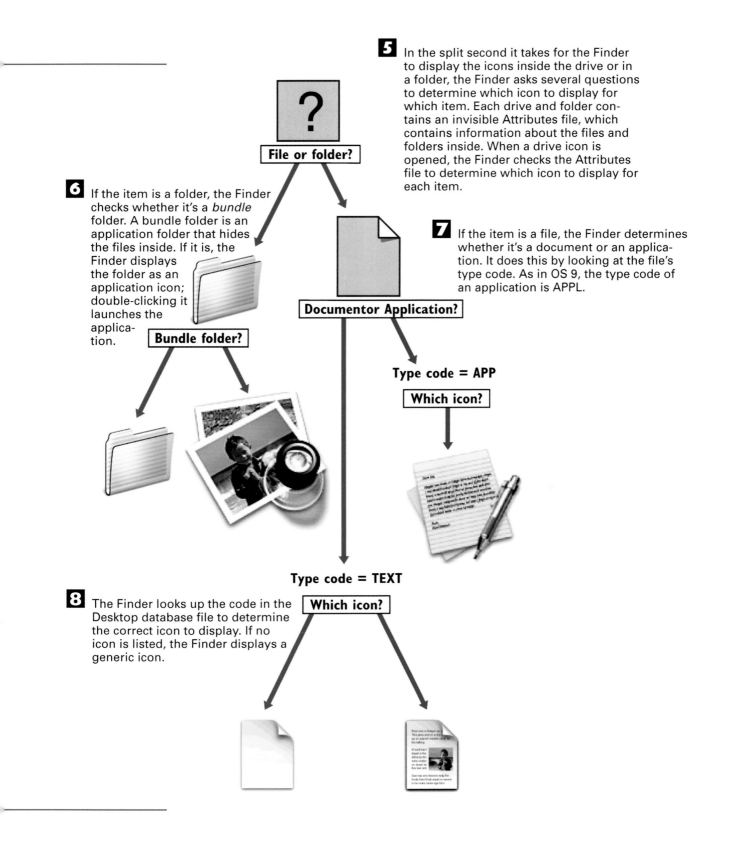

5 In the split second it takes for the Finder to display the icons inside the drive or in a folder, the Finder asks several questions to determine which icon to display for which item. Each drive and folder contains an invisible Attributes file, which contains information about the files and folders inside. When a drive icon is opened, the Finder checks the Attributes file to determine which icon to display for each item.

File or folder?

6 If the item is a folder, the Finder checks whether it's a *bundle* folder. A bundle folder is an application folder that hides the files inside. If it is, the Finder displays the folder as an application icon; double-clicking it launches the application.

Bundle folder?

Documentor Application?

7 If the item is a file, the Finder determines whether it's a document or an application. It does this by looking at the file's type code. As in OS 9, the type code of an application is APPL.

Type code = APP

Which icon?

Type code = TEXT

8 The Finder looks up the code in the Desktop database file to determine the correct icon to display. If no icon is listed, the Finder displays a generic icon.

Which icon?

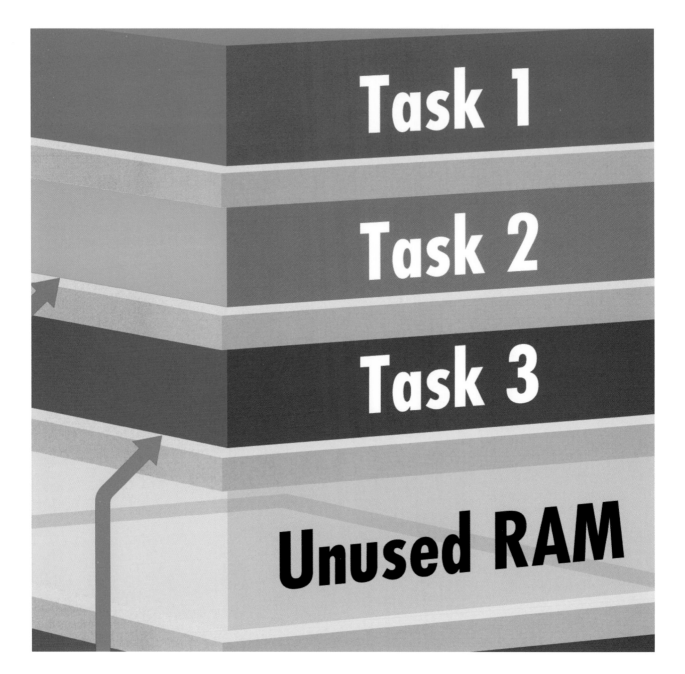

P A R T

3

PROCESSOR AND MEMORY

Chapter 7: Binary Numbers and Transistors

48

Chapter 8: How the Processor Works

52

Chapter 9: How RAM Works

60

Chapter 10: How Virtual Memory Works

68

Chapter 11: How a Cache Works

72

Chapter 12: How a RAM Disk Works

78

FOR all the metal, plastic, and glass that make up a computer, it's just a square inch of silicon that does the actual computing. This is the *processor*, the computer's engine. Getting its instructions from software, the processor juggles numbers by the millions to create complex graphics, calculate your spreadsheet results, and process the countless behind-the-scenes activities you can't see.

While processing components of computers of a few decades ago could fill a room, the processor in today's personal computers resides on a single chip called a *microprocessor*. The microprocessor used in Power Mac models is one of the PowerPC chips originally developed by IBM, Motorola, and Apple and built by Motorola and IBM.

But Macs don't run by processors alone. The processor works as part of a team with the main system memory, which resides on a set of silicon chips called *random access memory (RAM)*. The main system memory supplies the CPU with the software instructions and data it needs to do your work. The system memory receives the information from a permanent storage device, such as a hard disk, and temporarily holds it for the processor. Computers use RAM because it can pass information to the processor much more quickly than a hard disk can.

Functionally, the processor and main memory are quite different. Software tells a microprocessor chip to perform tasks and to request information from memory, but RAM chips are unintelligent storage vessels for information. At a microscopic level, however, microprocessors and RAM chips include the same primary component, the transistor.

Transistors are tiny, electronic switches typically measured in microns (millionths of a meter). These simple devices are certainly the single most important electronic device today. Cheap, reliable, and low-powered, you can find them in everything from TVs to telephones, from cars to karaoke machines.

In processors, RAM, and any other electronic component, transistors represent binary numbers—that is, numbers that use only the characters 0 and 1. A transistor represents 0 and 1 with two electronic states, on and off. A single transistor holding a 0 or 1 is a *bit*, short for *binary digit*. A series of transistors (or bits) represents numbers larger than 1.

The RAM that makes up your Mac's main system memory is an array of millions of transistors holding 0s or 1s. The Mac ROM chip mentioned in earlier chapters is similar to RAM chips. However, the values of 0 and 1 that the transistors hold in ROM are permanent.

A microprocessor chip is quite a bit more complicated than a RAM chip. Instead of merely storing bits, it executes millions of instructions every second based on information it gets from RAM. In a microprocessor chip, engineers combine the input and output signals of transistors in different ways to build tiny, integrated circuits inside a silicon chip. Microprocessors have many layers of thousands of integrated circuits.

Using integrated circuits, the processor adds and subtracts binary numbers at dazzling speeds set by the clock rate, measured in megahertz (MHz). This means the transistors inside a 500MHz microprocessor are opening and closing at a rate of 500 million times per second.

By operating at a speed that is far beyond the realm of everyday human experience, the processor eventually translates simple math into actions such as opening a window or displaying video on the Mac monitor. Similarly, everything you do with a Mac—from calculating a spreadsheet to using the Finder to find a file—turns into a series of binary numbers. The same is true of all software, which delivers its commands to the processor in the form of binary numbers. However, programmers don't write software as a string of 0s and 1s. We refer to software as *code* because programmers use high-level programming languages that in turn use the letters of the alphabet and English words to represent the 0s and 1s.

Of course, the processor and main system memory aren't the only electronic components in a computer. Besides main system memory, personal computers use RAM chips for other purposes. For example, video RAM stores the information used to display images on your monitor. A *cache* is a special type of RAM that speeds computer performance by keeping the processor from waiting for information. You'll find caches on the logic board, inside hard-disk and CD-ROM drives, and even inside the processor itself. Mac OS also can use standard Mac hardware components to perform some special memory tricks. *Virtual memory* is the trick that uses part of a hard disk as an extension of the main system memory. The Mac also can perform the opposite trick of creating a RAM disk by using RAM chips as a virtual hard disk.

Mac OS determines how efficiently the Mac will use the processor, main system memory, and the various other types of real and virtual memory in the Mac. Mac OS has had trouble keeping up with the increasing speed of microprocessors and RAM chips through the years. The problem is wasted time as the processor sits idly waiting for information.

Mac OS X is a major step forward in this respect because it eliminates this idle time, resulting in faster performance for the Mac. It requires more RAM and hard disk space than earlier versions, but this hardware has become much less expensive than in previous decades.

Eventually, Mac OS X will also need to be upgraded; hardware has traditionally stayed ahead of software's capability to take advantage of it. The hardware technology still has a long way to go before it hits a ceiling.

CHAPTER

7

Binary Numbers and Transistors

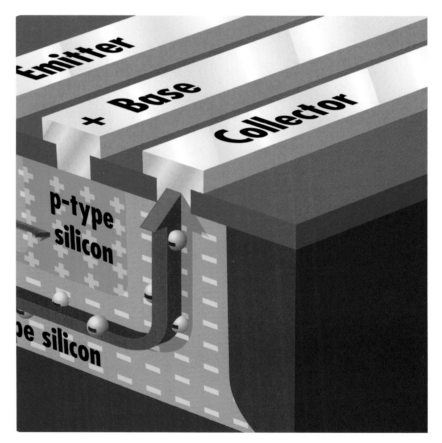

COMPUTERS use the binary number system to count. To understand why, let's look at some of the ways we can count. The most primitive method might be to assign a character—a vertical line (|), for instance—to each object we are counting. For example, if we had six sticks, we could represent them as:

| | | | | |

This numbering system, however, becomes unmanageable when the numbers grow large. To prevent massing a large number of characters, we could assign a unique character to every number, but we'd soon run out of characters and would have an awful lot to memorize as well.

The decimal system is a compromise: It uses ten characters for the first ten numbers (0 through 9) and combinations of these characters to represent larger numbers. We have a 1's place, a 10's place, a 100's place, and so on. Each place represents ten times the place to its right; for example, the number 126 tells us we have six 1's, two 10's, and one 100.

In the binary system, we only have two characters—0 and 1—so each place represents twice as much as the place to its right. This gives us a 1's place, a 2's place, a 4's place, an 8's place, and so on. The binary number 1011, then, tells us we have one 1, one 2, no 4's, and one 8. In the decimal system, that's 1 + 2 + 0 + 8, or 11.

In computer terminology, each binary place is called a *bit*, so 1101 is a 4-bit number. Bits are arranged in groups of 8, called *bytes*. The biggest 8-bit binary number, 11111111, is 255 in decimal (1 + 2 + 4 + 8 + 16 + 32 + 64 + 128), which isn't very big. However, today's Macs can handle numbers that are 4 bytes long, or 32 bits. The biggest 32-bit binary number (32 1's) is the decimal equivalent of 4,294,967,295—enough to add just about any two numbers in one step.

The reason binary notation is used in computers is that the electronics need only two types of electrical signals in different combinations to represent any number. The transistor is an ideal device to represent a single binary place, or bit. When a polarity is applied, we get a current flow, representing a 1. Reverse the polarity and the current stops—we have a 0.

Transistors are made from the element that gives Silicon Valley its name. Silicon, found naturally as silicon dioxide (aka silica) in quartz, agate, and sand, is an insulator—that is, it won't conduct an electric current. A process called *doping* turns silicon into a semiconductor—a material that is mildly conductive—by adding impurities. Silicon doped with phosphorus is called n-type and has a net negative charge. Silicon doped with boron, p-type, has a net positive charge.

A transistor consists of three layers of p- and n-type silicon. A metal lead is connected to each of the three layers, now called the base, emitter, and collector. In this chapter, we'll look at an npn transistor, the type used in most integrated circuits.

Binary Numbers and Transistors

To demonstrate how binary addition works, we constructed an imaginary binary adding machine. Each place, or bit, consists of a spinning sign with a 0 painted on one side and a 1 painted on the other. Attached to the side of the signs are levers. When the 0 side faces forward, the lever is in the down position. When the 1 side faces forward, the lever sticks straight out to the left, hitting the next sign. The decimal readout on the right displays the decimal equivalent of the binary number.

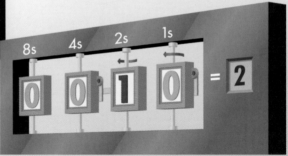

1 We start with 0000 and rotate the sign in the 1's place from 0 to 1. The lever hits the sign on the next column and stops.

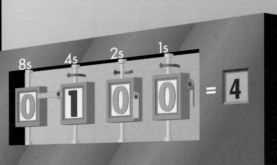

2 To increase the number by 1, we spin the 1's place sign again, returning it to 0. This causes the lever to flip the sign in the 2's place from 0 to 1.

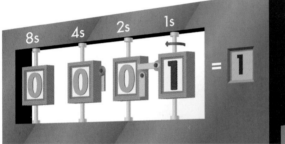

3 Increasing the number by 1 again causes the 1's place to advance from 0 to 1, but doesn't affect the 2's place.

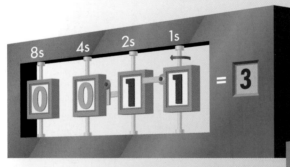

4 Adding another 1 to the 1's place causes the signs in both the 2's and 4's places to turn, giving us the binary number 0100, or decimal 4.

A Transistor

A transistor makes use of the fundamental physics principles that opposite charges attract and that electrons, which are negatively charged, will move from an area of more electrons to an area of fewer electrons. A flow of electrons is a *current*. Applying a small positive charge to the base causes a current to flow through a transistor, putting it in active mode, which can represent the binary numeral 1. By reversing the charge at the base connector to negative, electrons from the emitter are repulsed and no current flows. This case represents a 0.

1 The base of an npn transistor is made of p-type silicon, which normally has a net positive charge. If we apply a further positive charge to the base, we'll draw electrons from the n–type silicon, which normally has a few extra electrons.

2 If we apply a negative charge to the emitter, it becomes even more negative than normal, tending to push electrons into the p-type base region.

Electrons

Current Flow

3 Because the p-type silicon of the base is such a small region, most of the electrons are swept right through it into the n-type silicon of the collector. Because the collector does not have a negative charge applied to it, it is less negative than the emitter, which permits electrons to flow into it.

4 Some electrons stay in the p region. But because the p region is very thin (from .1 to 10 microns), the resulting current, called the trickle current, is much smaller than the current resulting from the electron flow from emitter to collector. In effect, the small trickle current controls the much larger current passing through the base from emitter to collector.

Emitter

Base

Collector

p-type silicon

n-type silicon

CHAPTER

8

How the Processor Works

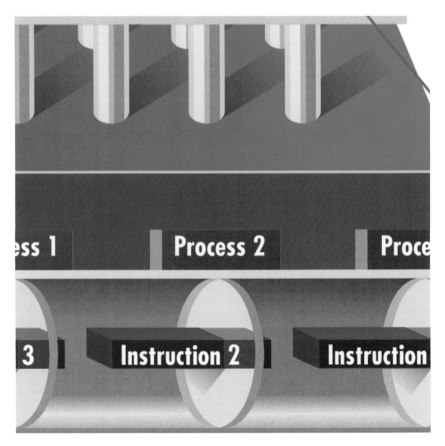

GROUP a few transistors together and you have a simple adding machine. Assemble a few adding machines together and you have a circuit performing complex functions. Combine enough of these circuits and eventually you'll wind up with millions of transistors switching on and off at hundreds of millions of times per second. You'd have a *microprocessor*—or just *processor* for short. The processor puts the computing in your computer. The rest of the Mac's components serve only to get information to the processor and the result of its efforts to you.

Today's Macs use either a PowerPC G3 or a PowerPC G4 processor. At least, that's what Apple calls them. The actual names of the processors are PowerPC 750 and PowerPC 7400, as designated by Motorola and IBM (the companies that build them). G3 stands for third-generation PowerPC, which is what the 750 is. The G4 (7400) is the fourth generation. The first-generation PowerPC processors used in Macs were the 601 and 603e. The second generation was the PowerPC 604. Before the PowerPC processors, early Macs used Motorola processors called the 68000, 68020, 68030, and 68040.

Inside a processor are tens of thousands of microscopic circuits, sometimes measuring only 0.15 millionths of an inch (*microns*) apart. In the G3 and G4, the circuits reside inside a wafer of silicon sitting inside a 1-square-inch protective ceramic case that is a little over 0.10" thick. The silicon wafer inside communicates with the Mac through dozens of pins at the bottom of the ceramic case. The G3 and G4 processors each have 360 pins. The signals are synchronized by a clock, which provides timing signals—called *cycles*—at a constant rate. The speed of the processor's clock is measured in *megahertz (MHz)*, or millions of cycles per second.

A common misconception is that the higher the MHz rating of a processor, the faster the computer is. Although this is true for Macs with the same processor, comparing the clock rate of different processors is like comparing the speed of cars by looking only at the RPM of the tachometer. For instance, a 400MHz G4 processor can be several times faster than a 400MHz G3 processor. Comparing clock rates of PowerPC processors in Macs and Pentium processors in PCs makes even less sense because of their radically different architectures. Apple says that when the G4's features are effectively used, a 500MHz G4 is more than twice as fast as an 800MHz Pentium III using Intel tests. That's because a PowerPC G3 or G4 can get more done in a clock cycle than a Pentium can. Clock rate is *not* horsepower.

How much work gets done in a clock cycle can be measured several ways. One way is to consider how many instructions can be accomplished in a clock cycle. *Instructions* are commands from the software. An instruction is a simple request, and a typical task usually consists of many instructions. Back in the first Macs, the old 68000 processor required 4 cycles to process an instruction. Today, through *parallel processing* (performing multiple tasks at one time), the PowerPC G3 and G4 can both issue 3 instructions for each clock cycle. However, the G4 goes even further and can execute up to 20 operations for each instruction. It does this using another type of parallel processing called *SIMD* (*single instruction-multiple data*).

Another factor that determines the speed of a processor is the number of *execution units*, which are the components of the processor that act upon instructions (the calculation engines). The G3 processor has six execution units, whereas the G4 has seven.

At the core of the execution units is the *integer unit*, also called the *fixed point unit*. Integer math is the most common type of calculation used by software. The G3 and G4 processors each have two integer units.

Another type of execution unit does *floating-point* calculations, a type of math popular with graphical and mathematical software. PowerPC processors have always been particularly good at floating-point calculations, and this is particularly true of the G3 and G4. In fact, the Power Mac G4 was the first personal computer to be capable of executing at least one billion floating-point operations per second—a *gigaflop*. For many years, the U.S. government used the capability to execute a sustained gigaflop as the definition of a *supercomputer*. Therefore, when the Power Mac G4 was first introduced, it was technically a supercomputer. In fact, the G4 has a theoretical peak performance over three gigaflops.

Despite the importance of floating-point math in graphics today, the old 68000 processor contained no floating-point unit. The 68020 (in 1987's Mac II) and the 68030 (introduced in the Mac SE/30) contained a floating-point processor as a separate chip. The 68040 was the first Mac process to include a built-in floating-point unit.

The PowerPC G4 introduced a new execution unit—a *vector processing unit*. This is a fast, highly parallel processing unit that is responsible for most of the high benchmark results for the G4. Motorola calls the vector execution unit, along with special instructions for it, the AltiVec technology. (Apple calls AltiVec the Velocity Engine. Both terms refer to the same technology.) AltiVec is similar in concept to Intel's MMX technology that is used in Pentium processors, except that it is much more parallel and can execute more instructions. Using the SIMD processing model mentioned earlier, the G4's vector unit can process data 128 bits at a time, as opposed to 64 or 32 bits in most processors.

The G4's AltiVec vector processing lends itself to demanding tasks, such as speech recognition and compressing or real-time encoding of video or MP3 sound. To take advantage of the AltiVec performance gains, application software must be written especially to use the AltiVec instructions. Adobe Photoshop is one application that can use AltiVec. Parts of Mac OS are also AltiVec-enabled.

Yet another factor that determines the speed of a processor is the amount of *cache* it has. Cache speeds things up by temporarily holding frequently used data and instructions, so that the processor doesn't have to import them from RAM or the Mac's hard disk. Cache inside a processor is called *Level 1*, or *L1*, cache. Most computers also have a Level 2 (L2) cache outside the processor to expand the size of the holding place. However, L2 cache is slower than the cache inside the processor because it must be fetched and imported into the processor when needed.

The PowerPC G3 introduced the performance-enhancing technique of *backside cache*. This is an L2 cache that sits on the same daughter card as the processor, instead of residing on the motherboard. The G3 and G4 processors include a special port to access the cache at a much higher speed than if it were on the motherboard. The G3 supports up to 1MB of backside cache, whereas the G4 supports up to 2MB.

With all these innovations in each generation of processor, it is amazing that the latest Macs can still run older software. I have a copy of FileMaker from 1987 that runs just fine on a Power Mac G4, for instance. One reason is that each new PowerPC processor is always backward-compatible with older versions. It can do everything the old models did plus some. However, this is not true for the 680x0 processors, for which my old copy of FileMaker was written.

However, Mac OS contains some software that acts as a 68040 emulator. The emulator software translates instructions from software written for the 680x0 Macs into PowerPC instructions. The old software thinks it is running on a 680x0 Mac. (This is the same principle behind Connectix's Virtual PC, which enables you to run Windows software on your Mac. Virtual PC emulates an Intel Pentium processor on a Mac.)

Finally, although the processor may be the brains of a Mac, it is not a free thinker; it does what it is told to do by software. Therefore, the operating system and applications must be well written for the processor to work at its maximum potential. As a more robust operating system, Mac OS X can squeeze more performance out of a processor than can Mac OS 9 and earlier. That's just one more thing to consider when comparing megahertz.

PowerPC G3 Microprocessor

1 Instructions and data from the Mac's RAM enter the bus interface unit, which prioritizes them to keep a steady supply to the execution units. Instructions and data are kept separate from each other so they can be processed simultaneously.

2 The memory management units (MMU) store tables of addresses to keep track of where information is in the process and in RAM. When virtual memory is turned on in the Mac OS Memory control panel, the MMUs keep track of data stored on hard disk as an extension to RAM.

4 New data and instructions that are on their way to the execution units are routed through the Level 1 caches (32K each). The next time the execution units need the same information, they fetch it from the caches instead of going out to the Mac's RAM. The data cache also holds intermediate results that require further processing.

6 Three instruction units feed instructions to the integer and floating-point execution units. The instruction unit retrieves instructions. The branch processing unit predicts when the computer must skip over to another part of a software program, keeping the branches in the software from interrupting the flow of instructions.

Mac System Bus

Bus Interface Unit

Data Cache

Data Memory Management Unit

Integer Unit

Integer Unit

Instruction Group

System Register Unit

Branch Processing Unit

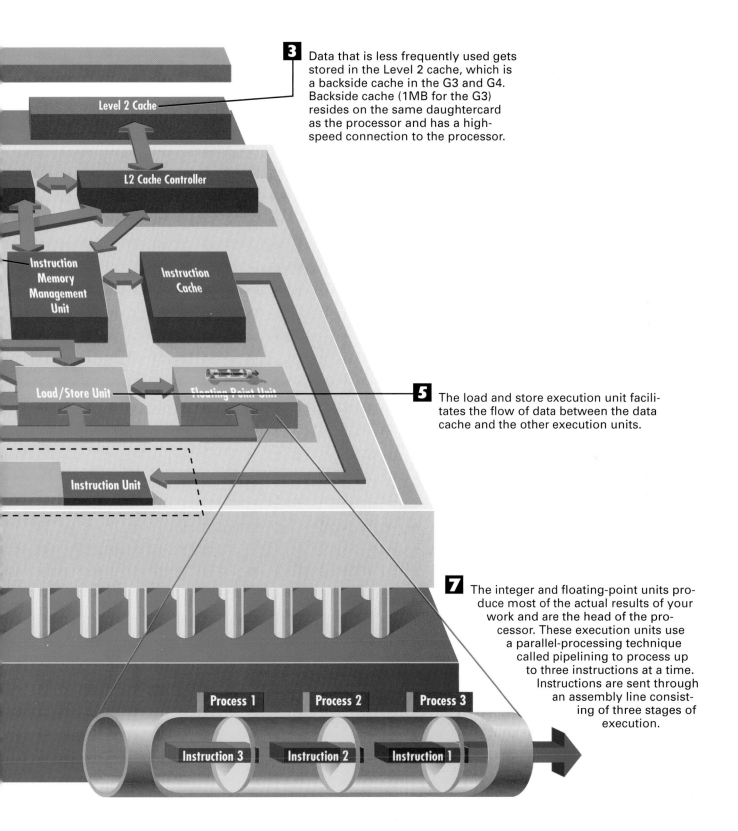

3 Data that is less frequently used gets stored in the Level 2 cache, which is a backside cache in the G3 and G4. Backside cache (1MB for the G3) resides on the same daughtercard as the processor and has a high-speed connection to the processor.

Level 2 Cache

L2 Cache Controller

Instruction Memory Management Unit

Instruction Cache

Load/Store Unit

Floating Point Unit

5 The load and store execution unit facilitates the flow of data between the data cache and the other execution units.

Instruction Unit

7 The integer and floating-point units produce most of the actual results of your work and are the head of the processor. These execution units use a parallel-processing technique called pipelining to process up to three instructions at a time. Instructions are sent through an assembly line consisting of three stages of execution.

Process 1   Process 2   Process 3

Instruction 3   Instruction 2   Instruction 1

PowerPC G4 Microprocessor

Mac System Bus

Bus Interface Unit

1 The PowerPC G4 works in much the same way as the G3. Instructions and data enter the bus interface unit and are passed through the Level 1 caches. Instructions go to the Instruction unit, and data goes to the Load/Store Unit.

Data Cache

Data Memory Management Unit

Integer Unit

Integer Unit

3 The Instruction unit fetches up to four instructions in every clock cycle and can hold them for a short time. The Dispatch unit sends instructions two at a time to the integer, floating-point, and vector execution units.

Dispatch Unit

Branch Processing Unit

MAC FACT

The Motorola MC68000 was the first processor used in Macs and was named after the 68,000 transistors it contained. By 1987, this amount more than quadrupled to 325,000 transistors in the MC68030. By 1990, Motorola was packing 1.2 million transistors into less than 1 square inch in the MC68040, which first appeared in Mac Quadras and Centrises. 1993's PowerPC 601 more than doubled this to 2.8 million transistors in a 1.7-square-inch area. The PowerPC G4 contains 10.5 million transistors, as many as in 154 68000 processors.

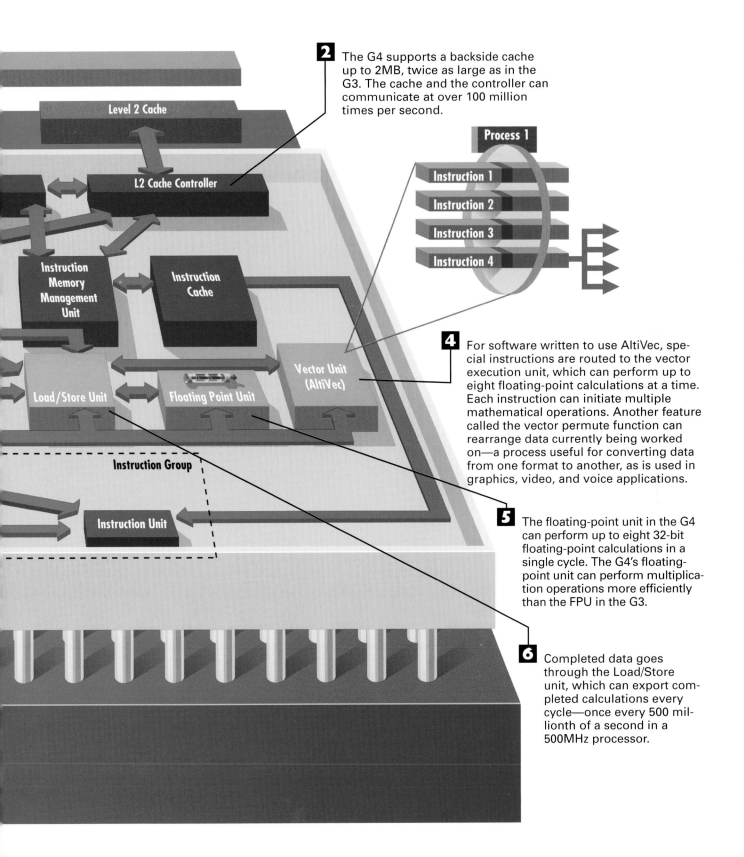

2 The G4 supports a backside cache up to 2MB, twice as large as in the G3. The cache and the controller can communicate at over 100 million times per second.

4 For software written to use AltiVec, special instructions are routed to the vector execution unit, which can perform up to eight floating-point calculations at a time. Each instruction can initiate multiple mathematical operations. Another feature called the vector permute function can rearrange data currently being worked on—a process useful for converting data from one format to another, as is used in graphics, video, and voice applications.

5 The floating-point unit in the G4 can perform up to eight 32-bit floating-point calculations in a single cycle. The G4's floating-point unit can perform multiplication operations more efficiently than the FPU in the G3.

6 Completed data goes through the Load/Store unit, which can export completed calculations every cycle—once every 500 millionth of a second in a 500MHz processor.

CHAPTER
9

How RAM Works

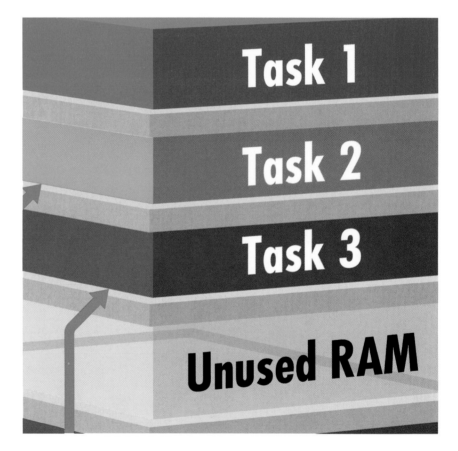

THE main system memory used in Macs and PCs is a type known as *dynamic random-access memory* (DRAM, or just RAM). It is called dynamic because the contents are constantly changing. Random-access means the processor can directly access information stored anywhere inside the chips, just as you can access any part of a phonograph record by dropping the needle down wherever you like on the disk. (A cassette tape, by comparison, is not a random-access medium because you have to wind through tape to get to a section in the middle.)

Most Macintosh memory consists of small cards called *dual inline memory modules (DIMMs)*. The industry standard DIMMs used in new Mac models changes every year or so as the technology evolves. SDRAM has an internal clock that is *synchronized* with the computer's clock so that it and the processor communicate at the same rate. The *SO* in SO-DIMMs stands for *small outline*, which means they are particularly small and are used in notebook Macs. Whether your DIMMs hold 32MB, 64MB, 128MB, or more, they usually contain the same number of memory chips—8 on each side. Regardless of how many DIMMs your Mac has or how much RAM is soldered on the logic board, all the RAM in a Mac acts as a single pool of memory.

The processor can access a piece of information stored in RAM by specifying an *address*, which is a number that identifies the location of a particular byte of information in RAM. Address 0 and the first several hundred address locations, referred to as *low memory*, are always taken by the system partition, which is created at startup. Applications, on the other hand, are loaded into the highest available addresses, referred to as *high memory*.

Mac OS 9.x and earlier allocates RAM to applications when they are launched. Multiple applications share the available RAM by running in memory partitions. You can set the size of an application's memory partition by selecting the application's icon in the Finder and choosing Get Info from the Finder's File menu. The suggested size is set by the software manufacturer, but you may want to enter a bigger number if you are working with large files. Up to the point where the entire application is loaded into memory, the bigger the application partition, the fewer times the application will need to go to disk and the faster its performance.

There's no need to do this in Mac OS X, however. The operating system loads only a small part of an application into RAM at one time, loading the rest whenever the application needs it. You also can open as many applications as you want. You'll never see an out of memory message in Mac OS X.

There's one other important memory feature in Mac OS X—*protected memory*. Mac OS 9 and earlier depend on software applications being well behaved and not writing data in the memory partition of another application. When an application misbehaves, it can cause a crash. In Mac OS X, the Mach kernel forbids bad memory behavior by creating protected memory to wall off sections of memory and prevents software conflicts. The result is a very stable operating environment.

Memory in Mac OS 9.x and Earlier

2 When an application is launched, the operating system assigns it a partition in high memory. Usually, only a portion of the application and document are loaded into the partition. When additional applications are launched, new partitions are created starting at the highest address and working down. The total amount of memory taken up by an application partition is determined by the memory size setting in the application's Get Info box in the Finder.

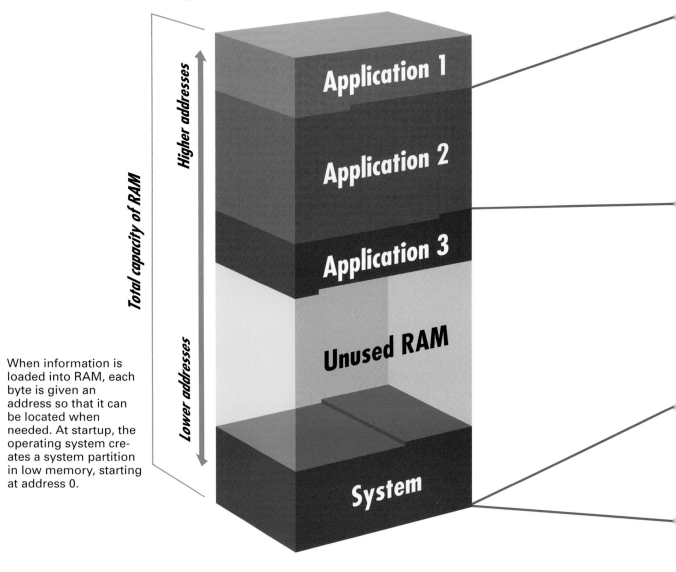

Higher addresses

Total capacity of RAM

Lower addresses

Application 1

Application 2

Application 3

Unused RAM

System

1 When information is loaded into RAM, each byte is given an address so that it can be located when needed. At startup, the operating system creates a system partition in low memory, starting at address 0.

3 Applications call their routines from the application jump table, which is a list of an application's routines and their memory addresses. The jump table is stored in the top part of an application partition, known as the A5 World, named after a part of the 68000 CPU called the A5 register. The A5 World also stores application global variables and parameters used by the Mac Toolbox and operating system.

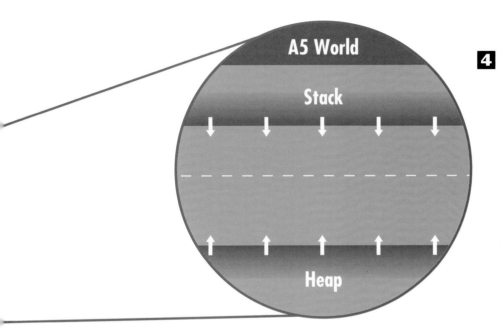

4 Most of the action occurs in the application stack, which holds temporary values, and in the application heap, which holds code segments, resources, and document data. The stack and the heap are dynamically allocated, constantly expanding into and retreating from an empty area of unallocated memory that sits between the two. The application stack can temporarily fill the entire unallocated space, but the heap can fill only a portion of it. The A5 World is static, never changing size while the application is open.

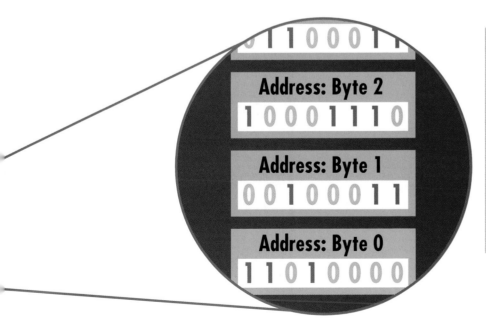

MAC FACT

If RAM is in short supply when you open an application, you may get a somewhat paradoxical message telling you that although there isn't enough memory to open the application, you may want to click OK and open it anyway. In this case, the Memory Manager will load the application by shrinking the unallocated space between the stack and heap, as well as by creating a smaller heap. However, you may not be able to open large files or perform all the functions you normally could, and performance could suffer.

Application Stack

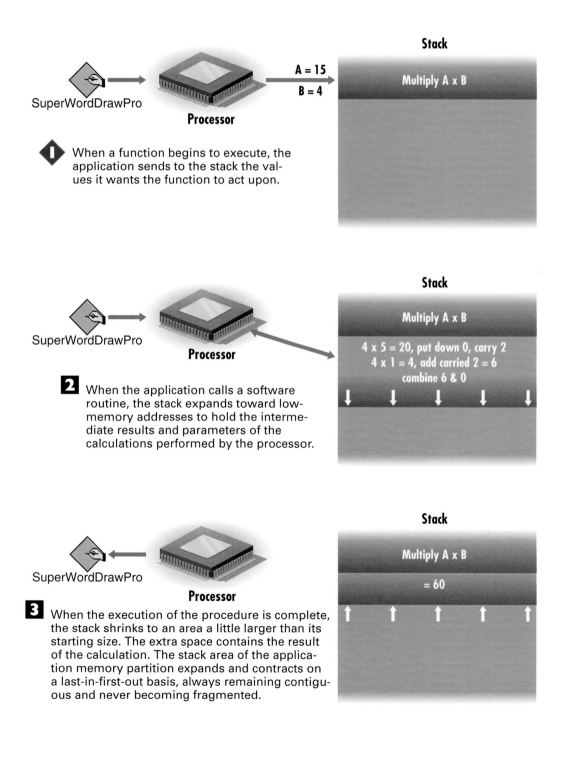

Stack

Multiply A x B

A = 15
B = 4

SuperWordDrawPro

Processor

1 When a function begins to execute, the application sends to the stack the values it wants the function to act upon.

Stack

Multiply A x B

4 x 5 = 20, put down 0, carry 2
4 x 1 = 4, add carried 2 = 6
combine 6 & 0

SuperWordDrawPro

Processor

2 When the application calls a software routine, the stack expands toward low-memory addresses to hold the intermediate results and parameters of the calculations performed by the processor.

Stack

Multiply A x B

= 60

SuperWordDrawPro

Processor

3 When the execution of the procedure is complete, the stack shrinks to an area a little larger than its starting size. The extra space contains the result of the calculation. The stack area of the application memory partition expands and contracts on a last-in-first-out basis, always remaining contiguous and never becoming fragmented.

Application Heap

1 When an application no longer requires a certain piece of information, such as a routine or piece of data, the Memory Manager releases the space occupied by the information. This is often in the middle of the heap.

2 When an application needs a resource, code segment, or data from a file, the information is loaded at the top end of the heap. If the heap grows to the heap limit, the Mac displays a message telling you that there is not enough memory to complete the action.

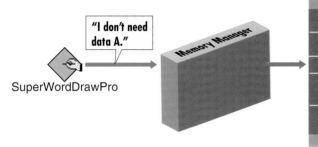

"I don't need data A."

Memory Manager

SuperWordDrawPro

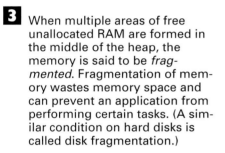

New data

Data A

3 When multiple areas of free unallocated RAM are formed in the middle of the heap, the memory is said to be *fragmented*. Fragmentation of memory wastes memory space and can prevent an application from performing certain tasks. (A similar condition on hard disks is called disk fragmentation.)

4 When fragmentation reaches a certain level, the Memory Manager *compacts* the heap by moving blocks of information into the empty spaces.

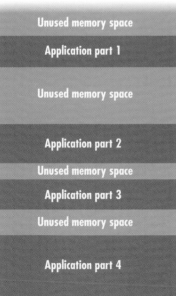

Unused memory space

Application part 1

Unused memory space

Application part 2

Unused memory space

Application part 3

Unused memory space

Application part 4

Unused memory space

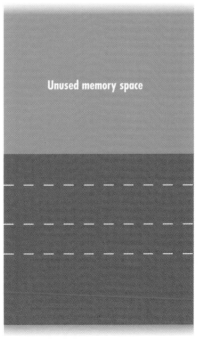

Unused memory space

MAC FACT

Most crashes on the Macintosh originate in RAM. Crashes will eliminate information in RAM, but don't harm the Mac hardware or data on the hard disk. If the stack grows into the space used by the heap, the heap can become corrupted, crashing the application. Applications can also crash if you've set the partition size too low. System crashes can occur when two programs think they each control the same segment of memory.

Protected Memory in Mac OS X

6 Applications and operating system processes can spin off tasks (such as graphics renderings or audio processing) into their own protected memory space.

3 Instead of filling up memory partitions, Mac OS X keeps a small fraction of an application in RAM, getting what it needs from the hard disk. It can keep adding more and more memory spaces. Adding RAM increases performance by requiring less hard disk access.

Hard disk

1 Instead of the one big, cooperative memory block of Mac OS 9.x and earlier, Mac OS X isolates memory partitions for applications or processes into their own protected memory space, walled off from other spaces. Each protected memory space has one or more tasks running in it.

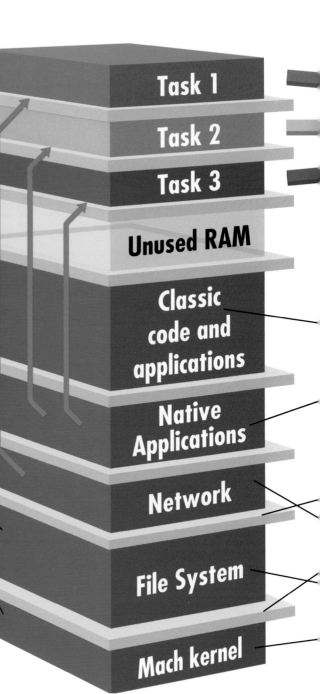

Task 1

Task 2

Task 3

Unused RAM

Classic code and applications

Native Applications

Network

File System

Mach kernel

7 In the cooperative multitasking of Mac OS 9, a task could voluntarily suspend itself to give processor time to other tasks. With pre-emptive multitasking, the operating system divides processor time among many tasks, enabling them to execute nearly simultaneously. Some processes can have a higher priority and get more processor time, but it is the OS that determines this, not the tasks themselves.

Pre-emptive tasking

Processor

8 The OS keeps a tight schedule for the processor, filling every tiny slice of empty time with instructions and data. In Mac OS 9 and earlier, small but numerous periods of time exist when the processor waits for information. This is one reason why Mac OS X is a faster operating system than previous versions.

5 The Classic environment, running the OS 9 interface and older applications, all runs in a single memory space—just like it does in Mac OS 9 and earlier. If something crashes here, the whole Classic environment crashes.

2 There is no negotiation for memory addresses, as there is in previous versions of Mac OS. Mac OS X protects each memory space from the others. If something inside one memory space crashes, it won't affect the other processes running in the other memory spaces, and it won't crash the whole Mac. Instead of restarting the computer, you just restart the task in that memory space.

4 The kernel, file system, and other important operating system functions are each isolated in their own protected memory space.

C H A P T E R

10

How Virtual Memory Works

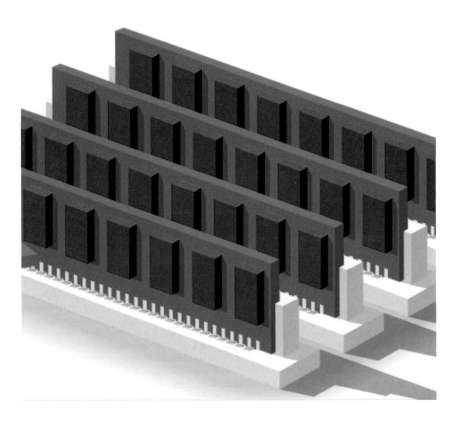

EVER need to open just one more application, but find you're short of RAM? This is when *virtual memory* comes in handy. A feature of Mac OS since System 7, virtual memory enables you to open more applications than you actually have room for in RAM. Virtual memory uses space on a hard disk as an annex to the main RAM to store information that hasn't been used recently by the processor. The processor treats virtual memory disk space as RAM.

In Mac OS 9, virtual memory is turned on by default. You can shut it off or change the amount of disk space used for virtual memory in the Memory control panel. With virtual memory turned on, the Mac acts as if you had added more RAM.

In Mac OS X, virtual memory is always on. No Memory control panel exists, and there is nothing to set. Virtual memory is an integral part of Mac OS X—much less of the software code is loaded into real RAM. Virtual memory in OS X is also faster and more efficient than in previous versions of Mac OS, and no need ever exists to turn it off (which is fortunate, because you can't).

In Mac OS 9.x and earlier, virtual memory can slow down the Mac's operation a little when running some applications. That's because access to a hard disk is slower than access to RAM, and the virtual memory management isn't as intelligent as in Mac OS X. Therefore, with OS 9 and earlier, you should use virtual memory according to some guidelines. First, set the amount of virtual memory for what you need, and not any more. Optimally, the currently active application should fit in real RAM.

In addition to being a feature of operating systems, the capability to use virtual memory is hardwired into processors, as you saw in Chapter 8, "How the Processor Works." The operating system code responsible for virtual memory controls part of the processor called the *memory management unit (MMU)*. The MMU in processors has improved greatly over the years. In fact, the first Macs, such as the Mac SE, Mac Classic, and PowerBook 100, could not use virtual memory because the 68000 processor had no MMU. In Macs with the 68020 processor, the MMU was a separate chip, the 68851. The 68030 and 68040 processors were the first to include built-in MMUs in Macs. Still, virtual memory was very slow in these old Macs, and most people kept it turned off. Mac virtual memory finally became practical with the introduction of the PowerPC processor.

The following pages describe virtual memory more specifically in Mac OS 9 and earlier. As you saw in the last chapter, virtual memory works somewhat differently in Mac OS X. However, the basic concept of swapping information between RAM and hard disk is the same for both operating systems.

An Application Using Virtual Memory

When you turn on virtual memory in the Memory control panel of Mac OS 9 and earlier and restart the Mac, the Virtual Memory Manager reserves a part of the hard disk as a virtual memory space. This space is not available for file storage, and you can't access information in this space.

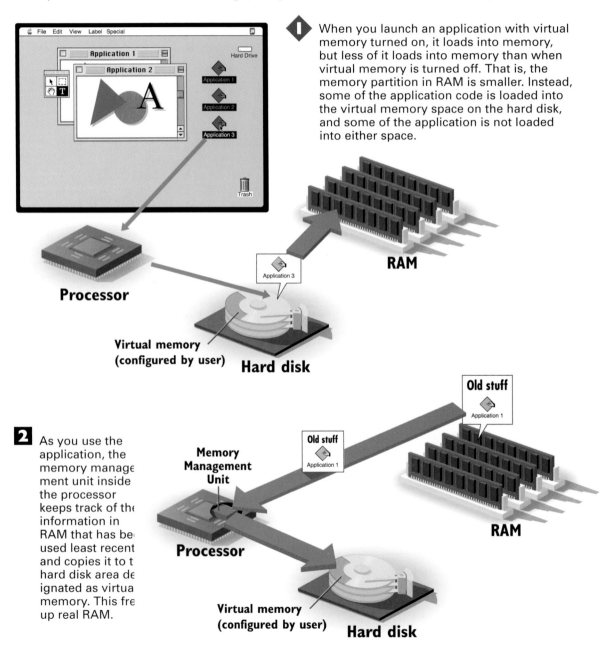

1 When you launch an application with virtual memory turned on, it loads into memory, but less of it loads into memory than when virtual memory is turned off. That is, the memory partition in RAM is smaller. Instead, some of the application code is loaded into the virtual memory space on the hard disk, and some of the application is not loaded into either space.

RAM

Processor

Virtual memory (configured by user)   **Hard disk**

2 As you use the application, the memory management unit inside the processor keeps track of the information in RAM that has been used least recently and copies it to the hard disk area designated as virtual memory. This frees up real RAM.

Old stuff

Memory Management Unit

Old stuff

RAM

Processor

Virtual memory (configured by user)   **Hard disk**

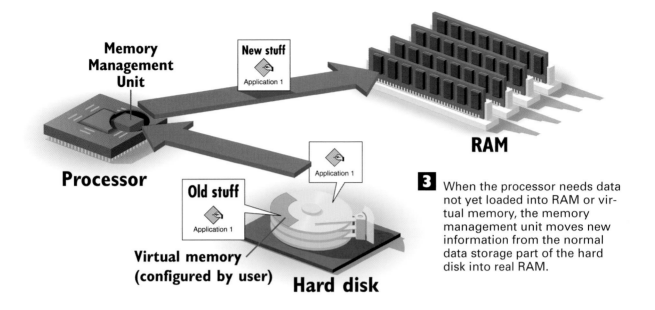

3 When the processor needs data not yet loaded into RAM or virtual memory, the memory management unit moves new information from the normal data storage part of the hard disk into real RAM.

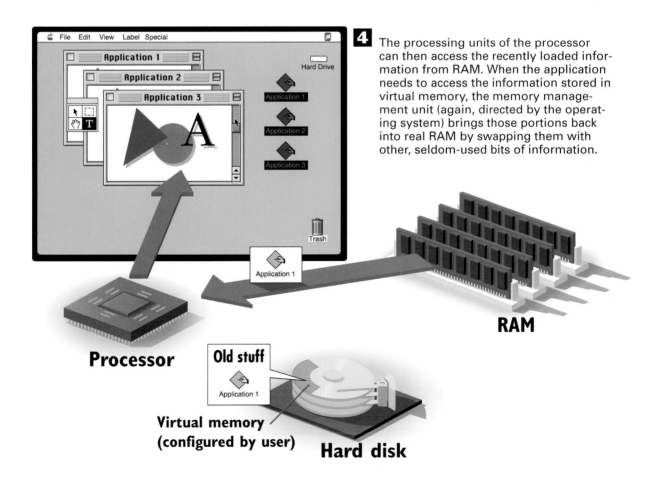

4 The processing units of the processor can then access the recently loaded information from RAM. When the application needs to access the information stored in virtual memory, the memory management unit (again, directed by the operating system) brings those portions back into real RAM by swapping them with other, seldom-used bits of information.

CHAPTER

11

How a Cache Works

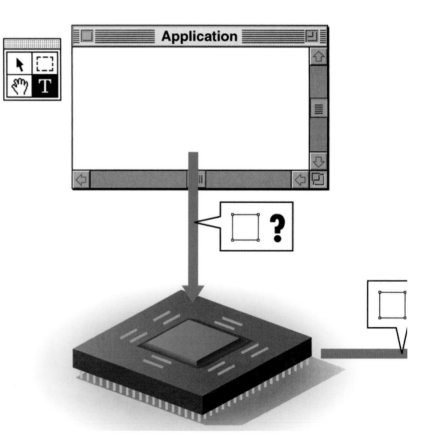

INFORMATION often moves from the hard drive to RAM and then to the processor. Yet, because the processor is faster than RAM, and RAM is faster than the hard drive, you might think the faster parts would have to wait around a lot for the slower media to feed them data. This would be the case were it not for *caching*. A cache is a temporary storage location that sits between a faster medium and a slower one. The purpose of a cache is to feed information as fast as it's requested.

Caches are used all over the Mac, with the processor, RAM, hard drive, CD-ROM drive, and even with your Web browser. We'll look at the two most import caches, the RAM cache and the disk cache. As the names imply, a *RAM* cache speeds up RAM access, and a *disk* cache speeds up disk access.

We've already mentioned RAM cache in Chapter 8, "How the Processor Works," under the name L2 cache (short for level 2 cache). (The name comes from the fact that a cache is also inside the microprocessor itself and is called the level 1 cache.) On Macs with a G3 or G4 processor, the RAM cache is also called a *backside* cache because of its high-speed connection to the processor. On older Macs, the level-2 RAM cache was not backside, but was located on the motherboard. This wasn't as fast as backside cache, but it still speeded Mac operation by 15–60 percent.

The reason caching works is that the cache medium is faster than the medium from which it is caching. A RAM cache is often made of high-speed static RAM, which is at least four times faster than the dynamic RAM used in main memory. Therefore, it is faster for the processor to get information from the cache than from RAM.

A disk cache uses a piece of the Mac's RAM to temporarily hold information from a disk storage device. Performance is improved because it is faster to access information from dynamic RAM than from a hard disk. Disk caching is built into the Mac's system software. (System 6 erroneously labeled it a RAM cache, which caused a lot of confusion. Apple corrected this in System 7.) You can set the size of the cache you want to use in the Memory control panel, but you can't shut it off. The optimal disk cache setting varies with the type of application you use, but Apple recommends 32K of disk cache for every megabyte of RAM installed.

Your Web browser's cache works the same way, using a faster media to temporarily store information. In this case, the cache is a folder on your hard disk and the slow media is the Internet. When you access a Web page, the graphics for that page are temporarily copied to the cache folder. If you access the page again soon, it is faster for the browser to get the graphics from this folder on your hard drive than out to the Internet again.

A RAM Cache

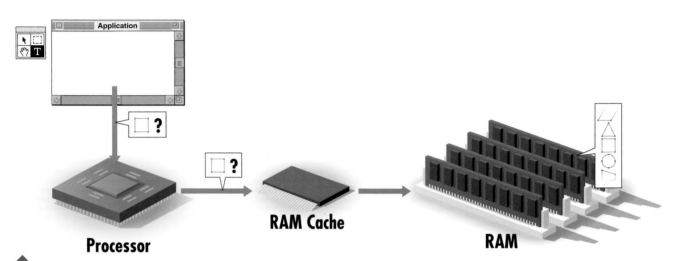

Processor   **RAM Cache**   **RAM**

1 When an application requests a piece of information (program code, file data, a resource, or anything else stored in RAM), the processor sends a query to RAM. The RAM cache intercepts the request and searches itself for the information. If it does not have the requested information, it passes the query along to RAM.

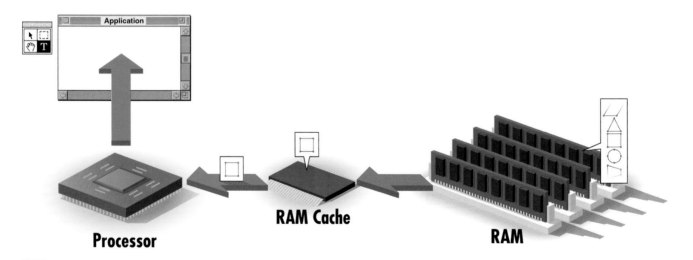

Processor   **RAM Cache**   **RAM**

2 RAM passes a copy of the information to the processor, but it is first intercepted by the cache. The cache makes and keeps a copy, and passes a copy to the processor.

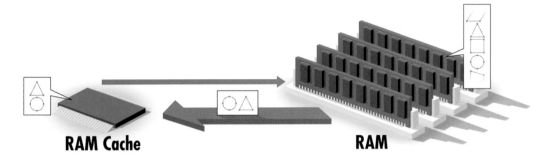

RAM Cache   **RAM**

3 The processor often requires pieces of information that are grouped together in RAM within a short period of time. When the processor is not being used, the RAM cache fetches information from the RAM addresses near the addresses of the information last requested by the processor.

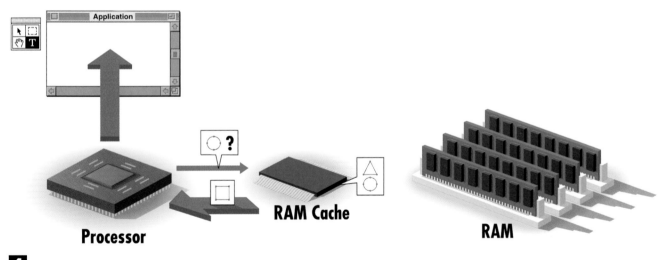

Processor   **RAM Cache**   **RAM**

4 When the application requires another piece of information, the processor sends out another query, which once again is intercepted by the cache. This time, the cache has the requested information and sends it along without having to access RAM.

A Disk Cache

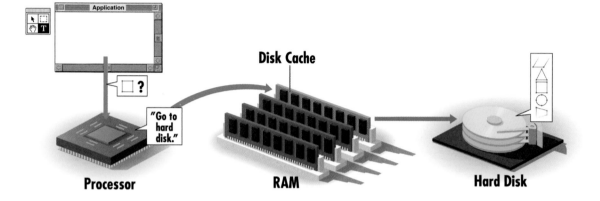

Mac OS sets aside 1/32 of the system RAM to be used as a disk cache. (The user can change this amount.) This space is not available to be used as main memory. When an application makes a request for information residing on a hard disk, the disk cache intercepts the request and searches itself for the information. If it does not have the requested information, it passes the query along to the disk.

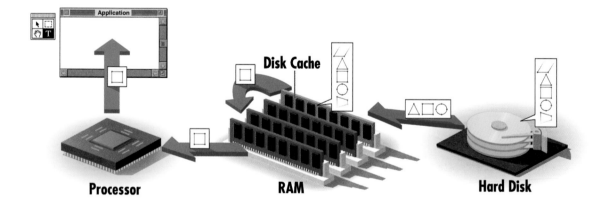

2 The disk cache reads the requested information from the disk, along with information residing in nearby addresses. The disk cache stores the fetched information in its portion of RAM and copies the requested information into main memory, where it is retrieved by the processor.

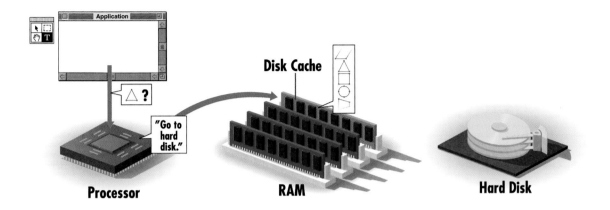

3 When the application requires another piece of information, the processor sends out another query, which once again is intercepted by the cache.

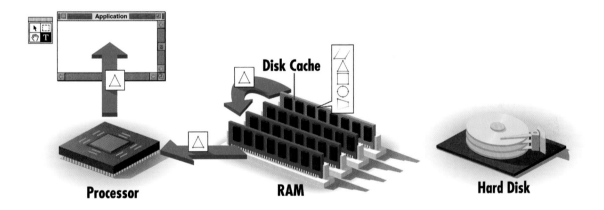

4 If the disk cache has the requested information, it does not forward the request to the disk. Instead, the disk cache copies the information into main memory, where it is retrieved by the processor.

MAC FACT

The use of RAM as disk cache shows up as part of the Mac OS memory (as seen in the About this Computer window of the Apple menu). If Mac OS is using 32MB of RAM, 2MB of that is the disk cache if your Mac has 64MB RAM in it.

CHAPTER

12

How a RAM Disk Works

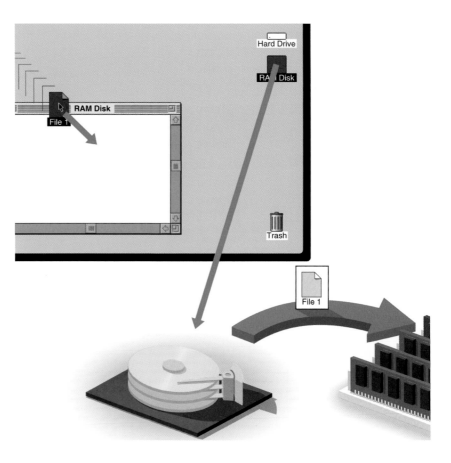

A RAM *disk*, sometimes called a *virtual disk*, is the flip side of virtual memory. Whereas virtual memory takes away a part of a disk and uses it as RAM, a RAM disk takes away part of RAM and uses it as a bootable, desktop-mountable disk. To the user, a RAM disk looks and acts like an ordinary disk drive; you can mount it on the desktop and drag files to and from it. A RAM disk gives you the speed of RAM with the easy accessibility of a disk drive. You can create a RAM disk in the Memory control panel.

One way to get an idea of the comparative performance of RAM disks and disk drives is to consider *seek time*, which is the time it takes the storage device to locate a piece of data within it. For moderately fast hard disk drives, the seek time is usually in the 10-millisecond range. Because RAM has no moving parts, a RAM disk's seek time is almost zero. The lack of moving parts also means that a RAM disk uses far less power than a hard disk, making it a great way to add hours of battery life to PowerBooks and iBooks.

The principle behind the RAM disk is similar to that of a disk cache (discussed in Chapter 11, "How a Cache Works") in that both use part of the system RAM. However, a user can't access a disk cache directly, as one can with a RAM disk. The data stored in a RAM disk is not as temporary as data in a cache, which starts erasing old data as soon as it fills up. However, RAM disk data is not as permanent as disk drive data, because a RAM disk loses everything stored within it when the computer's power is shut off.

To get around this problem, the Memory control box has a check box called Save on Shutdown. When you check this, Mac OS automatically copies the contents of a RAM disk to the hard drive when you shut down. When you start up, the Mac copies everything back to the hard disk, as if it were there all the time.

A restart of your Mac will not erase the contents of a RAM disk. That's because the power remains on when you restart. The same is true when your Mac goes into sleep mode. Power continues to supply the RAM disk even though it turns off the hard drive and display. However, a system crash will erase the RAM disk, so it is vital that you copy the files on the RAM disk to your hard disk before you put a Mac to sleep.

RAM Disk

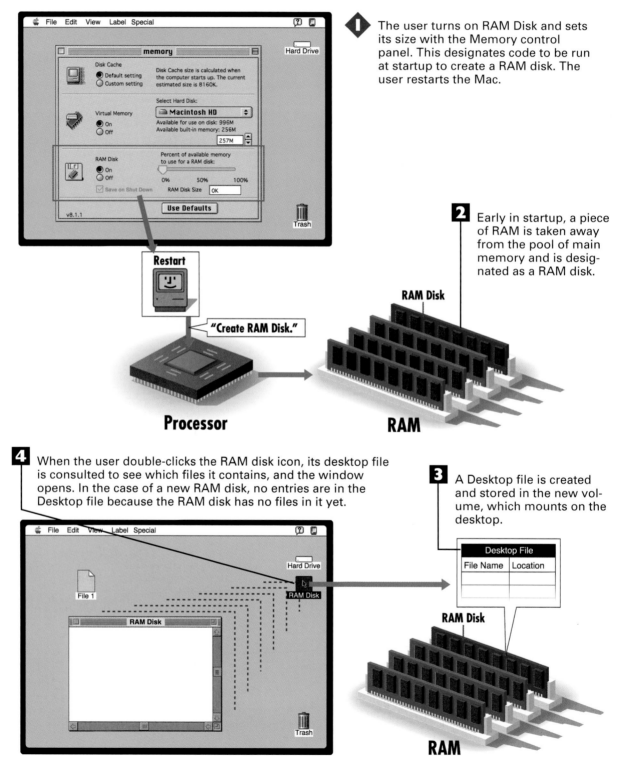

1 The user turns on RAM Disk and sets its size with the Memory control panel. This designates code to be run at startup to create a RAM disk. The user restarts the Mac.

2 Early in startup, a piece of RAM is taken away from the pool of main memory and is designated as a RAM disk.

4 When the user double-clicks the RAM disk icon, its desktop file is consulted to see which files it contains, and the window opens. In the case of a new RAM disk, no entries are in the Desktop file because the RAM disk has no files in it yet.

3 A Desktop file is created and stored in the new volume, which mounts on the desktop.

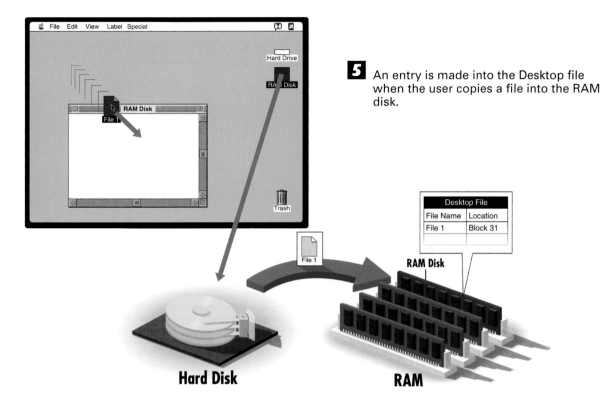

5 An entry is made into the Desktop file when the user copies a file into the RAM disk.

Desktop File	
File Name	Location
File 1	Block 31

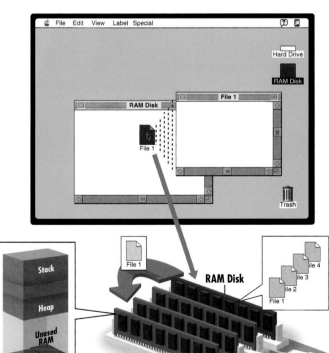

6 Double-clicking a file in a RAM disk loads the file from the RAM disk portion into real RAM. The RAM disk stores the file as a document, just as disk drives do, rather than in the stack/heap format of an application's partition in main memory.

MAC FACT

To get the most out of a RAM disk, keep a copy of the application you use most on the RAM disk and work from it. If you have a lot of RAM to spare, you also can create a slimmed-down System folder on the RAM and make it the startup disk. Because the System folder contains resources used by applications, putting a System folder on the RAM disk prevents the applications from accessing the hard disk. This improves overall performance and increases the battery life of PowerBooks and iBooks.

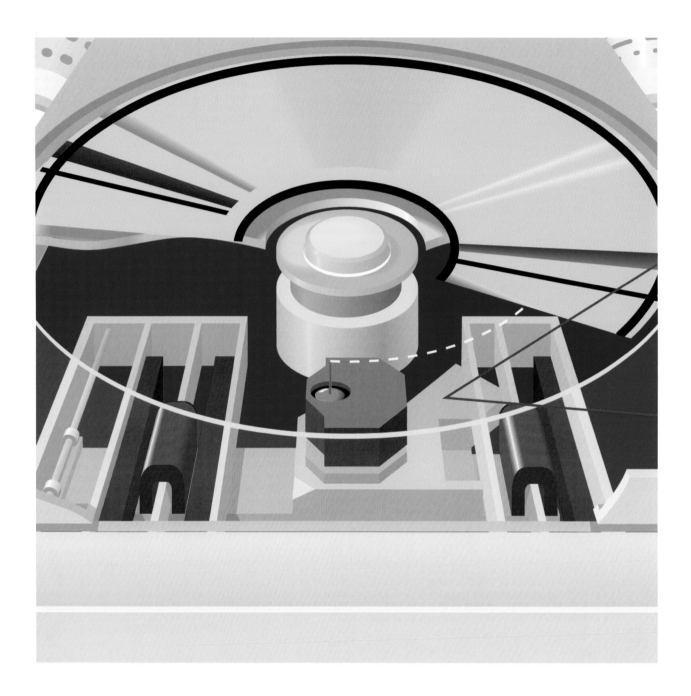

P A R T

DISK STORAGE

Chapter 13: How a Floppy-Disk Drive Works
86

Chapter 14: How a Hard-Disk Drive Works
90

Chapter 15: How Optical and Zip Storage Works
96

FOR long-term memory, the Mac uses the spinning disks inside disk drives, which save data even after the power goes off and the disks stop spinning. These include the hard disks; Zip cartridges; CD-ROMs and DVDs; and other types of disks that you use to store your software, work, and entertainment.

Disk drives come in a variety of capacities, sizes, speeds, and purposes. Some types of disks offer speed, whereas others offer storage that will last a long time. You can remove some disks (such as CD-ROMs and Zip cartridges) from their drives for easy transporting. The disks in hard drives are sealed inside an airtight enclosure. Therefore, trying to get to them will ruin the drive and void the warranty.

Hard disk drives are the workhorses of mass storage. They are the fastest type of long-term storage media, delivering information to RAM faster than other types of disks. This is why they are the main place you keep your data, applications, and system software. Using multiple platters, hard disks are also some of the largest-capacity storage devices available. Even 3 1/2-inch drives can hold several dozen gigabytes.

Although every personal computer today has one or more hard-disk drives, the original Mac did not have any—the System folder and applications of 1984 could fit on a single 400K floppy disk. Today, a typical control panel file can be bigger than the first Mac's startup disk. Floppy disk drives are no longer included in Macs because even 1.44MB disks just don't hold that much data. You can connect external floppy drives to a Mac's USB port for compatibility with PCs, which still have floppy drives. Some floppy drives, such as the iMation SuperDisk, also can use disks that hold more data than floppies.

For distributing software, CD-ROM discs have long replaced floppy disks. These discs can hold 650MB, the equivalent of hundreds of floppy disks. Some Macs have a DVD drive that can read both CD and DVD discs. The capacity of a DVD—up to 5.2 *gigabytes*—makes it possible to distribute storage-intensive forms of data, such as video and sound.

CD-ROM/DVD drives are fundamentally different from hard drives, floppy drives, and Zip drives in the way they store information. Hard disks, floppies, and Zip cartridges are made of magnetic media; the drives use electromagnets to read and write the 1s and 0s that make up the data. CD-ROM and DVD drives are optical in nature, using laser light to read data from the disc. Optical media is immune to the effects of stray magnetic fields, which can corrupt or erase data on magnetic media. This makes optical media a more permanent type of storage than magnetic media.

In fact, CD-ROM is a read-only media; you can't copy anything to it or erase anything from it. DVD-ROM drives are also read-only. The *ROM* in both stands for *read-only memory*. (DVD movie discs are DVD-ROM discs.) However, some Power Macs have DVD-RAM drives, which let you write data. These erasable optical discs come in the form of a cartridge rather than a naked disc like the CD-ROM and DVD-ROM. You also can buy external CD-W and CD-RW drives, which also enable you to copy data to the discs.

If your Mac doesn't have a Zip drive, you can buy an external drive. Other magnetic removable cartridges are available as well, such as Jaz and SuperDisk. Data written on magnetic removable cartridges is more vulnerable than data on optical cartridges, and magnetic cartridges don't have the large capacities of some DVD cartridges. Zip and Jaz drives are less expensive than DVD drives, but the cartridges cost quit a bit more per megabyte than those for DVD or CD-RW.

This optical storage is better suited for the storage of large amounts of data and for archiving data for long periods of time. Generally, people use removable magnetic cartridges for the short-term moving of files or for moving data between machines.

Regardless of their differences, all disk drives behave similarly when connected to a Mac. Each disk appears on the Finder's desktop as on icon called a *volume*. With any disk, whether hard drive, Zip, CD, or DVD, you can use the Finder to view files and folders located on a disk. You also copy files to and from a writable disk using the same drag-and-drop technique.

A process called *formatting* arranges the data on all disks in a manner that the Mac OS File Manager can understand. Most disks for the Macintosh come preformatted from the manufacturer according to a standard called the *extended hierarchical file system (HFS Plus)*. CD-ROM and DVD discs also can be formatted with their own special formats. The File Exchange control panel enables the Finder and File Manager to recognize and mount disks that use PC formats, as well.

Drives connect to the Mac motherboard in several different ways. Most hard drives and other internal optical drives in Macs use the IDE/ATA interface (Integrated Drive Electronics/ Advanced Technology Attachment). Power Macs have the option of using SCSI (small computer system interface hardware, pronounced "scuzzy") with an add-in card. SCSI enables you to connect seven disk drives to your Mac by simply daisy-chaining one to the other with cabling. SCSI is also a little faster than IDE/ATA. Power Macs, some iMacs, and recent PowerBooks also enable you to connect hard drives to FireWire, another fast port. You can plug slower external drives, such as Zip, CD-RW, and floppy drives, into a Mac's USB port.

CHAPTER

13

How a Floppy-Disk Drive Works

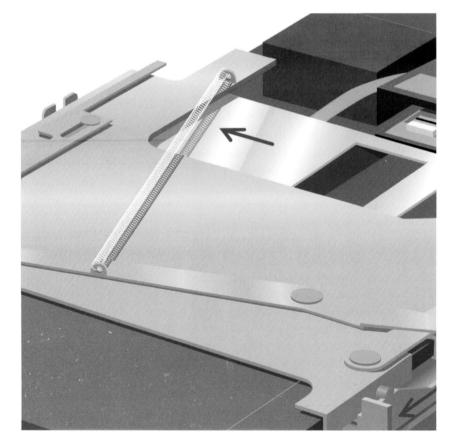

THE lowly floppy disk (known more demurely as a *diskette*), appears to be neither floppy nor disk-shaped. However, if you break open the 3 1/2-inch stiff plastic case, you'll find a thin, flexible, plastic disk that is indeed floppy.

Floppy disks are historical storage devices to many of us because Macs no longer come with one. The iMac was the first Mac to abandon the floppy. But as soon as the iMac shipped, companies began selling external floppy drives to plug into it. It seems that people found a use for the old workhorse.

In the original Macintosh, the floppy-disk drive was the only storage device available. Some of the early Mac models even had two internal floppy drives, and some had a special external floppy port to connect an additional floppy disk drive. Those first Macs used a floppy that was single-sided and held 400KB. Apple replaced the 400KB disk drive in the Mac 512KE with a drive that reads a double-sided, 800KB disk. During the middle of the Mac SE's production run, this was replaced by the double-sided, double-density disk, which holds 1.44MB. Today's external USB floppy drives can read only 1.44MB floppies, which PCs still use as well.

Floppy disks were never known for their speed. They spin as fast as 360 revolutions per minute, which is 1/20 the rate (or less) at which hard disks spin. Floppy-disk drives connect to a Mac through the USB port, the slowest port in today's Macs. Older Macs with built-in floppy drives used a very slow serial connection to communicate with the logic board.

Mechanically, however, floppy-disk drives are quite sophisticated. Their internal process for inserting and ejecting floppies resembles the operation of a Rube Goldberg device: a gear moves a lever, which fits into a slot, which releases a spring-loaded pin, which slides a sled, and so on. These machinations support the Mac's automatic ejection feature, which shoots the disk out at you when you drag the floppy icon to the Trash. Of course, nothing works perfectly all the time, so the drive also supports a manual method of ejecting a floppy. Experienced Mac users will recognize this procedure as the paper-clip trick: Insert the end of a paper clip into the small hole at the right side of the floppy-disk drive, and the disk pops out. It's low-tech, but effective.

Mac Floppy-Disk Drive

1 When a floppy disk is inserted correctly, the diagonally cut corner (not shown) on the disk case moves aside a pin on a lever, letting the disk pass farther into the drive. If the disk is inserted backward or upside down, the pin will hit the straight edge of the disk and prevent it from entering the drive.

2 When the disk is almost inside the drive, the edge of the disk's shutter door hits a pin attached to a spring-loaded lever. As the disk moves farther in, the lever pivots clockwise, pushing the pin to open the disk's metal shutter and exposing the thin, flexible disk inside.

3 This same pivoting lever moves another pin that holds the lower sled in place. With the pin moved, springs move the lower sled toward the front of the drive, causing the spring-loaded upper sled to fall. This moves the floppy below the level of the insertion slot.

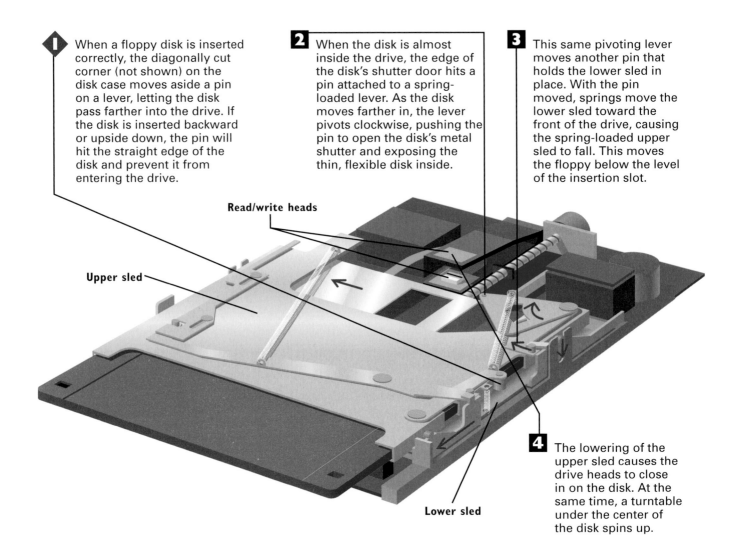

Read/write heads

Upper sled

Lower sled

4 The lowering of the upper sled causes the drive heads to close in on the disk. At the same time, a turntable under the center of the disk spins up.

MAC FACT

The Macintosh was the first computer to feature 3 1/2-inch drives. Before the Mac, the vast majority of personal computers used flexible 5 1/4-inch floppies, which are not as convenient or sturdy.

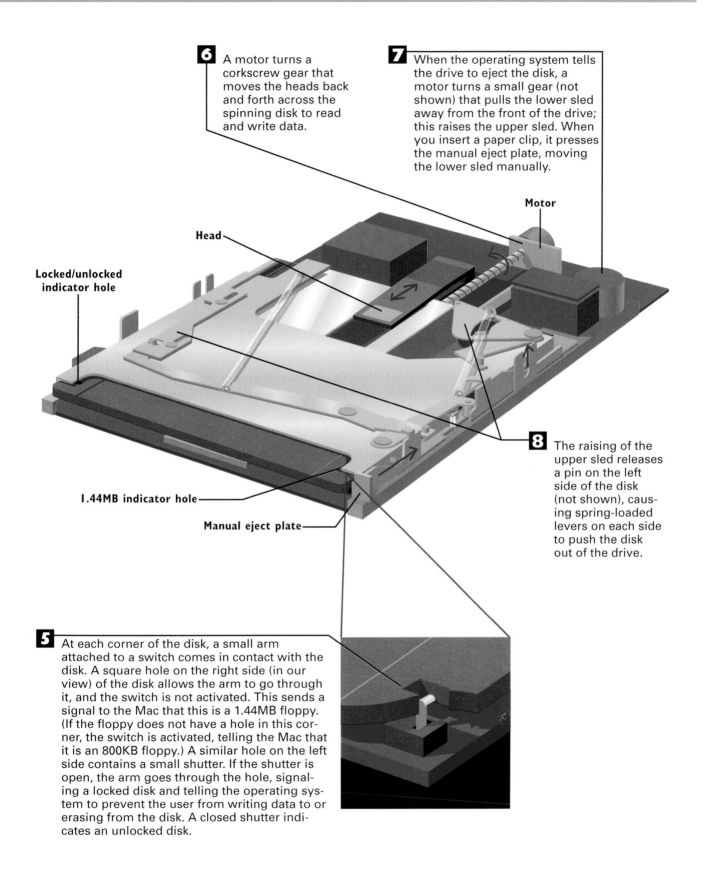

6 A motor turns a corkscrew gear that moves the heads back and forth across the spinning disk to read and write data.

7 When the operating system tells the drive to eject the disk, a motor turns a small gear (not shown) that pulls the lower sled away from the front of the drive; this raises the upper sled. When you insert a paper clip, it presses the manual eject plate, moving the lower sled manually.

Motor

Head

Locked/unlocked indicator hole

8 The raising of the upper sled releases a pin on the left side of the disk (not shown), causing spring-loaded levers on each side to push the disk out of the drive.

1.44MB indicator hole

Manual eject plate

5 At each corner of the disk, a small arm attached to a switch comes in contact with the disk. A square hole on the right side (in our view) of the disk allows the arm to go through it, and the switch is not activated. This sends a signal to the Mac that this is a 1.44MB floppy. (If the floppy does not have a hole in this corner, the switch is activated, telling the Mac that it is an 800KB floppy.) A similar hole on the left side contains a small shutter. If the shutter is open, the arm goes through the hole, signaling a locked disk and telling the operating system to prevent the user from writing data to or erasing from the disk. A closed shutter indicates an unlocked disk.

CHAPTER

14

How a Hard-Disk Drive Works

EVERY computer user depends on a *hard-disk drive* to hold and retrieve software and data files. A high-precision machine, the hard-disk drive is the fastest mechanical storage device available, second only to RAM (which is not mechanical), but far less expensive per megabyte of storage.

Inside a humming hard-disk drive are several spinning rigid aluminum platters, coated on both sides with a magnetic material containing particles of oxides of iron or metals. The 0s and 1s of binary information are written by magnetizing areas on the disks' surfaces, similar to the way information is recorded on audio- and videotape.

The disks spin together at a constant rate of about 7,200 revolutions per minute (rpm), although this rate increases with each new generation of drive technology. Moving rapidly back and forth over the surface of the disks are tiny electromagnets called *heads*, which read and write data. The precision movement of the heads can locate a spot on the disks, which pass under the head at 75 miles per hour. (This is for a 3 1/2-inch disk spinning at 7,200rpm.)

Similar to a car crash at these speeds, a *head crash* is very destructive. A head crash occurs when a head plows into a platter. This can occur when a platter wobbles due to old age or from a jolt to the drive. This is one reason not to drop an iBook while it's turned on.

The distance between head and platter is only a matter of several dozen microns (millionths of a meter). At this scale, a speck of dust is a huge boulder that can carve a trench in the disk media, ruining swaths of data. To keep dust out, the platters and heads are permanently encased in an airtight metal case, which also conducts heat away from the disks.

The platter-and-head assembly is attached to a circuit board containing the drive's controlling electronics, which together are referred to as the *hard-disk mechanism*. The mechanism can be placed directly inside the Mac or in an external case along with a power supply and sometimes a fan.

Before any data can be written, the drive must be *formatted*. This is usually done before you buy the drive, but you can reformat a drive with Apple's Drive Setup utility or with other software. Formatting sets up a sort of organizational grid on the disks that will hold the data. Formatting also creates information on the disk that is loaded into RAM at startup. This information helps the Mac locate files stored on the drive's grid.

The Macintosh formatting standard for magnetic storage such as Zip, Jaz, and hard drives is called the *Hierarchical File System (HFS)*. Today's Macs come with drives formatted with an improved version called HFS Plus (also called HFS Extended). HFS Plus is more efficient than the original HFS, in that it puts more of the disk space to actual use, especially on large drives.

Hard-Disk Drive Formatting

Physical and Logical Formatting

HFS formatted disk

1 *Physical formatting* creates concentric rings called *tracks* on each platter, similar to the individual songs on a vinyl phonograph record but much thinner. Hard-disk platters can contain 600 tracks per inch or more. Tracks are divided into *sectors*. All sectors on a disk contain the same amount of data, usually 512 bytes of data each.

2 *Logical formatting* creates *blocks*. A block is the smallest amount of data transferred at one time by the drive. A block is usually several sectors, but never a fraction of a sector.

Wasted disk space

File

3 Sectors that contain defective media are not assigned to blocks and are ignored by the drive.

4 The size of a block is larger on bigger disk drives. Unfortunately, the bigger blocks waste more disk space. This is because two files can't occupy one block; any block space left over at the end of a file is wasted. For instance, a 3.5K file that occupies four 1K blocks takes up 4K of disk space, wasting 0.5K. On a bigger drive, the same 3.5K file might require three 1.5K blocks (for a total of 4.5K of disk space), wasting 1K of disk space.

HFS Plus formatted disk

5 HFS Plus raises the maximum number of blocks from 65,536 (16-bit) to 4,294,967,296 (32-bit), which enables you to have a much smaller block size. For instance, on a 4GB volume, HFS uses a 64K block, while HFS Plus uses a 4K block. This can save quite a bit of disk space on volumes with a large number of small files.

Partitions

6 Most formatting software can create *partitions*, which are sections of a disk drive that act as separate Mac volumes. A disk partitioned into three volumes will appear as three hard-disk icons on the Finder's desktop.

Wasted disk space

1GB partition

3GB partition

6GB partition

Files

7 As with drives, bigger partitions yield bigger block sizes. Smaller partitions (which use smaller blocks) tend to be more efficient than larger partitions, for the same reasons described in step 4.

8 Accessing a file on a partitioned drive is faster than on a unpartitioned drive. This is because the drive searches only the partition, not the entire drive, so it has fewer blocks to search through.

Invisible Disk Data

9 Several small, invisible partitions contain software and information about the drive. Invisible data exists on your visible partitions, as well. This all loads into RAM to tell the Mac where to find files. These areas take up disk space, which is why a formatted disk with no files on it doesn't have its full capacity available to the user.

10 One invisible partition contains the *driver* software, which communicates between the drive and Mac OS. Another invisible partition contains the *partition map*, which keeps track of where all the partitions begin and end.

11 The *boot blocks*, always the first blocks of the user volume, contain information used during startup. The boot blocks identify the user partition as a Macintosh volume.

12 The *volume information blocks*, which follow the boot blocks, contain the name you give to your drive or partition and the number of files stored.

13 The *volume bitmap* identifies used and unused blocks.

16 The *data area* takes up most of the disk and is where you store your files.

14 The *extents directory* contains the location of blocks that are next to each other, called *contiguous* blocks. When you copy a file to the drive, the extents directory looks for contiguous blocks to which to write the file.

15 The *catalog tree* is a directory that stores the locations of files on the platters. The Mac operating system uses the catalog tree to locate files when needed.

Hard-Disk Operation

2 Drives store incoming write commands in a write cache to speed up performance. The *write cache* holds the write commands while telling the Mac's processor that the task has been completed, and it writes the data when it gets a chance. The benefit is that the processor doesn't have to wait for the actual writing to take place before sending more commands.

3 The drive's logic board sends an electric current to the head actuator motor to move the heads rapidly back and forth over the spinning platters. All the heads are connected to the same actuator, and they move in unison. The actuator is held by a spring. When the current increases, the heads move toward the center of the spinning disks. When the current decreases, the spring pulls the heads back toward the outer edge of the disks.

1 A command comes in from the IDE or SCSI bus ordering the drive to perform a task, such as writing data to the disk. The command is received by the drive's controller circuitry on the logic board, which processes the command.

4 Sector boundaries are marked by strongly magnetized lines. The heads count these boundaries to determine which sector they are currently over and to keep from wandering from correct locations.

Data

To SCSI or IDE Bus

9 Data retrieved from the disk goes into the drive cache, which saves the most recently requested information. If the Mac asks for information already in the cache, the drive sends the data without having to access the platters.

5 When the specified sector passes under a head, a current flows through the coil to produce a magnetic field, turning the head into a magnet. The head magnetizes a small area of the disk under the head, so that north poles of the magnetic particles in the area are all facing in one direction. This magnetized area represents 1 bit.

6 Reversing the direction of the current in the coil under another area on the platter reverses the magnetic field, causing the north pole of the area to face the opposite direction. An area with a north pole oriented in one direction represents a 1, and an area with a north pole oriented in the opposite direction represents a 0.

7 The volume bitmap, now in RAM, is used to locate free blocks on the disk. The extents tree looks for blocks that are next to each other to write the file. If most of the files on the disk are stored in noncontiguous blocks, the disk is said to be *fragmented*. A fragmented disk is slower because the heads must wait for the disk to spin farther between blocks when reading a file. Disk optimization software defragments a disk by moving data around so that files are contiguous.

8 Reading data is the reverse of the process described in step 7: The catalog directory loaded into RAM is used to find the blocks on the disks where the data is stored. When the heads pass over the magnetized bits, a current is produced in the coil. Current flowing in one direction is read as a 0, whereas current produced in the opposite direction is read as a 1. This technique of moving magnetic material near wire coils to produce an electric current exploits the same electromagnetic phenomena used to produce electricity in power plants.

CHAPTER

15

How Optical and Zip Storage Works

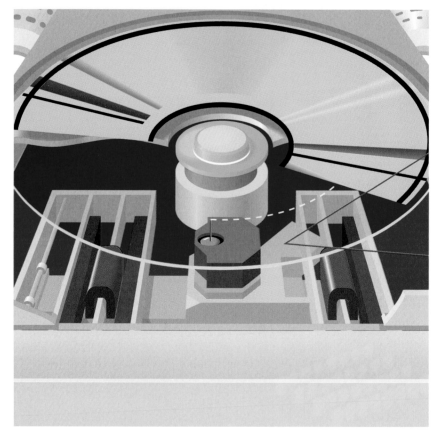

YOU *can* take it with you. Replace the hard drive's multiple platters with a single disk, put it in a removable cartridge, and you have mass storage that fits in your pocket. Magnetic removable cartridges come in several formats, holding 100MB–2GB of data. The most popular, the Zip drive, uses cartridges just slightly bigger than a floppy.

Other removable storage is not magnetic at all, but *optical*. Optical drives use a system of lenses and mirrors that guides a tiny laser beam to microscopic areas on a single rotating disc. Precise aiming of the laser enables data bits to be written more closely together than on magnetic disks, which in turn enables optical discs to hold more information than removable magnetic discs such as Zip and Jaz.

Many types of optical storage are available, but the types found in Macs all use a 120-millimeter, shiny disc. We first saw it used for CD audio; then CD-ROM, DVD-ROM, and DVD-video; and most recently for the erasable DVD-RAM. CD-ROMs can hold up to 680MB of data, or about 200,000 pages of text. Today, DVD-ROM drives have replaced CD-ROM drives in most Mac models. DVD-ROM drives can read everything that CD-ROM drives can, including audio CDs, photo CDs (which hold digital images of photographs), and CD-RW. In addition, DVD-ROM drives can also read DVD-ROM discs, which can hold up to 17GB on a double-sided disc. That's over 13 CDs on each side.

All this space is put to good use on DVD-video discs, which are DVD-ROM discs containing feature-length movies. To play the movie, the Mac must decode the MPEG-2 video and Dolby AC-3 digital sound stored on the disc. Some Macs, such as the blue and white Power Mac G3 and some PowerBooks, did this with special hardware. But today's Macs decode DVD movies purely in software.

With the Power Mac G4, Apple offers the option of DVD-RAM (digital versatile disk-random access memory). DVD-RAM drives can read everything that DVD-ROM can. In addition, you can read, write, and erase data, as you do with a hard disk or Zip cartridge. For this, you need a DVD-RAM cartridge, which contains a CD-sized disc. A double-sided DVD-RAM cartridge holds 5.2GB, which is equivalent to 52 Zip cartridges. DVD-RAM drives are slow, but the media is very economical, costing less than a tenth of a cent per megabyte and dropping all the time.

Another type of optical drive, CD-RW (CD read/write), can be found connected to the external ports of many users' Macs. These drives enable you to create (or *burn*) 650MB CD-ROM discs and audio CDs. The cost of the drive and media is fairly low, although it's a higher cost per megabyte than DVD-RAM. The main advantage of CD-RW is mass distribution—everyone has a drive that can read CD-ROMs.

CD/DVD-ROM Storage

8 The smallest pits on CD-ROM discs are 0.834 micron. DVD-ROM pits are half that size at 0.4 micron. The tracks on DVD-ROM discs are also closer together, at 0.74 micron compared to 1.6 micron on CD-ROM. This close spacing is one reason why DVD-ROM discs hold more data than CD-ROMs. Another is that DVD-ROMs can have a second layer of pits and lands on top of the first.

1 Power Macs, PowerBooks, current iMacs, and iBooks all have different DVD/CD-ROM drives. The drive shown here is the Power Mac drive, which sits behind a hinged front panel. You place a CD-ROM, DVD-ROM, or audio disc in a tray called a *sled* that you can push into the drive. More recent iMacs don't have a tray, but are *slot loading*—you insert a disk in a slot and the disk triggers a mechanism that grabs it by the edge and pulls it inside. In any Mac, data is read from the bottom side of the disc.

2 A *read head* moves on tracks back and forth under the disc and directs a beam of light from a laser diode through a series of lenses and mirrors. (In PowerBooks and the first iMacs, the read head sits in the sled itself. This is also true for iBooks, which have CD-ROM drives.) DVD drives have two lenses: one for reading CDs and one that focuses on the two layers.

MAC FACT

Similar to Mac hard drives, CD-ROM and DVD-ROM can be formatted using the Mac's HFS format. But to use a disc with both Mac OS and Windows, you need a format that both operating systems can understand. High Sierra was the first multiplatform CD-ROM standard, hammered out by manufacturers and software publishers near Lake Tahoe in California's Sierra Nevada. High Sierra was later formalized in an international standard called ISO 9660. The multiplatform standard format for DVD is Universal Disk format (UDF).

4 Data is recorded as pits pressed into the disc. The pits absorb light, while the *lands* reflect light.

0   1   0   1   0   1   1   0   0

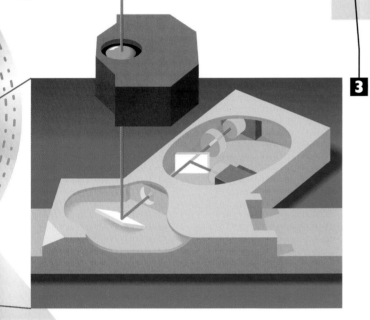

3 Light passes through a protective plastic layer on the CD and is reflected off a recording layer, usually made of aluminum. (Premium discs sometimes have a gold recording layer for longer life.)

5 The photosensitive detectors in the heads can detect the beginning or end of a pit, which represents a 1. Areas where no change in elevation occurs represent 0s.

6 Unlike hard disks, CD-ROM and DVD-ROM discs contain a single spiral track beginning near the center of the disc and ending at the outer edge. Sectors near the outside of the disc are the same length as those near the inside.

7 While hard disks spin at a constant rotational speed, the rotational speed of CD-ROM/DVD-ROM drives varies. As the head moves toward the edge of the disc, where more sectors per revolution exist, the disc rotation slows to keep constant the number of sectors passing under the head every second. This is called *constant linear velocity*.

Zip Storage

2 Similar to a floppy, the drive pushes aside the metal door on the cartridge to expose the disk. Unlike a floppy, however, this end of the cartridge is held tightly against the drive head assembly to prevent dust from entering during operation.

3 The motor grabs a hub at the center of the disk to spin it at 3,000rpm : over 8 times faster than a floppy, but still less than half the spin rate of hard drives.

4 The drive's two read-write heads extend over each side of the disk, moving back and forth to read data using a mechanism similar to that in a hard drive. At one-tenth the size of floppy heads, the Zip heads are closer in size to those of a hard drive head. This enables them to read more data per square inch than floppies.

1 Zip drives combine elements of floppy technology for low cost with hard drive technology for higher capacity storage. Inside the Zip cartridge is a flexible, plastic disk coated with a magnetic material, similar to a floppy or an iMation SuperDisk.

CD-RW

Similar to Zip storage, CD-RW (read-write) combines technologies. It mimics the disc size, layout, and data reading techniques of CD-ROM, while using the data writing and erasing technology found in DVD-RAM called *phase change*, which can rewrite data up to 100,000 times.

Instead of pits and lands, a CD-RW disc has less-reflective patches in its shiny surface. To ordinary CD-ROM drives, these only *appear* to be pits and lands.

1 When you *burn* a CD to write data, the CD-RW laser does not actually burn a pit in the disc. Instead, it changes its structure from a normally shiny, crystalline state to a less-reflective amorphous state. The data writing layer, made of antimony, indium, silver, and tellurium, melts and loses its crystalline structure when heated to 900–1300 degrees Fahrenheit by the laser.

Amorphous State

Crystalline State

2 Erasing data changes the less-reflective, amorphous state back into the shiny, crystalline state, which simulates a CD-ROM land. This is done with a lower-power laser that heats the media to only 400 degrees Fahrenheit. This energy is enough to re-create the crystal, but is not enough to melt it.

Track

Track

Track

3 To read data, a low-power laser is used. Similar to CD pits, the amorphous patch absorbs light. And similar to CD lands, the shiny crystalline areas reflect light. CD-RW uses a single spiral track, as does CD-ROM.

Laser

DVD-RAM

DVD-RAM discs are encased in a protective cartridge similar to that on a Zip disk, only bigger. Disks can be single-sided (2.6GB) or double-sided (5.2GB).

The disc is arranged into 24 annular rings called *zones*, which you can actually see with the naked eye. Each zone has 1,888 tracks where the data is written. The disc rotates at a constant speed within a recording zone, but this speed varies from zone to zone.

Zone

24 Zones

Sector

Within each zone are sectors framed by headers. You can see these headers with the naked eye as short lines. The headers contain read-only information that identify the sectors to help locate data. The innermost zone has 17 sectors per track. Each zone adds 1 sector, so that the outside zone has 40 sectors per track.

Read-only information also is in the inner ring of the disc. This contains information that identifies it as a DVD-RAM disc.

Each track alternates as a pressed groove and a raised land. This helps to guide the laser servo mechanism, keeping the heads on track.

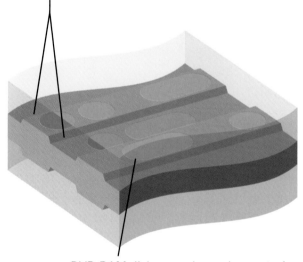

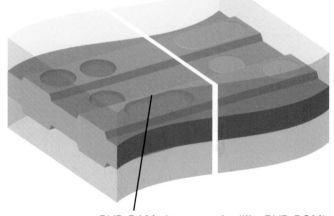

DVD-RAM disks use phase change technology to write data marks, just like CD-RW (see previous page). A 1 indicates a change between the shiny crystalline surface and dull amorphous surface. The data marks are much smaller than in CD-RW, averaging 0.42 micron in size.

DVD-RAM also uses pits (like DVD-ROM) for its read-only data in the sector header. The pits are created when the disk is manufactured.

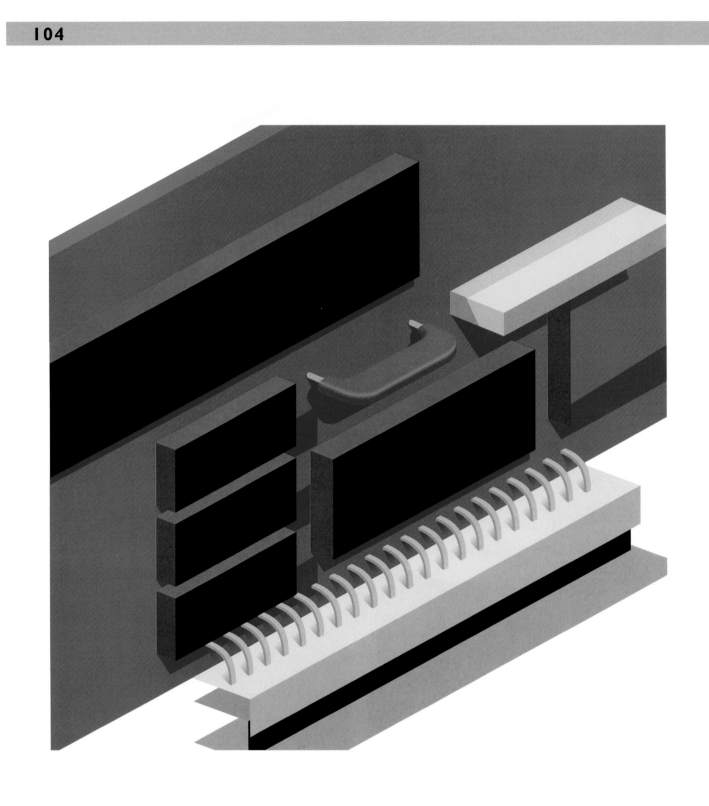

P A R T

5

GETTING INFORMATION IN AND OUT

Chapter 16: How USB Works

108

Chapter 17: How FireWire Works

112

Chapter 18: How the Keyboard, Mouse, and Trackpad Work

116

Chapter 19: How SCSI Works

122

Chapter 20: How Expansion Slots Work

126

Chapter 21: How Multimedia Works

136

CABLES are all about communication. They connect the peripheral devices that enable us to have a two-way conversation with the Mac's processor. We send commands and data through a keyboard, mouse, joystick, scanner, microphone, or video camera. The Mac sends information to use through video monitors, printers, and speakers. Moving data between the processor and these devices is known in geek speak as *input/output*, or simply *I/O*.

Other I/O devices expand the capabilities of the processor, communicating with it even when you are not. Hard-disk and optical disc drives store massive amounts of data for when the processor needs it. In addition, modems and network connectors enable your Mac to communicate with other computers. To the processor and RAM, however, it doesn't matter what type of device is doing the talking—it's all I/O to them, with bits coming in and bits going out.

The various I/O devices we can connect to the Mac plug into several different types of *ports*. A port consists of a connector and the circuitry on the logic board that sends and receives signals to and from the devices. Most ports have connectors on the outside of the Mac, but some have connectors on the inside.

One type of internal port is an *expansion slot*. Instead of plugging in a cable, you plug an expansion card into the slot to expand the capabilities of your Mac. For example, you can add an AirPort card to add any of today's Macs to add it to a wireless network. PowerBooks have PC Card Bus slots, which accept credit-card–sized expansion cards from the side of the machine. Power Macs have the most expansion capabilities, containing three full-sized peripheral component interconnect (PCI) slots. You can use these for a variety of functions, such as importing and exporting video to a camera and VCR and adding a fast SCSI card for access to the fastest hard drives. Power Macs also have an AGP slot specifically for a graphics card.

Each port and expansion slot uses a uniquely shaped connector that prevents you from plugging the wrong device into it. Not only would a device not work if it were plugged into the wrong port, but the wrong voltages going to the wrong connector pins would also harm both the peripheral device and the Mac's circuitry. Fortunately, this is very hard to do.

Most of the external ports found on Macs, including USB, FireWire, and SCSI, are *buses*. With bus ports, only one of the multiple devices can communicate with the processors at any given moment. All the devices on a bus constantly negotiate with each other or with the Mac to determine which one will do the talking. You can do two things at once—for instance, move your mouse and type on the keyboard—because each device sends data at intervals that are a fraction of a second in length.

Most of the Mac's ports move more than one signal at one time through the various pins on the connectors. Some of these lines of communication transmit electrical power to the peripheral device. Others, called *address lines*, provide timing and signaling information. *Data lines*, on the other hand, move the information with which you are working. All together, a port can move millions of signals per second across a connector.

To keep track of all the lines of communication, each port has an I/O controller chip that regulates the flow of traffic across a port. The controller chip reads the address lines to determine from which peripheral device a signal is coming from or heading to. The port circuitry also translates the various types of signals running back and forth across the connectors into a form the processor and RAM can read. Usually one part of the operating system manages this port hardware, keeping track of the devices connecting to it. Another piece of software, called a *device driver*, facilitates communication between the operating system and the devices connected to the port.

All the ports communicate with the processor and RAM through a master bus called the *system bus*, which is a data superhighway on the logic board. A set of managers in the operating system directs the traffic flowing across the system bus and in and out of the Mac. Higher-level system software can then direct the processor to properly process and display large amounts of complex data, such as multimedia movies and sound.

A key feature of all ports and expansion slots on the Mac is ease of setup. Installing a peripheral device usually involves nothing more than plugging it in and sometimes dragging files to the System folder. Usually there are no DIP switches to set or jumpers to remove. This is because each device carries information about itself. The ports and expansion slots can recognize a device, read this information, and respond appropriately. The ports and slots know which device is in which connector or slot. This means no conflicts exist between devices, which is often the case with Windows-based PCs. The design of the peripheral devices is partly responsible for the Mac's easy setup, but most of the credit goes to the design of the ports and their tight integration with I/O system software.

CHAPTER

16

How USB Works

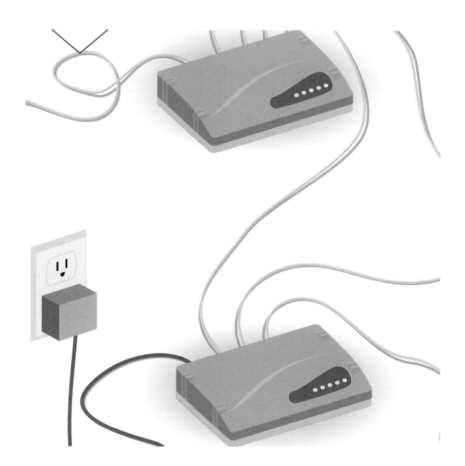

USB (Universal Serial Bus) is the Mac's *first port*—you use it every time you turn on your iMac or Power Mac from the keyboard. You also use it whenever you type or click the mouse. In addition, the *U* in USB stands for *universal* because you can plug almost anything into it: scanners, printers, digital cameras, Zip or SuperDisk drives, speakers, and Palm OS devices, among other things. USB is Mac's first port because it is the most likely port you would use to connect most types of external devices to your iMac, iBook, PowerBook, or Power Mac.

The idea of the USB began at Intel, which started the push for USB as an industry standard. However, USB didn't really catch on until Apple popularized it by putting it in the iMac and then in the other Mac models. Now, USB is in many PCs, as well as in hundreds of peripheral devices.

The basic idea of USB was to replace several special-purpose ports with a single general-purpose port. USB doesn't really care what type of data it transmits—it's all just 1s and 0s. On Macs, USB replaced several serial ports and ADB (the Apple Desktop Bus), which supplied the keyboard and mouse port on Macs for more than 10 years.

USB and ADB have some things in common. Each is a type of *bus*, a hardware and software system that enables several entities to share a common pathway to move information. In this case, the entities involved are keyboards, mice, and joysticks. Additionally, in the case of USB, cameras, scanners, and dozens of other peripherals are included. But whereas ADB enabled you to connect up to 16 devices, USB enables you to plug in 127 devices. If your Mac has 2 USB buses (as does the Power Mac G4), you can plug in up to 254 devices. Hubs enable the use of all these devices. *Hubs* are boxes that give you multiple USB ports. Some USB peripherals have hubs built into them.

The main reason that USB can use all these different types of devices (and a large number of them) is that it can move a lot more data than ADB can. USB devices can run at 1.5Mbps or 12Mbps, or both, as is the case when you are using a keyboard and camera at the same time.

USB and ADB both also supply a small amount of power over the cable. This means low-power devices, such as joysticks, can get all the power they need from the USB cable. If a USB device, such as a printer, needs more than 500mA (at 5 volts) of current, you'll have to plug it into the wall socket for AC power.

Unlike ADB, USB is *hot-pluggable*. That means you can connect or disconnect a device while the Mac is on and without having to restart because the Mac's USB circuits will recognize a device when you plug something into a USB port.

USB (Universal Serial Bus)

1 When the operating system or an application needs to communicate with a USB device, they ask the driver software (in the Extensions folder) to communicate with the USB controller. Some drivers are specific for a certain USB device, such as a printer. Apple Class drivers, which come with Mac OS, work with a variety of devices. A class driver is available for keyboards and mice and another is available for storage drives.

8 The USB controller in the Mac recognizes the change in voltage. Through the controller, the Mac OS USB Manager asks the drive for identification. The Mac OS USB Manager then assigns the device a unique USB address.

USB Controllers

KeyLargo

2 The USB controller communicates with the devices. iBook and PowerBook have a single USB controller chip. Current iMacs and Power Macs have two USB controllers inside an integrated circuit chip called KeyLargo, which also includes controller circuits for the internal hard drive and CD/DVD drive, sound hardware, and other input/output hardware. Because two USB buses exist, you can move a lot of data on one port without affecting the performance of the other port.

7 When you plug in a new USB device, it causes a change in the voltage of either the Data+ or Data- lines to announce its presence. A signal on Data+ indicates it is a high-speed device, such as a drive, and will operate at 12Mbps. A signal on Data- indicates a low-speed device, such as a keyboard, and will operate at 1.5Mbps.

6 The Mac keyboard has a built-in hub with two ports, which is why you can connect a mouse and any other USB device into it.

4 Inside the shielding are four wires. The two wires twisted together, known as Data+ and Data-, are both used for data and control signals. The two straight wires are used for power (5 volts) and ground.

10 The USB controls peripheral devices that are dependent on the controller for communications in a master/slave relationship. Only one master can exist, which is why you can't connect two Macs to one USB device, as you can in FireWire.

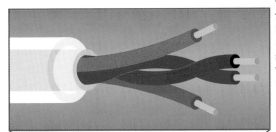

3 The Mac's clear plastic USB cables look silver. What you're seeing is shielding the USB signals from stray electromagnetic fields. This is often aluminum-coated Mylar wrapping. The Mac keyboard cable uses a tinned copper mesh for shielding.

5 A *hub* enables you to add more USB ports at any point. *Powered hubs* plug into an AC wall socket to provide power to the 5-volt line in each of the USB ports it provides. When you first plug in a hub, the hub waits for a signal from the controller before becoming active.

9 The Mac OS USB Manager keeps a list of which devices are on the bus, at what speed they operate, and what *priority* they have. The highest priority, *isochronous*, permits a continuous stream of data without interruption, as is necessary for audio speakers. Keyboards and mice have *interrupt* priority: They can send small amounts of information occasionally. The lowest priority allows interruption at any time, such as when you are copying files to a Zip disk.

CHAPTER

17

How FireWire Works

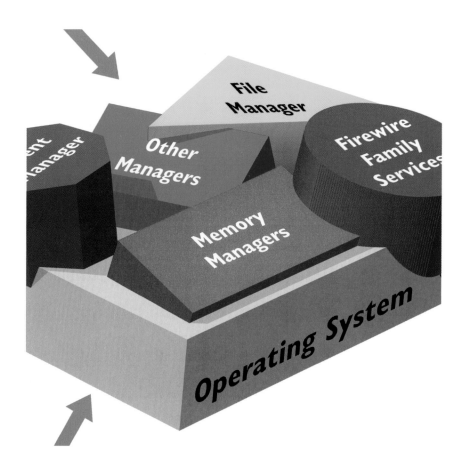

WHAT if USB were 33 times faster and enabled multiple Macs to share a device? Then you might be talking about FireWire, the high-speed port that can move 400 megabits of data every second. You use FireWire to connect your Mac to high-speed devices, including digital cameras and camcorders, hard drives, and top-end printers and scanners.

Apple invented FireWire back in 1986, but it wasn't until 1995 that it became an industry standard, known as IEEE 1394 High Performance Serial Bus. At that time, FireWire began to be used in digital camcorders, where it is very common today. Apple first put FireWire in a Mac in 1998's blue and white Power Mac G3. Today, FireWire ports are found in many iMac models, PowerBooks, and the Power Mac G4. You can add FireWire to older Macs and PowerBooks by adding a FireWire card.

Similar to USB and SCSI, FireWire is a *bus*—up to 63 devices per port share a common communications pathway. Also similar to USB, FireWire is a serial device: It sends one bit at a time. So why is FireWire so much faster than USB? For one thing, it has a more complex communications protocol than USB and an extra pair of data wires in the cables. FireWire also has a faster signaling rate than USB. The drawback, however, is that FireWire is more expensive to build into peripherals. This is why Macs have two ports, FireWire for high-speed, heavy-data devices and USB for lower-speed, inexpensive peripherals.

The increased complexity of FireWire provides other advantages over USB as well. Unlike USB, FireWire does not need to control peripheral devices in a master/slave relationship. Instead, FireWire devices communicate on a *peer-to-peer* basis and don't need to get permission from the Mac to communicate. This enables devices to communicate directly with each other. For instance, you can copy digital video from one camcorder to another, even when the Mac is turned off. The lack of a bus master also enables you to connect several Macs to one FireWire device, such as a printer, in order to share it.

FireWire also supplies more DC power to devices than USB—up to 15 watts at 10-to-24 volts, which is enough to power a hard drive. This keeps down the cost and size of FireWire hard drives because they don't need their own power supplies to plug into an AC outlet. A FireWire hard drive also can fit in your shirt pocket. Unlike SCSI drives, FireWire drives don't have ID switches or terminators, and they sport tiny 6-pin cable connectors.

FireWire also allows *daisy chaining* of devices, which enables you to add a new device simply by plugging it into a FireWire device already connected to the Mac. You can connect up to 16 devices to 1 FireWire port before you must buy a hub.

FireWire

1 Most FireWire devices have two ports. You can connect one to the Mac and the other to another FireWire device. This is called a *daisy-chain*. You also add FireWire hubs at any point to add multiple ports, as you can with USB. (You should not use any cables longer than 15 feet.)

5 The Mac doesn't have to be turned on for devices to communicate with each other. The Mac has built-in repeaters that enable FireWire devices to pass signals between the Mac and external devices. Devices with external power supplies will provide 1 watt of power to the Mac's repeater through the FireWire cable.

4 In a chain, you should put the fastest devices first. Slower devices pass data through them more slowly and create bottlenecks. In this case, the faster hard drive is connected before the slower printer.

Application

7 A part of Mac OS called *FireWire Family Services* enables the Mac to recognize devices plugged into the FireWire chain while the Mac is on. It keeps track of all the devices that are turned on. It also accepts requests to transfer data to or from the Mac.

9 *Isochronous* transport in FireWire guarantees data transport at a specific rate, without interruption. This is used in viewing video or other real-time data.

"Here comes a movie."

File Manager

Event Manager

Other Managers

Firewire Family Services

Memory Managers

Operating System

"Okay, send the data."

FireWire transceiver and repeater

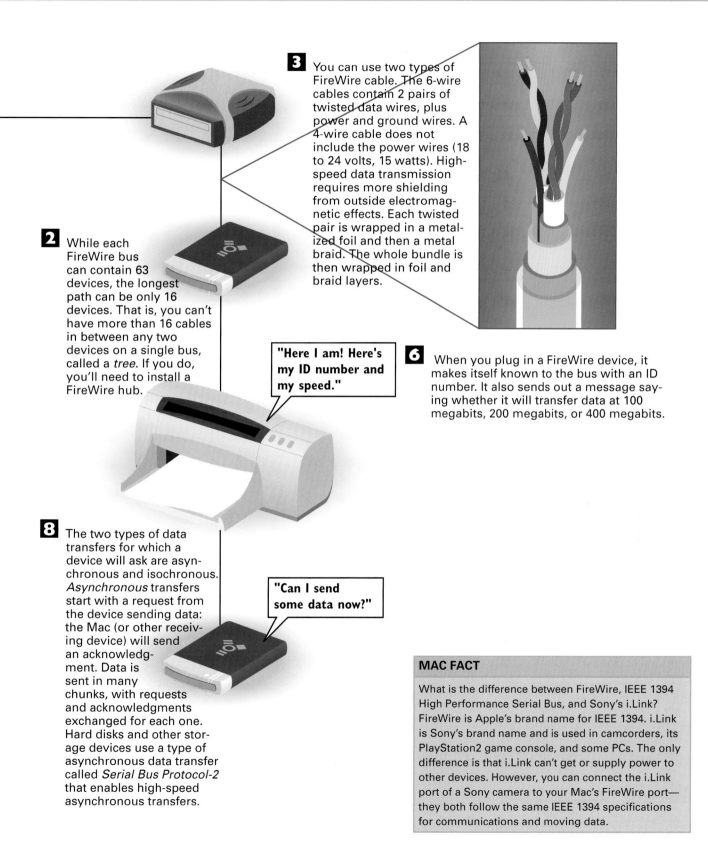

3 You can use two types of FireWire cable. The 6-wire cables contain 2 pairs of twisted data wires, plus power and ground wires. A 4-wire cable does not include the power wires (18 to 24 volts, 15 watts). High-speed data transmission requires more shielding from outside electromagnetic effects. Each twisted pair is wrapped in a metalized foil and then a metal braid. The whole bundle is then wrapped in foil and braid layers.

2 While each FireWire bus can contain 63 devices, the longest path can be only 16 devices. That is, you can't have more than 16 cables in between any two devices on a single bus, called a *tree*. If you do, you'll need to install a FireWire hub.

"Here I am! Here's my ID number and my speed."

6 When you plug in a FireWire device, it makes itself known to the bus with an ID number. It also sends out a message saying whether it will transfer data at 100 megabits, 200 megabits, or 400 megabits.

8 The two types of data transfers for which a device will ask are asynchronous and isochronous. *Asynchronous* transfers start with a request from the device sending data: the Mac (or other receiving device) will send an acknowledgment. Data is sent in many chunks, with requests and acknowledgments exchanged for each one. Hard disks and other storage devices use a type of asynchronous data transfer called *Serial Bus Protocol-2* that enables high-speed asynchronous transfers.

"Can I send some data now?"

MAC FACT

What is the difference between FireWire, IEEE 1394 High Performance Serial Bus, and Sony's i.Link? FireWire is Apple's brand name for IEEE 1394. i.Link is Sony's brand name and is used in camcorders, its PlayStation2 game console, and some PCs. The only difference is that i.Link can't get or supply power to other devices. However, you can connect the i.Link port of a Sony camera to your Mac's FireWire port—they both follow the same IEEE 1394 specifications for communications and moving data.

CHAPTER

18

How the Keyboard, Mouse, and Trackpad Work

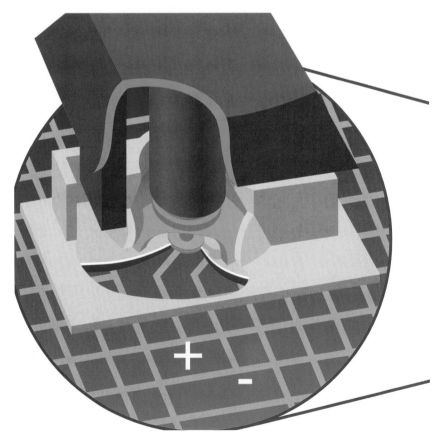

THE Mac's number-one peripheral device is not a drive. It's not a printer, scanner, hub, or network. It's you, the user. At least, that's how the Mac sees you. The Mac won't do anything until it receives command signals from you.

Because you can't enter commands in the Mac's language of voltages representing 0s and 1s, you must use the keyboard and mouse, or, in iBooks and PowerBooks, the trackpad. You can think of these devices as collections of hardware standards that define the interface between you and the Mac.

The keyboard uses the oldest standard in a Mac—the Qwerty layout of the keys is over 125 years old. (Q-W-E-R-T-Y are the first six letters at top left of the keyboard.) Qwerty was created in 1873 by typewriter inventor Christopher Latham Sholes. The layout was a modification of the one on his 1868 typewriter, which had an alphabetical layout that would constantly jam. Sholes looked at which pairs of letters were most commonly used, and moved the keys apart to prevent jamming. A few years later, Sholes added the Shift key, which physically shifted the position of the carriage to switch between capital and lowercase letters.

Despite the many myths about the Qwerty standard, the fact is no competing keyboard layout was able to replace Qwerty. In "The Fable of the Keys" (*Journal of Law and Economics*, 1990), economists Stan Liebowitz and Stephen Margolis point out that even the highly praised Dvorak keyboard (from the 1930s) was not sufficiently superior to warrant abandoning Qwerty. The standard has also proven useful in languages other than English; most of the world outside the United States has adopted Qwerty.

In addition to the alphanumeric and punctuation keys of the nineteenth century, today's 108-key Apple keyboard includes keys that perform functions, such as Control or Option. When you press a key, the keyboard translates your action into a unique electrical signal that is sent to the Mac. Each key's signal represents a letter, number, punctuation, or function.

The mouse is a more recent invention—the early 1960s brainchild of Doug Engelbart, who was then a scientist at the Stanford Research Institute. In 1966, Engelbart conducted a NASA-funded study that showed the mouse to be the most efficient device for positioning a computer cursor onscreen. The Stanford Research Institute later licensed the idea to Apple, which then popularized the mouse by using it in the first Macintosh. Apple used Engelbart's basic mechanical design for 16 years. The Apple Pro Mouse, introduced in 2000, uses optical technology which has no moving parts.

The trackpad in the iBook and PowerBook performs the function of the mouse, although in this case your finger is the only moving part. Your finger changes the electrical characteristics of the trackpad, enabling the iBook or PowerBook to detect the placement and movement of your finger. Fortunately, if you still believe in Englebart's and NASA's assessment, you can plug a mouse into any iBook or PowerBook. As the Mac's number one peripheral device, it's your decision.

How the Keyboard Works

8 The Mac USB controller sends an interrupt signal to the processor, which lets the operating system know that data is incoming.

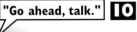
"Go ahead, talk."

10 The Mac sends the keyboard a talk command.

KeyLargo

9 The operating system's USB manager uses the USB controller to poll each device to see which one is requesting attention. The keyboard responds.

3 Each key is supported by a column that sits on a plastic bubble, as well as a pair of guideposts that fit into slots.

2 Under each key is a round, metal pad on the circuit board. The pad is connected to the grid.

1 Under the keys is a circuit board spanning the length and width of the keyboard. The board is criss-crossed with a sensor grid in which signals are moving from left to right and top to bottom.

4 When you press a key, its column presses the bubble down until a raised point on the underside of the bubble touches a metal disc on the keyboard's circuit board. This changes the pad's *capacitance*, the difference in voltage between positively and negatively charged elements. When you release the key, the bubble pops up.

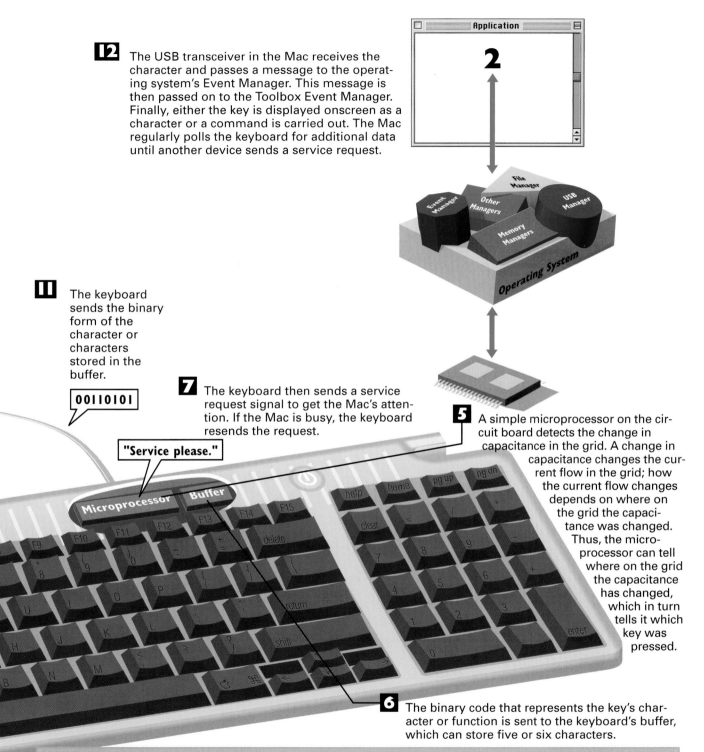

12 The USB transceiver in the Mac receives the character and passes a message to the operating system's Event Manager. This message is then passed on to the Toolbox Event Manager. Finally, either the key is displayed onscreen as a character or a command is carried out. The Mac regularly polls the keyboard for additional data until another device sends a service request.

11 The keyboard sends the binary form of the character or characters stored in the buffer.

00110101

7 The keyboard then sends a service request signal to get the Mac's attention. If the Mac is busy, the keyboard resends the request.

"Service please."

5 A simple microprocessor on the circuit board detects the change in capacitance in the grid. A change in capacitance changes the current flow in the grid; how the current flow changes depends on where on the grid the capacitance was changed. Thus, the microprocessor can tell where on the grid the capacitance has changed, which in turn tells it which key was pressed.

6 The binary code that represents the key's character or function is sent to the keyboard's buffer, which can store five or six characters.

MAC FACT

From the original 128K Mac to the Mac Plus, the keyboard port used synchronous transmission, in which signals were sent on a timed schedule according to a clock on the logic board. The need to perform the complex task of synchronizing signals from multiple devices prevented users from daisy-chaining additional devices. Synchronous communication was abandoned in favor of the asynchronous approach of the Apple Desktop Bus introduced in the Mac SE and used in USB keyboards today.

USB Mouse

4 Pressing the mouse button activates a switch, which sends a signal to the mouse's microprocessor. The switch is deactivated when you take your finger off the button. The Mouse also transmits a signal representing whether the mouse button is up or down.

3 The mouse's microprocessor interprets these pulse signals and sends the data to the Mac's USB controller.

Microprocessor

1 Two capstans at right angles to each other are in contact with a rubber-coated, steel ball that partially protrudes from the bottom of the mouse. When you move the mouse, the ball rotates the two capstans, which measure the up-and-down and side-to-side motion of the mouse, as well as the speed of the mouse in each direction.

2 Each capstan turns an interrupt wheel, a disk with 96 slots around the edge. For each slotted wheel, a tiny infrared lamp sends a beam of light through the moving wheel to a detector on the other side of the wheel. When a slot lines up with a lamp and detector, the beam is received and an electrical pulse is generated. When a slot does not, the light is blocked and no pulse is generated.

Apple Pro Mouse

The Apple Pro Mouse has no moving parts; it has optics. A small LED lights the surface under the mouse. A camera lens focuses light bouncing off the surface. The camera takes 1,500 microscopic pictures per second. The mouse's digital signal processor compares the images and calculates the position and velocity of the mouse from the differences in the pictures. The digital signal processor sends the data to a controller chip in the mouse, which converts the information into standard mouse data and transmits to the Mac over the USB cable.

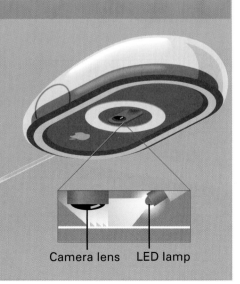

Camera lens   LED lamp

Trackpad

2 Placing your finger on the trackpad disturbs the electrical field, which in turn alters signals going through the conductors. This is called *field distortion sensing* or *capacitance-sensing*.

3 A controller chip receiving the altered signals calculates where the center of your finger is and makes it the control point for the cursor.

1 A trackpad has no moving parts. Under the trackpad's top protective layer, two layers of electrical conductors form a grid. A high-frequency AC current passes through the conductors in the grid, creating an electrical field.

4 The controller chip measures how far and fast you move your finger across the grid. On some PowerBook models, the controller interprets a tap on the trackpad as a mouse click.

5 The Mac's USB controller receives signals from a mouse and passes them on to the processor. The operating system and user interface toolbox decode the USB signals back into numbers for left-right and up-down motion and move the cursor.

KeyLargo

MAC FACT

The trackpad's field distortion is similar to the keyboard's capacitance-sensing grid used to detect key presses. However, the field distortion was used much earlier, in the 1920s-era electric instrument called the *theremin*. This instrument was used for the sound effects in the Beach Boys' "Good Vibrations" and in many 1950s science fiction movies. Whereas the trackpad sends out cursor control signals when you move your finger on it, the theremin changes pitch when you move your hand next to an antenna.

CHAPTER 19

How SCSI Works

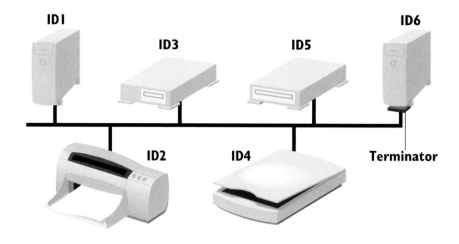

IT was an engineer's sense of humor that applied a disreputable epithet to a fast input/output method, *SCSI* (pronounced "scuzzy"). Short for small computer system interface, SCSI was a standard port in Macs for many years. It was used for connecting up to seven hard disks, removable drives, and scanners. Today it is used mostly for the fastest hard drives.

Before the release of the Mac Plus in 1986, the only way you could connect a hard disk to a Mac was through a slow serial connection. The addition of SCSI was *much* faster. SCSI is still the fastest method of moving data to a hard disk and is considered an upgrade from the standard IDE/ATA connections that are standard today for Mac hard disks. It is also faster than FireWire. The type of SCSI available in the Power Mac G4, Ultra2 SCSI, can move 80MB of data per second.

However, SCSI connections require more care than serial connections—if you have multiple devices, getting the cabling to work can require a little trial and error. SCSI is also more expensive than IDE/ATA or FireWire. The reason for the complexity and cost—as well as the high speed—is the fact that SCSI is a *parallel* technology, moving many bits at the same time over different wires. USB and FireWire are among the fastest types of serial connections (which send data one bit at a time), but are not as fast as SCSI.

For these reasons, Apple removed SCSI from Mac motherboards. Today, SCSI is available only as an option in Power Mac G4, as an expansion card sitting in a PCI expansion slot. The SCSI card enables you to connect both internal SCSI drives and external devices.

To plug multiple external devices into a SCSI port, you simply connect each new SCSI peripheral into the back of the last peripheral, forming a string of devices called a *SCSI chain*. Similar to USB and FireWire, SCSI is a *bus*, which is a common pathway shared by multiple devices. The SCSI controller circuitry on the SCSI card sends out signals that pass from one device on the chain to the next.

One of the complicating factors of SCSI is that a terminating resistor is required on the first and last devices on the bus. These identify the extent of the bus and prevent signals from reflecting back on the bus after reaching the last device. You usually must plug a terminator connector into a device's SCSI connector, although some hard drives have internal terminators.

Signals from the Mac are sent out on the SCSI bus by the operating system's SCSI Manager, which commands the SCSI controller chip on the SCSI card. Each peripheral has a SCSI driver that is loaded into the Mac's system partition in RAM at startup. With the drivers loaded into the Mac's RAM, the Mac knows for which devices to look on the SCSI bus.

SCSI Chain

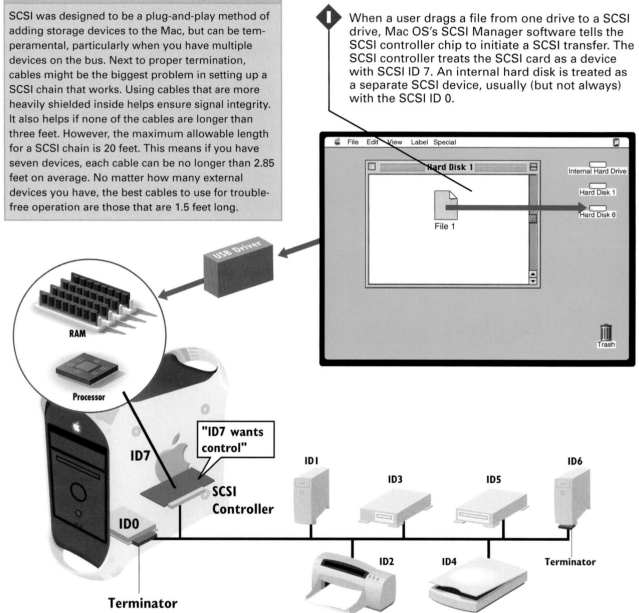

MAC FACT

SCSI was designed to be a plug-and-play method of adding storage devices to the Mac, but can be temperamental, particularly when you have multiple devices on the bus. Next to proper termination, cables might be the biggest problem in setting up a SCSI chain that works. Using cables that are more heavily shielded inside helps ensure signal integrity. It also helps if none of the cables are longer than three feet. However, the maximum allowable length for a SCSI chain is 20 feet. This means if you have seven devices, each cable can be no longer than 2.85 feet on average. No matter how many external devices you have, the best cables to use for trouble-free operation are those that are 1.5 feet long.

1 When a user drags a file from one drive to a SCSI drive, Mac OS's SCSI Manager software tells the SCSI controller chip to initiate a SCSI transfer. The SCSI controller treats the SCSI card as a device with SCSI ID 7. An internal hard disk is treated as a separate SCSI device, usually (but not always) with the SCSI ID 0.

2 Because only one SCSI transaction can occur at a time, the SCSI controller monitors for a free bus. If it detects a transaction occurring, it waits. When it hears nothing, the SCSI controller sends out a signal to gain control of the bus. If no termination signal is detected, it can't see any of the other SCSI devices. If more than one SCSI device seeks control at the same time, the one with the highest number wins, and the SCSI Manager queues the requests from the other devices. Because the SCSI controller has the highest possible ID number, it always wins.

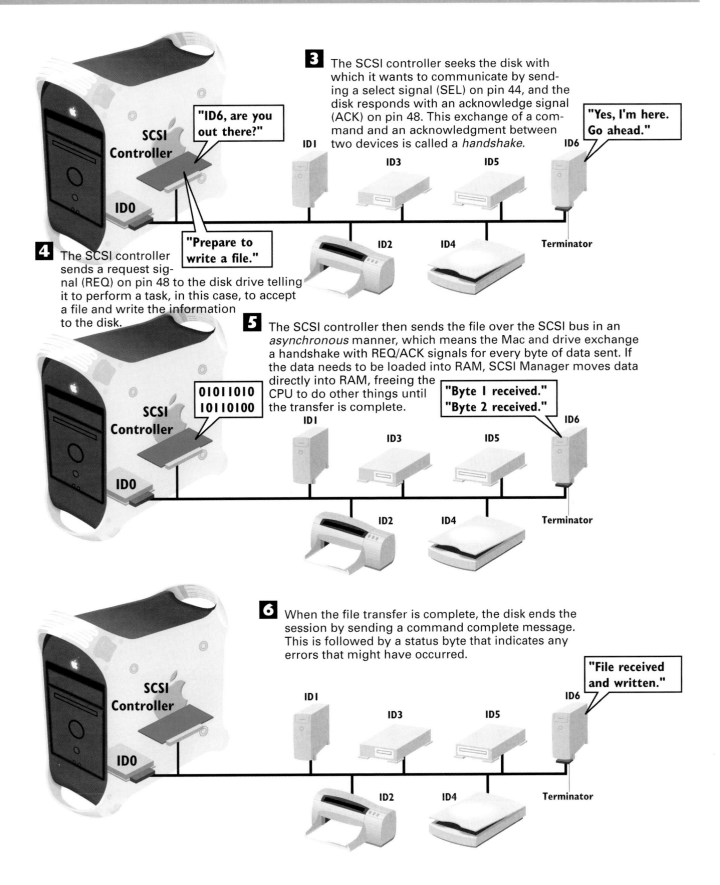

3 The SCSI controller seeks the disk with which it wants to communicate by sending a select signal (SEL) on pin 44, and the disk responds with an acknowledge signal (ACK) on pin 48. This exchange of a command and an acknowledgment between two devices is called a *handshake*.

"ID6, are you out there?"

"Yes, I'm here. Go ahead."

"Prepare to write a file."

4 The SCSI controller sends a request signal (REQ) on pin 48 to the disk drive telling it to perform a task, in this case, to accept a file and write the information to the disk.

5 The SCSI controller then sends the file over the SCSI bus in an *asynchronous* manner, which means the Mac and drive exchange a handshake with REQ/ACK signals for every byte of data sent. If the data needs to be loaded into RAM, SCSI Manager moves data directly into RAM, freeing the CPU to do other things until the transfer is complete.

01011010
10110100

"Byte 1 received."
"Byte 2 received."

6 When the file transfer is complete, the disk ends the session by sending a command complete message. This is followed by a status byte that indicates any errors that might have occurred.

"File received and written."

CHAPTER

20

How Expansion Slots Work

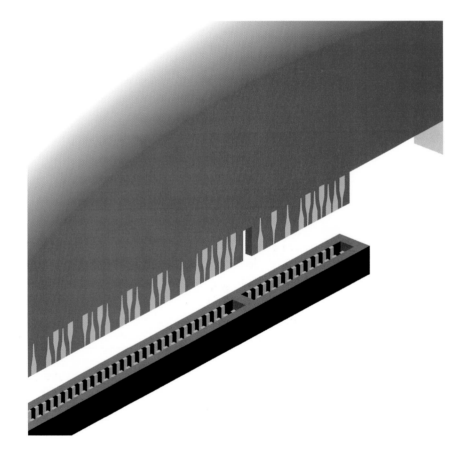

MACS are comprehensive machines. The electronics necessary for drive control, sound, modem, networking, and other functions are all built into the Mac's logic board. Ports enable you to connect cameras, storage drives, and other devices that expand the Mac's capabilities.

Yet, for some people, that's not enough. That's why Power Macs and PowerBooks contain general-purpose expansion slots, which are connectors on the motherboard that enable you to add new electronics inside the Mac. As you saw in the first three chapters, every Mac has slots for specific purposes, such as adding RAM or an AirPort wireless networking card. But the expansion slots of Power Macs and PowerBooks enable you to add all sorts of boards, such as a high-speed video processing board; another graphics card for a second monitor; or a SCSI card for connecting to SCSI hard drives, scanners, or other SCSI devices. You also can use expansion slots to update an older Mac. For instance, you can add FireWire to an older PowerBook G3 that doesn't have a built-in FireWire port.

Actually, an expansion slot is much more than just a connector on the motherboard. Expansion slots include electronics on the motherboard that provide the expansion card with operating power and access to the Mac's RAM. Part of these electronics is controller hardware, which regulates and interprets the flow of signals between the card and the rest of the Mac. The slot hardware on the motherboard and software in Mac OS enable Mac expansion cards to be self-configuring and are designed to be just as easy to use as the rest of the Mac. Just plug them in and they work.

Power Macs and PowerBooks use slots that suit the needs of the computer. Power Macs come with three or four PCI (peripheral component interface) slots that can hold expansion cards up to 12 inches long. Power Mac G4s include three PCI slots and an AGP (accelerated graphics port) slot—a special type of PCI slot adapted for high-speed graphic controller cards. PowerBooks use special miniature expansion slots called CardBus slots, which you can access without opening the PowerBook.

All three slots are industry standards that are also used in PCs. This means that the expansion cards that fit the slots can be run in either Macs or PCs. Some cards might require special software drivers installed on the Mac or PC to run, but others do not.

PCI, AGP, and PC CardBus are buses, which means that multiple devices can share a common data pathway. In fact, PCI is an integral part of the logic board architecture because it is the main system bus used to move information between the processor, RAM, ports, and expansion slots. Even iMacs, iBooks, and PowerBooks have PCI as their main system bus and AGP as their graphics bus, even though they don't have the expansion slots.

Given the primary role that PCI plays in Macs today, it's interesting to note that the PCI standard was created by Intel. It is now controlled by the PCI Local Bus Special Interest group, of which Apple is a member. The same is true with AGP, now a standard based on PCI.

Although AGP slots are modeled after PCI slots, they are designed to be faster in order to support large data transfers of 3D graphics and video. Whereas the PCI slot can transfer data at a maximum rate of 132MB per second, the AGP slot can move data up to 528MB per second. (With both buses in actual operation, the numbers for sustained throughput are smaller.) The AGP bus also provides faster access to main memory than previous designs using the PCI bus.

One reason for this is that the processing circuitry for the PCI slots adds some delays that AGP tries to avoid. For instance, PCI combines the data and address lines, whereas AGP keeps them separate. Address lines specify the memory location of each piece of data. Keeping the address information separate enables the AGP bus to pipeline the address—process several of them at the same time. (Pipelining is also used in the PowerPC G3 and G4 processors.)

Addresses and data are transferred between the PCI/AGP cards and the motherboard through metal fingers on each side of the card's edge, similar to those used on RAM DIMMs. These fingers are called pins, but are actually strips of tin-lead alloy, sometimes plated with a thin layer of gold. Fingers are prone to wearing out if you frequently remove and replace the card, which is something you aren't very likely (or advised) to do. The advantage of the finger-style pins is that you can't accidentally bend them, making the cards easier to install.

PC Card and CardBus

PC Card and CardBus cards don't have pins, either—they have sockets. When you insert a card, the sockets meet 68 pins inside the PowerBook, safely out of reach.

These credit card–sized expansion cards were originally named *PCMCIA cards*, after the group in charge of the specification (the Personal Computer Memory Card International Association). Fortunately, the unwieldy acronym was eventually dropped in favor of *PC Card*.

CardBus is a newer version of the PC Card standard. The difference between the two is simple: PC Cards transfer data 16 bits at a time, whereas CardBus cards are 32-bit. The first PowerBook G3 model contained two PC Card slots. Since then, PowerBook G3s have come with CardBus slots, which also support the older 16-bit PC Cards.

Both the older and newer standards hold three different sizes of cards. Type I cards are only 3.3 millimeters thick and aren't very common. The Type II cards are 5 millimeters thick, and Type III cards are 10.5 millimeters thick and fill the space of both slots. However, the current generation of PowerBook G3 supports only Type I and II. Despite their small sizes, PC Cards and CardBus cards can provide a number of functions, including supplying an extra hard disk and giving your PowerBook a SCSI port.

Similar to PCI slots, CardBus slots can move data at a maximum rate of 132MB per second. They also use the same protocols (the signaling language) as PCI slots. In fact, relative to the processor, RAM, and main system bus, the CardBus slots reside in the same position on the PowerBook motherboard that the PCI slots do on the Power Mac G4. In fact, the two motherboards of these two radically different Macs are remarkably similar.

However, one major difference between CardBus and PCI/AGP does exist—CardBus cards are hot-swappable. As with USB devices, you can plug in and eject CardBus cards while the PowerBook is on, and you don't have to restart. You should never plug in or unplug a PCI or AGP card in a Power Mac while the Mac is running.

Older Expansion Ports

While AGP is a fairly new technology, PC Card and PCI slots have been around awhile. When I wrote the first edition of *How Macs Work* back in 1992, I made a prediction that PCI would completely replace something called NuBus in Macs within a few years. These days, it seems as though only the old-timers remember NuBus.

NuBus was the very first expansion slot used in Macs, debuting in the Macintosh II in 1987. That year, another defunct slot, the PDS (processor direct slot) first appeared in the Mac SE. Before that, Macs didn't have expansion slots.

NuBus was invented by Texas Instruments and is specified by an industry standard called IEEE 1196. It was slower than PCI slots, which was probably okay because the Macs were pretty slow back then as well. The main problem was that PCs didn't use it, which meant that NuBus expansion cards tended to be expensive.

PDS were even more unique. Not only was this a Macintosh-only expansion slot, but the PDS slot was not standard across all Mac models that contained them. This meant that many PDS cards worked only in a specific Mac model.

Still, PDS was a faster slot than NuBus, and even had some things in common with the high-tech AGP slot. For instance, it kept data and address lines separate. It also had a direct connection to the system bus that was, in some ways, similar to the AGP bus.

PCI Expansion Slot

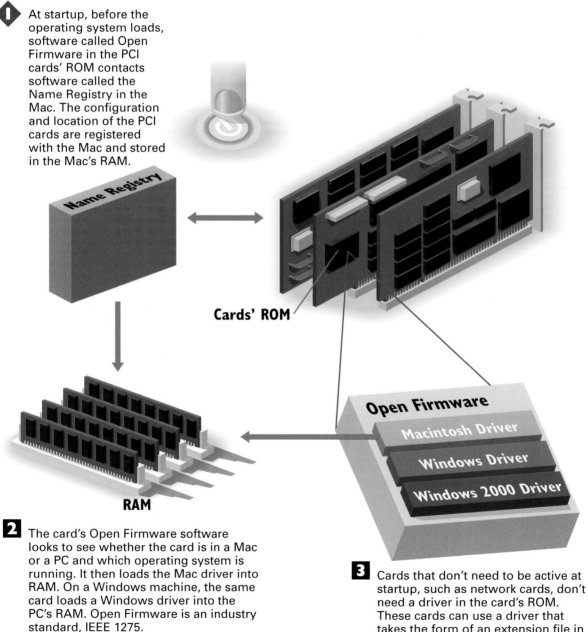

1 At startup, before the operating system loads, software called Open Firmware in the PCI cards' ROM contacts software called the Name Registry in the Mac. The configuration and location of the PCI cards are registered with the Mac and stored in the Mac's RAM.

Name Registry

Cards' ROM

RAM

Open Firmware

Macintosh Driver

Windows Driver

Windows 2000 Driver

2 The card's Open Firmware software looks to see whether the card is in a Mac or a PC and which operating system is running. It then loads the Mac driver into RAM. On a Windows machine, the same card loads a Windows driver into the PC's RAM. Open Firmware is an industry standard, IEEE 1275.

3 Cards that don't need to be active at startup, such as network cards, don't need a driver in the card's ROM. These cards can use a driver that takes the form of an extension file in the System folder, which is loaded later in the startup process.

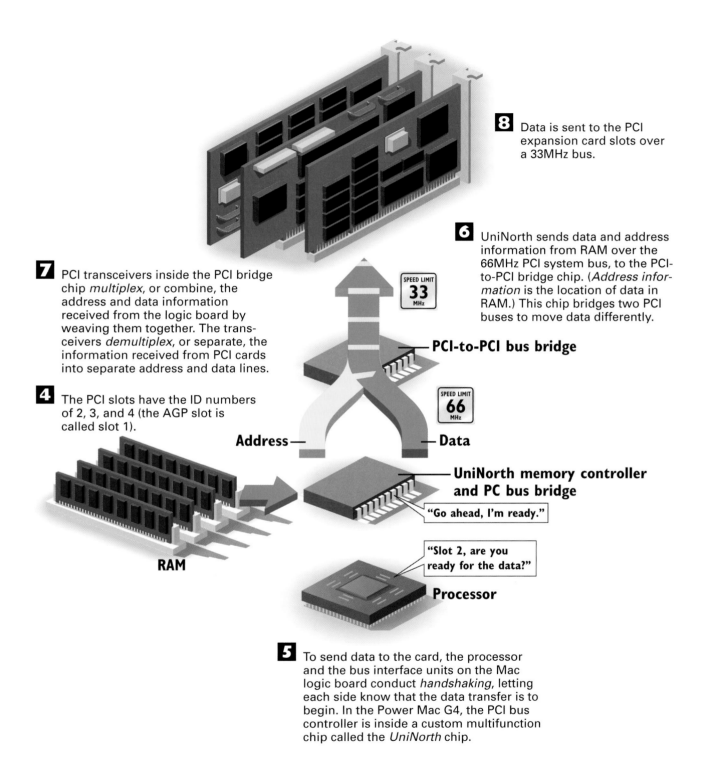

8 Data is sent to the PCI expansion card slots over a 33MHz bus.

6 UniNorth sends data and address information from RAM over the 66MHz PCI system bus, to the PCI-to-PCI bridge chip. (*Address information* is the location of data in RAM.) This chip bridges two PCI buses to move data differently.

7 PCI transceivers inside the PCI bridge chip *multiplex*, or combine, the address and data information received from the logic board by weaving them together. The transceivers *demultiplex*, or separate, the information received from PCI cards into separate address and data lines.

4 The PCI slots have the ID numbers of 2, 3, and 4 (the AGP slot is called slot 1).

SPEED LIMIT **33** MHz

PCI-to-PCI bus bridge

SPEED LIMIT **66** MHz

Address — — **Data**

UniNorth memory controller and PC bus bridge

"Go ahead, I'm ready."

"Slot 2, are you ready for the data?"

RAM

Processor

5 To send data to the card, the processor and the bus interface units on the Mac logic board conduct *handshaking*, letting each side know that the data transfer is to begin. In the Power Mac G4, the PCI bus controller is inside a custom multifunction chip called the *UniNorth* chip.

AGP Slot in the Power Mac G4

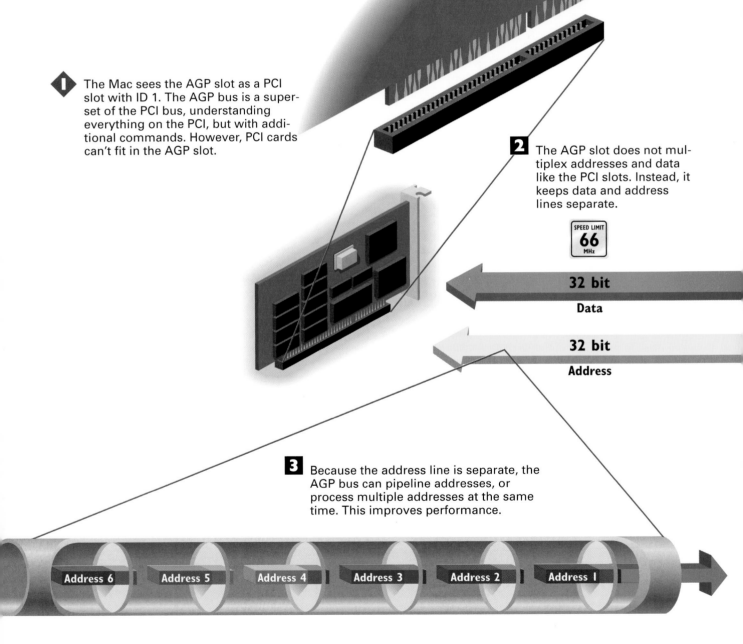

1 The Mac sees the AGP slot as a PCI slot with ID 1. The AGP bus is a superset of the PCI bus, understanding everything on the PCI, but with additional commands. However, PCI cards can't fit in the AGP slot.

2 The AGP slot does not multiplex addresses and data like the PCI slots. Instead, it keeps data and address lines separate.

SPEED LIMIT
66
MHz

32 bit
Data

32 bit
Address

3 Because the address line is separate, the AGP bus can pipeline addresses, or process multiple addresses at the same time. This improves performance.

Address 6   Address 5   Address 4   Address 3   Address 2   Address 1

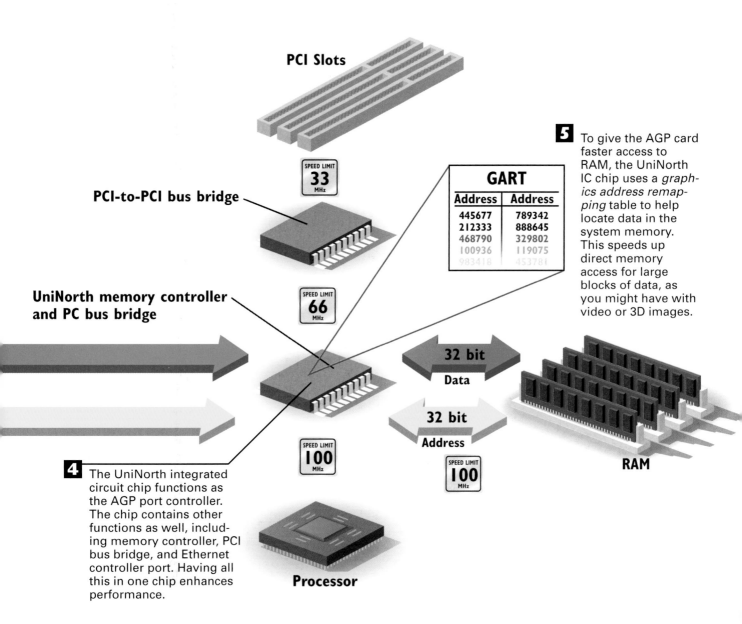

PCI Slots

SPEED LIMIT
33
MHz

PCI-to-PCI bus bridge

**UniNorth memory controller
and PC bus bridge**

SPEED LIMIT
66
MHz

5 To give the AGP card faster access to RAM, the UniNorth IC chip uses a *graphics address remapping* table to help locate data in the system memory. This speeds up direct memory access for large blocks of data, as you might have with video or 3D images.

GART

Address	Address
445677	789342
212333	888645
468790	329802
100936	119075
983418	453781

32 bit
Data

32 bit
Address

SPEED LIMIT
100
MHz

SPEED LIMIT
100
MHz

RAM

4 The UniNorth integrated circuit chip functions as the AGP port controller. The chip contains other functions as well, including memory controller, PCI bus bridge, and Ethernet controller port. Having all this in one chip enhances performance.

Processor

CardBus Slot in PowerBook

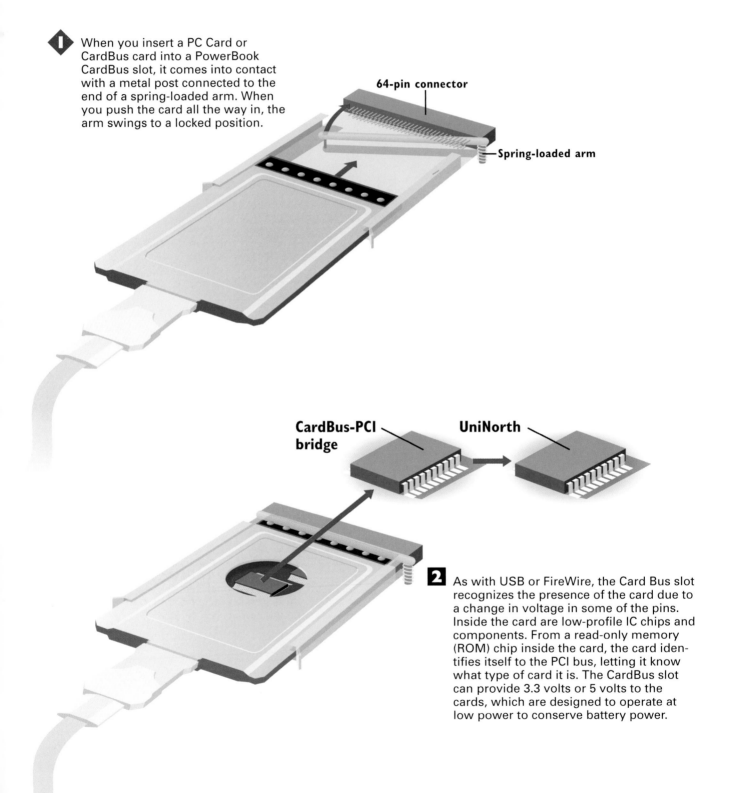

1 When you insert a PC Card or CardBus card into a PowerBook CardBus slot, it comes into contact with a metal post connected to the end of a spring-loaded arm. When you push the card all the way in, the arm swings to a locked position.

64-pin connector

Spring-loaded arm

CardBus-PCI bridge

UniNorth

2 As with USB or FireWire, the Card Bus slot recognizes the presence of the card due to a change in voltage in some of the pins. Inside the card are low-profile IC chips and components. From a read-only memory (ROM) chip inside the card, the card identifies itself to the PCI bus, letting it know what type of card it is. The CardBus slot can provide 3.3 volts or 5 volts to the cards, which are designed to operate at low power to conserve battery power.

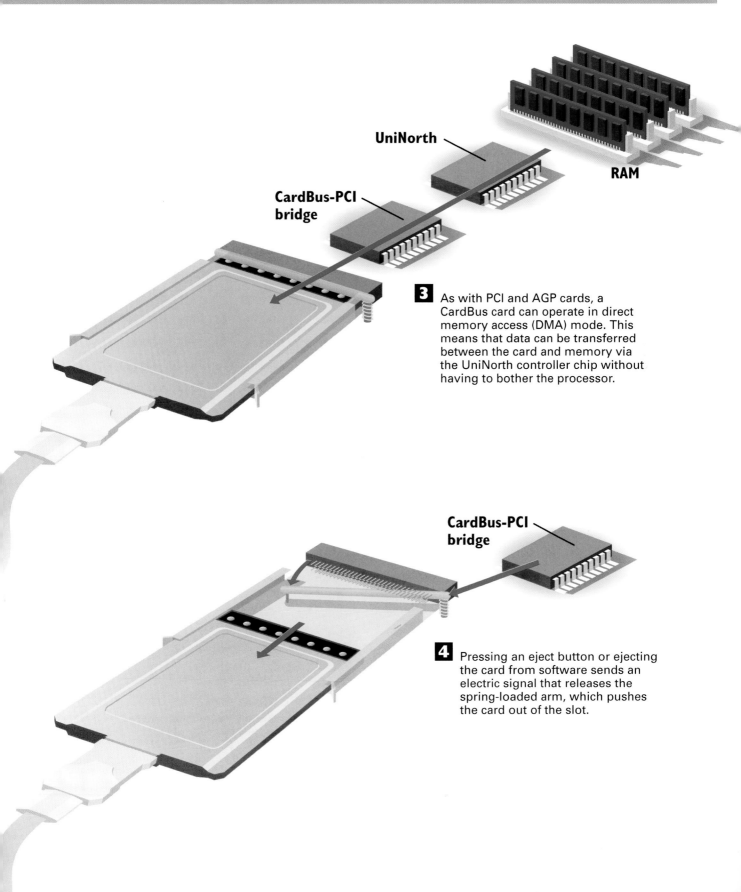

UniNorth

RAM

CardBus-PCI bridge

3 As with PCI and AGP cards, a CardBus card can operate in direct memory access (DMA) mode. This means that data can be transferred between the card and memory via the UniNorth controller chip without having to bother the processor.

CardBus-PCI bridge

4 Pressing an eject button or ejecting the card from software sends an electric signal that releases the spring-loaded arm, which pushes the card out of the slot.

CHAPTER

21

How Multimedia Works

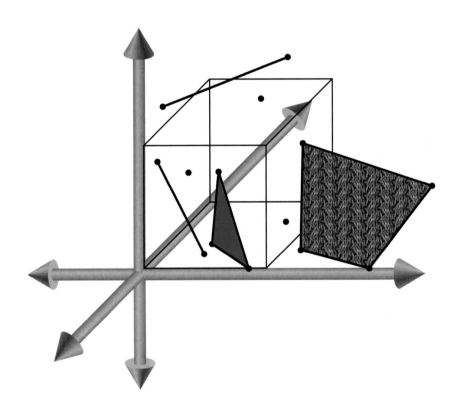

THE original Macintosh was a multimedia machine. In addition to text, the first Mac could show you pictures and simple animations and play multiple sounds. Even these earliest Macs enabled you to easily combine three media—text, graphics, and sound—at a time when most computers were text-only machines.

Multimedia has grown up with the Mac. Sound, music, video, still graphics, animation, 3D images, and, of course, text all can be mixed together in different communications media. Your Mac can even talk to you, and with the right software, you can talk to your Mac and have it do your bidding.

Today, a lot more storage methods for multimedia are available than in the old days, such as audio CDs, DVD movies, stereo systems, musical instruments, CD-ROM discs, analog VCRs and video cameras, digital cameras, microphones, digital files created on your Mac, and the Internet. On these different media, you'll find a number of different formats ranging in quality and storage requirements. They'll often use different compression standards as well. Fortunately, you don't need to keep up with all the standards or know what every component is. For the most part, you plug in the media, double-click a file, and it plays.

That's because multimedia is incorporated throughout the Mac. Every Mac has a core set of multimedia hardware and software that can handle the different media and formats. It also has a hardware and software infrastructure that can handle any additional hardware or software you'd care to use. You plug in a digital camcorder, and it becomes an extension of your Mac.

Consider that sound is everywhere in a Mac. Your Mac reads you alert messages. Synthesizer circuits on the logic board can create multiple sounds at the same time. Mac OS's QuickTime Player can play sound files, including MIDI files created by music synthesizers. Every Mac ever produced can play sophisticated sounds through built-in speakers. Macs have sound output and input ports, and some even come with built-in microphones. You also can connect speakers to the USB ports. On recent models, these sound ports can play or record 16-bit, 22KHz per channel CD-quality sound, either from audio CDs or CD-quality MP3 files you download from the Internet.

When you play a sound from a file, the Mac is converting digital information (1s and 0s) into the analog form (constantly fluctuating voltages) that produces sound. The opposite happens when you capture a sound with a microphone and turn it into a file. In that process, you are *digitizing* it, turning the analog data into digital form.

You perform the same kind of conversions with video (which often includes sound). You play digitized video when you watch DVD movies, download clips from the Internet, or watch your own home movies using iMovie. Digital video is almost always compressed when stored in a file or on disc. (Video and sound files are huge and would quickly fill a hard-disk drive if it weren't for compression.) When you watch video, your system software is decompressing the video stream and displaying it onscreen. The Mac OS DVD software performs the decompression for DVD movies.

Much of the other video decompression is performed by Mac OS's QuickTime software. QuickTime uses several Apple and industry standard compression/decompression algorithms (CODECs), including JPEG (Joint Photographic Experts Group) for photos and MPEG (Motion Picture Experts Group) for video. Each new version of QuickTime supports new CODECs as they come along. You don't have to upgrade your application software to use new compression standards; QuickTime takes care of that as well.

QuickTime Player, the application that enables you to play movies and sound files, is just one small part of QuickTime. Most of QuickTime is behind-the-scenes system software that gives Mac applications, such as Web browsers, the capability to use digitized audio, video, graphics, and animation files created by a variety of software. QuickTime provides a standard way for applications to handle all these multimedia elements. For instance, QuickTime enables you to view video movies in a word processor or to look at still images in SimpleText. When you double-click on PC WAV and AU sound files, QuickTime automatically converts to formats your software can read. Additionally, QuickTime enables you to cut, copy, and paste movies and sounds between documents of different applications.

QuickTime also provides a standard file format for sharing various types of multimedia. This is called the Movie format. Files written in the Movie format can contain video clips with synchronized sound, animation, or just sounds. An application supporting the Movie format can play each of these types of multimedia. QuickTime also supports other formats, including the Windows AVI movie format used on the Internet.

One special type of movie format is called QuickTime VR (the VR is short for virtual reality). It lets you navigate around in a photo-realistic scene at your own discretion. Instead of passively watching a video pan around a room, you can move 360 degrees around in a scene. You can also "look" above you and below you. Another QuickTime VR feature enables you to "pick up" an object in a scene, bring it into close view, and turn it completely around. Unlike video clips, QuickTime VR scenes are actually a series of still images stitched together so that they wrap completely around to form a complete panoramic view. Because no real video is involved, QuickTime VR files are very small, with a typical panoramic scene occupying several hundred kilobytes (not megabytes) of disk space. You don't need special goggles, wired gloves, or add-in cards to use QuickTime VR. You don't even need a particularly speedy Mac. All you need is a mouse.

Another type of 3D graphics technique, 3D *rendering*, is used to create the virtual reality worlds used in games. Mac OS includes an industry-standard 3D rendering technology called OpenGL, which was created by Silicon Graphics. A favorite programming environment for 3D developers, OpenGL is used in the most graphics-intensive 3D games, as well as in the special effects created for movies.

OpenGL consists of graphics-generating routines that applications can use to create interactive 3D environments. It can produce realistic-looking worlds complete with lighting and shading effects, translucency, reflective objects, and even atmospheric effects such as fog or smoke.

OpenGL works together with the 3D graphics acceleration hardware that all Macs have included for several years. The 3D graphics co-processor performs the calculations necessary for turning mathematical models into pixels to be displayed onscreen. OpenGL is a high-performance graphics engine that uses the hardware efficiently.

The rest of this chapter gets inside four of the Mac's multimedia technologies: the generation of sound, the use of digital video movies, the multimedia infrastructure that QuickTime system software provides, and OpenGL.

Playing Sound

The simplest sounds, the system alerts, are stored as sound resources in the System file. Others are stored as sound files, such as the high-quality MP3 (MPEG3) files or the earlier and simpler AIFF (audio interchange file format), which easily can be shared by various applications. The Mac also can play CD audio files, QuickTime Movie sound files, and PC WAV files. Whatever the format, the sound is stored in digital format.

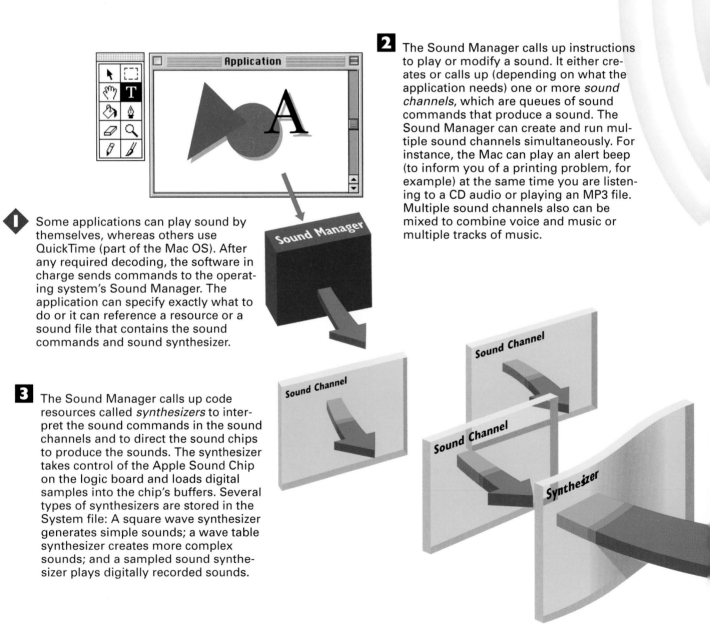

2 The Sound Manager calls up instructions to play or modify a sound. It either creates or calls up (depending on what the application needs) one or more *sound channels*, which are queues of sound commands that produce a sound. The Sound Manager can create and run multiple sound channels simultaneously. For instance, the Mac can play an alert beep (to inform you of a printing problem, for example) at the same time you are listening to a CD audio or playing an MP3 file. Multiple sound channels also can be mixed to combine voice and music or multiple tracks of music.

1 Some applications can play sound by themselves, whereas others use QuickTime (part of the Mac OS). After any required decoding, the software in charge sends commands to the operating system's Sound Manager. The application can specify exactly what to do or it can reference a resource or a sound file that contains the sound commands and sound synthesizer.

3 The Sound Manager calls up code resources called *synthesizers* to interpret the sound commands in the sound channels and to direct the sound chips to produce the sounds. The synthesizer takes control of the Apple Sound Chip on the logic board and loads digital samples into the chip's buffers. Several types of synthesizers are stored in the System file: A square wave synthesizer generates simple sounds; a wave table synthesizer creates more complex sounds; and a sampled sound synthesizer plays digitally recorded sounds.

Diaphragm

Coil

7 The speaker contains an iron magnet with a fixed magnetic field. In front of it is a coil of thin wire. The analog signals travel through the coil, creating a constantly fluctuating magnetic field; stronger voltages create a stronger magnetic field, and negative voltages reverse the magnetic field.

8 The fluctuating magnetic field is repelled by or attracted to the stationary iron magnet, causing the coil to rapidly vibrate. The vibrating coil is attached to a cone of paper called the *speaker diaphragm*, which moves rapidly in and out with the coil. A damper prevents the diaphragm from moving erratically.

9 The motion of the diaphragm compresses the air, creating sound waves, just as a pebble creates water waves in a pond. Low-pitched sounds are created by vibrations as slow as 50 times per second (50 hertz); high-pitched sounds are created by vibrations as high as 22,000 hertz.

Stereo Minijack

USB Port

5 Two analog processing chips (one for each stereo channel) smooth the signals from the Apple Sound Chip to complete the D/A (digital-to-analog) conversion. The analog chips then amplify the signals and regulate the volume. The resulting analog signals travel simultaneously to the Mac's speaker(s) and stereo minijack.

Amplifier

Volume Control

Analog Sound Chip

4 For built-in speakers or speakers connected to the sound ports, Apple Sound Chip synthesizes complex sounds as directed by the synthesizer resources. It converts the digital 1s and 0s into analog, electronic waves of constantly fluctuating voltages. A constant sound fluctuates at a constant rate—for instance, 440 times per second for the musical note middle A above middle C.

Digital Signal 1 0 0 1 1 **Analog Signal**

Buffers

Apple Sound Chip

USB Controller

6 In the case of USB speakers, the Apple Sound Chip is bypassed and the Sound Manager passes its output to the USB controller. The digital signals are sent along the USB port to the external speaker, which has its own synthesizing and amplifier chips.

Viewing Video

You can view video on a Mac from several different sources. Here we'll look at DVD movies, digital camcorders, and analog camcorders. We'll look at playing movie files, such as QuickTime, later in the chapter and pick up Internet video in Chapter 29, "How Internet Connections Work." Whatever the source, digital video uses a lot of data, so data compression is always involved.

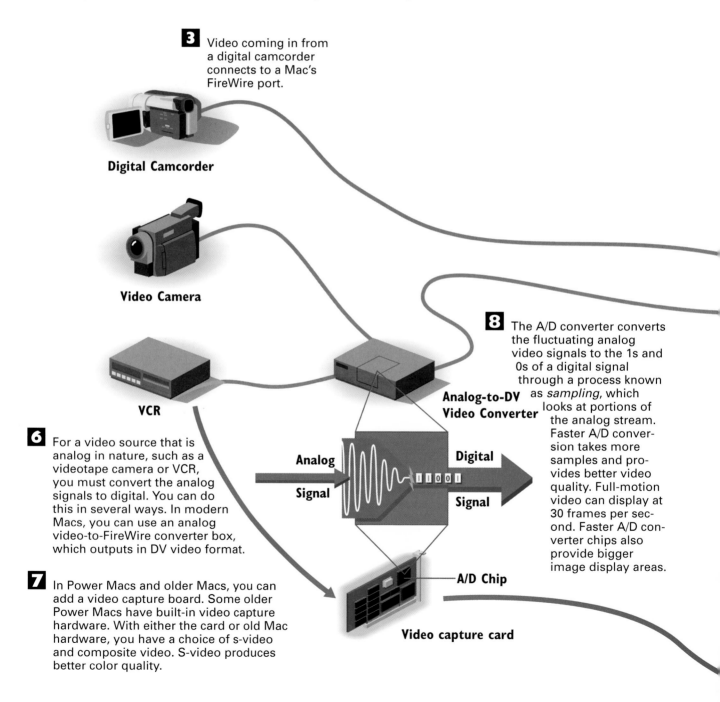

3 Video coming in from a digital camcorder connects to a Mac's FireWire port.

Digital Camcorder

Video Camera

VCR

Analog-to-DV Video Converter

8 The A/D converter converts the fluctuating analog video signals to the 1s and 0s of a digital signal through a process known as *sampling*, which looks at portions of the analog stream. Faster A/D conversion takes more samples and provides better video quality. Full-motion video can display at 30 frames per second. Faster A/D converter chips also provide bigger image display areas.

6 For a video source that is analog in nature, such as a videotape camera or VCR, you must convert the analog signals to digital. You can do this in several ways. In modern Macs, you can use an analog video-to-FireWire converter box, which outputs in DV video format.

Analog Signal

Digital Signal

A/D Chip

7 In Power Macs and older Macs, you can add a video capture board. Some older Power Macs have built-in video capture hardware. With either the card or old Mac hardware, you have a choice of s-video and composite video. S-video produces better color quality.

Video capture card

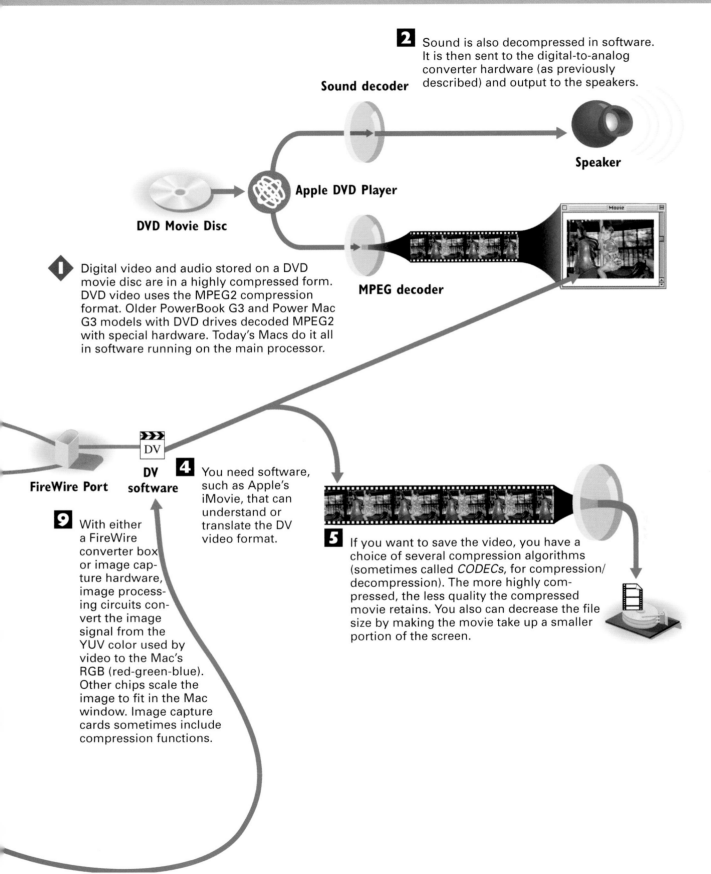

2 Sound is also decompressed in software. It is then sent to the digital-to-analog converter hardware (as previously described) and output to the speakers.

Sound decoder

Speaker

Apple DVD Player

DVD Movie Disc

MPEG decoder

1 Digital video and audio stored on a DVD movie disc are in a highly compressed form. DVD video uses the MPEG2 compression format. Older PowerBook G3 and Power Mac G3 models with DVD drives decoded MPEG2 with special hardware. Today's Macs do it all in software running on the main processor.

FireWire Port

DV software

4 You need software, such as Apple's iMovie, that can understand or translate the DV video format.

9 With either a FireWire converter box or image capture hardware, image processing circuits convert the image signal from the YUV color used by video to the Mac's RGB (red-green-blue). Other chips scale the image to fit in the Mac window. Image capture cards sometimes include compression functions.

5 If you want to save the video, you have a choice of several compression algorithms (sometimes called *CODECs*, for compression/decompression). The more highly compressed, the less quality the compressed movie retains. You also can decrease the file size by making the movie take up a smaller portion of the screen.

QuickTime

1 QuickTime enables any application that supports it to play a variety of video, graphic, and sound formats. When a user presses the play button of a movie or sound, the application sends a call to the Movie Toolbox.

2 The Movie Toolbox asks the Mac operating system to retrieve the compressed movie data, which consists of sound and compressed video, from the hard-disk drive and send it to the QuickTime extension loaded into RAM.

QuickTime

Movie ToolBox

Video

Image Compression Manager

Operating System

3 The Movie Toolbox separates the sound from the video. The sound is sent to the Sound Manager in the Mac Toolbox, and the video is sent to the Image Compression Manager.

VDIGs

4 QuickTime's Component Manager uses video digitizer components (VDIGs) to enable QuickTime to work with any add-in compression cards that might be in the Mac (Power Macs and earlier models only).

7 QuickDraw displays the video in the application onscreen while Sound Manager plays the audio through the Mac's speaker. The QuickTime extension ensures that the sound and video are played in sync. If the Mac hardware is too slow to handle the amount of data being displayed, the QuickTime Manager drops out frames from the video to keep the sound and video synchronized. This is why QuickTime movies sometimes appear jumpy on earlier Mac models.

Speaker

6 If the sound is compressed, QuickTime can access audio algorithms from the Sound Manager to decompress the sound. If the file is a PC sound file in the WAV or AU format, QuickTime uses the Sound Manager audio algorithms to convert it to the QuickTime format.

Sound Manager
QuickTime
Sound Data
Image Data
Toolbox

5 The Image Compression Manager decompresses the video (and compresses a video movie when it is being saved to disk) using a video compressor/decompressor algorithm (CODEC). The Image Compression Manager can detect which one of dozens of supported CODECs was used to save the file. It then sends the decompressed video to QuickDraw.

Component Manager

CODECs
Apple Animation
Apple Compact Video
Apple Graphics
Apple JPEG/Photo
Apple Video

3D Graphics with OpenGL

1 OpenGL stores mathematical models of images in a three-dimensional space. In this space, OpenGL first constructs *geometric primitives*—points, lines, and polygons, as well as 2D images that can cover the 2D surfaces. By default, OpenGL fills in all the polygons by drawing all the pixels within the boundary. Some images are filled with *texture bitmaps*, pixel drawings made to look like uneven surfaces, such as brick, wood, wallpaper, and other surfaces.

2 OpenGL arranges the objects in 3D space to create 3D objects. All 3D objects, including people, monsters, and spaceships, are built out of 2D polygons. Later, final rendering will smooth out the edges.

3 Multiple objects are arranged in the 3D space. Objects closer to the front will obscure objects farther back. OpenGL assigns a depth value with each pixel to decide whether it is to be displayed or obscured. Hidden surfaces are removed from the model and are not drawn. This saves processing power. The depth of each pixel is constantly examined as an image is animated and redrawn.

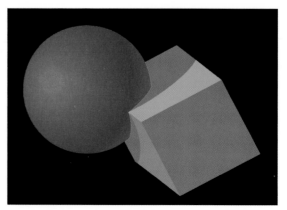

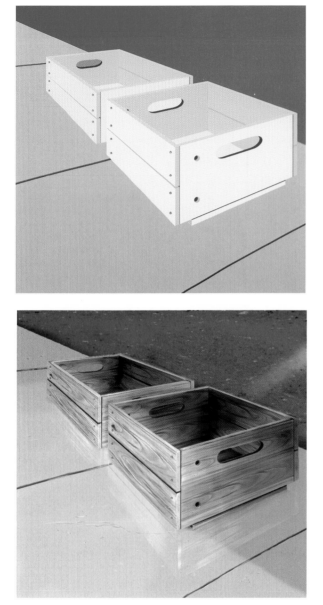

4 Through OpenGL, the user software selects a viewing angle and perspective to display the scene. In a perspective view, objects farther away from the front appear smaller than those closer.

5 Lighting and reflections are added to the model next. OpenGL can render effects due to lighting, reflections, and shadows, and texturing within the scene. With this information, OpenGL calculates the exact colors necessary to produce these effects.

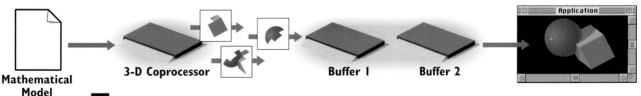

Mathematical Model → **3-D Coprocessor** → **Buffer 1** → **Buffer 2** → **Application**

6 OpenGL converts the mathematical descriptions of the objects and their colors into pixels onscreen. This is called *rasterization.* OpenGL uses the 3D co-processor chip on the Mac's logic board or graphics card to perform the calculations. It uses a technique known as *double buffering.* One buffer holds image for the frame of an animation that is being fed to the display screen. At the same time, another holds the image of the next frame that is being constructed.

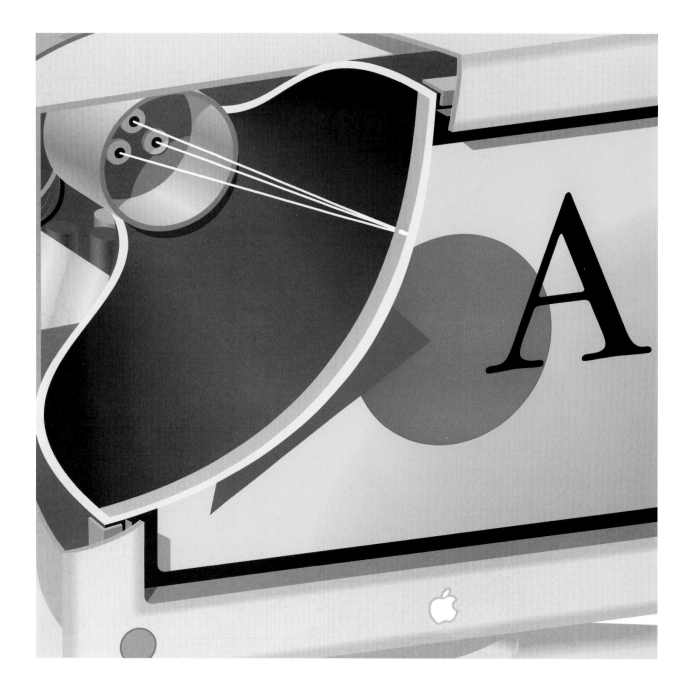

P A R T

6

DISPLAY

Chapter 22: How QuickDraw Works
152

Chapter 23: How Aqua Works
160

Chapter 24: How a CRT Display Works
164

Chapter 25: How Flat-Panel Displays Work
168

COMPUTERS are not TV sets. It's true that TV sets and some computer monitors share some basic technology, but the similarity ends there. Computer displays give you better resolution, crisper colors, and sharper images than even the best television screens.

The main difference between TV and computer displays is that TVs are analog devices based on decades-old technology. Computer displays are digital affairs. Behind the screen that presents the Finder and your documents is a complex system of digital electronics that produces the images, as well as system software that tells the hardware what to do. The main piece of imaging system software in Mac OS 9 is QuickDraw, a group of graphics routines in the Macintosh Toolbox. QuickDraw is the director of the whole show. In Mac OS X, Quartz takes over as the display system software for drawing two-dimensional graphics. Mac OS X also comes with OpenGL, industry-standard software for accelerated three-dimensional graphics.

Computer displays are also more versatile than TV displays. For instance, TV screens are locked into a 3:4 aspect ratio at one size, often cutting off the left and right sides of movies. Today's cathode-ray tube displays enable you to select the number of *pixels* (the basic dots that make up an image), so that if you want to see more of a document at one time, you can switch from 800×600 pixels to 1,024×768 pixels. You also can choose the number of colors you want. Additionally, some applications will change the number of colors for you if they require a certain setting.

Display monitors have had many shapes and sizes, from the modest 9-inch built-in screens of the first Macs to the high-tech, 22-inch Apple Cinema Display. The latter display, as well as those in iBooks and PowerBooks, use a type of screen called a *flat-panel LCD* (liquid crystal display), which is more like the readout on a microwave oven than the display on a television set. If one display isn't big enough, most desktop Macs and PowerBooks let you add more, enabling you to use them together as if they were one. You also can connect desktop and laptop Macs to large projection display systems for presentations in front of live audiences. And, with a special adapter cable, many Mac models enable you to connect monitors used with PC-compatible computers.

Monitors also vary in the number and type of shades they can display. The first Macs had monochrome displays, as did the first PowerBook models. *Monochrome* displays use only two colors, black and white. *Grayscale* presents many shades of gray between black and white for a more realistic rendition of graphic images. Technically, so-called black-and-white photographs and television programs are actually grayscale images.

Color Macs have been available since 1987, and the first color PowerBooks were introduced in 1992. Color monitors can display in color, grayscale, and monochrome. The maximum number of gray values or colors that a particular Mac model can display usually varies between 256 and more than 16 million. Macs that can display millions of colors can produce images with photographic realism. The Mac's system software contains the monitor's control panel, which lets you select fewer colors to improve screen performance when you don't need the colors. On some displays, you also can choose to display grayscale to further improve performance.

Displays also consume a lot of energy—in fact, they use most of the energy your Mac consumes. You can always safely turn off a monitor while you leave a Mac turned on, although Macs can do this for you. The Energy Saver control panel will turn off the display after a specified period of inactivity. You can turn the display back on again when you hit the keyboard. Some monitors have their own energy-saving features that put them in various *sleep* modes when they're not being used.

The Mac uses a color display technology called *RGB video*, short for red, green, and blue. RGB video creates every displayable color by mixing red, green, and blue light in different amounts. Software applications might use different color systems to enable users to set colors, but the Mac translates them into RGB values for displaying the colors onscreen.

You can expand on the Mac's display capabilities in many cases. On some iMac and PowerBooks and all Power Macs, you can add a second display monitor. Similar to other parts of the Mac, the display system is plug-and-play. Replacing a monitor or adding additional monitors is simply a matter of plugging in a second display to the graphics port, or, in the case of Power Macs, adding a second display card. No switches need to be set, and no programming is required. Installing a Mac monitor is not quite as simple as plugging in a television set; but it's not as hard as programming your VCR.

CHAPTER

22

How QuickDraw Works

QUICKDRAW plays a key part in Macintosh graphics. In OS 9 and earlier, it acts as the supervisor for the other graphics managers in the system software and video hardware to create the text and graphics you see onscreen. QuickDraw provides consistent display for all applications and is responsible for the Mac's what-you-see-is-what-you-get (WYSIWYG, pronounced *wiz-ee-wig*) display. With WYSIWYG, an inch onscreen is an inch on printed paper, and lines of text will end in the same place onscreen as on paper.

Mac OS X replaces most of QuickDraw with a new graphics technology called Quartz (described in Chapter 23, "How Aqua Works"). However, OS X still contains parts of QuickDraw to enable developers to easily port earlier software to Mac OS X. These ported applications, known as *carbon* applications, use QuickDraw in their own windows to display two-dimensional shapes, pictures, and text.

QuickDraw has been a part of the Mac system software since the first Mac, where it resided in the original Mac's ROM. Apple revamped QuickDraw to add color in 1987. When Apple released System 7 in 1991, it expanded QuickDraw to enable it to move in and out of RAM 32 bits at a time.

When your monitor is set to its WYSIWYG resolution, QuickDraw displays information by drawing 72 dots per linear inch. This might sound like a random number, but the size was chosen to match a unit of measure, called a *point*, in typography, which is 1/72 of an inch in size. When you have a ruler displayed in your word processor or drawing program, QuickDraw always displays 72 dots per inch as measured by that ruler, regardless of what your monitor is set at.

Each dot onscreen is called a *pixel* and is the smallest possible area that can be drawn. The number of colors that can be displayed is often given in bits per pixel. As you might remember from Chapter 7, "Binary Numbers and Transistors," a *bit* is a binary digit. One bit represents 2 binary numbers, 0 and 1, so 1 bit per pixel would give you 2 shades—black and white. The original Macintosh had a 1-bit-per-pixel display and could not even display grays, just black and white. Two bits give you 4 binary numbers available—00, 01, 10, and 11—to represent 4 colors. Similarly, 8-bit video can use 256 colors, and 32-bit video can provide over 16 million colors, which is more than the number of pixels onscreen. In 32-bit video, 24 bits are used for colors; the extra 8 bits are used to represent other information.

The extra bits needed to display more colors require more processing power. For graphic-intensive functions, such as animation and image processing, QuickDraw isn't so quick. That's one reason Quartz replaced QuickDraw in Mac OS X. But Quartz is the topic of the next chapter. For now, let's take a look at what QuickDraw can do.

The QuickDraw Coordinate Plane

1 The Monitors control panel is a user interface for QuickDraw. You can set the number of colors or grays to be displayed; 256 shades or colors is 8 bits per pixel. Thousands refers to 65,536 colors, or 16 bits per pixel, and the Millions setting refers to the 16 million colors available at 24 bits per pixel.

-640, 480

Mon

File Edit View Special Help

Monitors (1)

Monitor   Arrange   Color   Preferences

Arrange Monitors

To rearrange the monitors: drag them to the desired positions.
To make duplicate monitors: drag one onto another.
To stop duplication: drag the monitors apart.
To relocate the menu bar: drag it to a different monitor.
To change the startup screen: drag the smiling face to a different monitor.

Identify the monitors   ☐ **Identify the startup screen**

Use Defaults

-32,767

-640, 0

2 QuickDraw's Extended Desktop mode can display a continuous desktop across multiple monitors. You up the physical location of one monitor with respect to the other by dragging the windows representing each monitor to the position you desire.

3 QuickDraw creates a giant hyper-desktop area—a coordinate plane of numbered points. This plane is 65,535 points tall by 65,535 points wide (the binary number 11111111,11111111, which takes up 16 bits). The points are numbered in both horizontal and vertical directions, so a pair of numbers represents a point. QuickDraw measures the locations of objects and their motion in terms of this coordinate system.

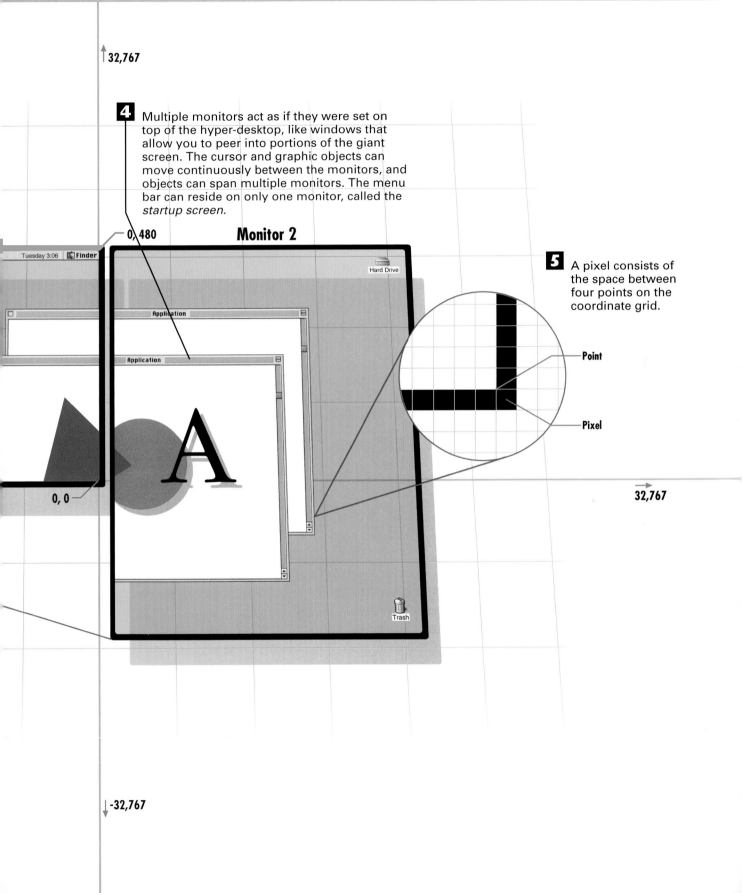

↑ 32,767

4 Multiple monitors act as if they were set on top of the hyper-desktop, like windows that allow you to peer into portions of the giant screen. The cursor and graphic objects can move continuously between the monitors, and objects can span multiple monitors. The menu bar can reside on only one monitor, called the *startup screen*.

0, 480   **Monitor 2**

5 A pixel consists of the space between four points on the coordinate grid.

Point

Pixel

0, 0

32,767

↓ -32,767

The RGB Color Model

QuickDraw and Macintosh video hardware and monitors use the RGB (red, green, and blue) color model to specify colors; the model is based on the way colored light behaves. Some software can use other color models. CMYK (cyan, magenta, yellow, and black), used in color publishing, is based on the way colored inks behave, and HLS (hue, lightness, and saturation) is sometimes used in graphic arts. Although software can use these other models, QuickDraw converts them to RGB values for display.

1 The Color Picker is the QuickDraw user interface for color selection. It enables users to specify new colors for objects within applications. The user can select a color by either clicking a color on the color wheel or typing in number values for the red, green, and blue components of the color. The Color Picker also provides the equivalent values for hue, saturation, and brightness (an alternative method for describing a color in the RGB model).

3 The values for red, green, and blue components correspond to an imaginary three-dimensional plot called a *color space*. Three axes exist: one red, one green, and one blue.

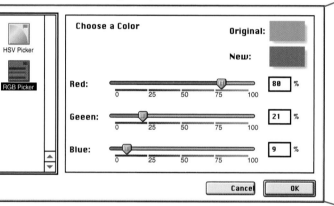

2 In the RGB model, any color can be created by mixing red, green, and blue in different amounts. The color is additive: The more of each color you add, the closer you get to white. With no amount of any of the colors, you get black, like a room with the lights turned off.

MAC FACT

With 48 bits' worth of numbers to play with, the Color Picker can specify over 280 trillion colors—far more than the Mac can display or the human eye can see. QuickDraw allows this many possible colors to best match any conceivable color that can be created by video hardware.

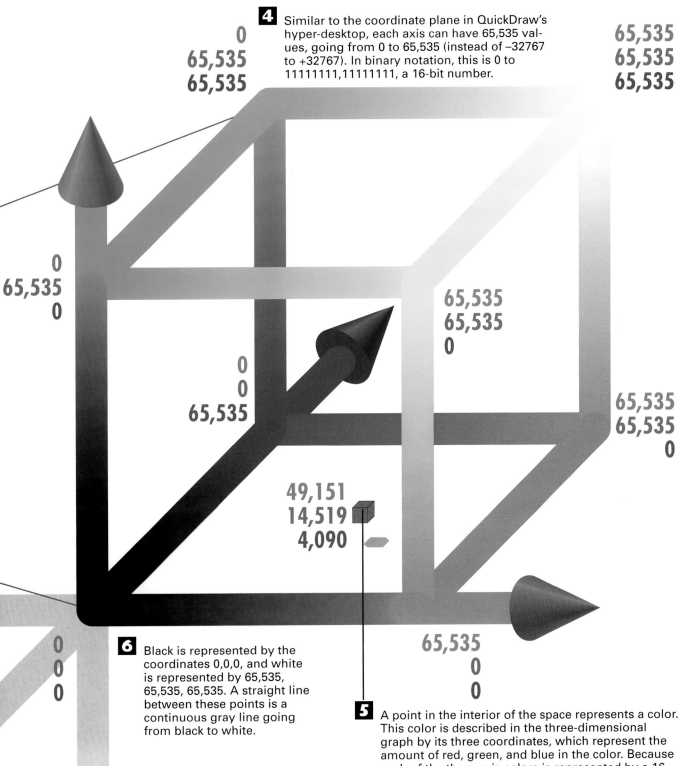

4 Similar to the coordinate plane in QuickDraw's hyper-desktop, each axis can have 65,535 values, going from 0 to 65,535 (instead of –32767 to +32767). In binary notation, this is 0 to 11111111,11111111, a 16-bit number.

0
65,535
65,535

65,535
65,535
65,535

0
65,535
0

65,535
65,535
0

0
0
65,535

65,535
65,535
0

49,151
14,519
4,090

0
0
0

65,535
0
0

6 Black is represented by the coordinates 0,0,0, and white is represented by 65,535, 65,535, 65,535. A straight line between these points is a continuous gray line going from black to white.

5 A point in the interior of the space represents a color. This color is described in the three-dimensional graph by its three coordinates, which represent the amount of red, green, and blue in the color. Because each of the three axis colors is represented by a 16-bit number, the composite color is fully represented by a 48-bit value.

QuickDraw at Work

Most of what QuickDraw draws is created from mathematical descriptions of objects. QuickDraw can also use a technique called *direct pixel*, or bit image, which is faster but requires more RAM. QuickDraw manages the translation of a color chosen by the user into a color the hardware can create.

1 A user draws or types in an application window. In this example, the user draws a box with a filled pattern and chooses a color for it.

3 The application makes calls to QuickDraw routines to draw the figure and use a color.

2 The application consults the Color Picker for the color the user has chosen. The Color Picker returns with a 48-bit RGB description of the color.

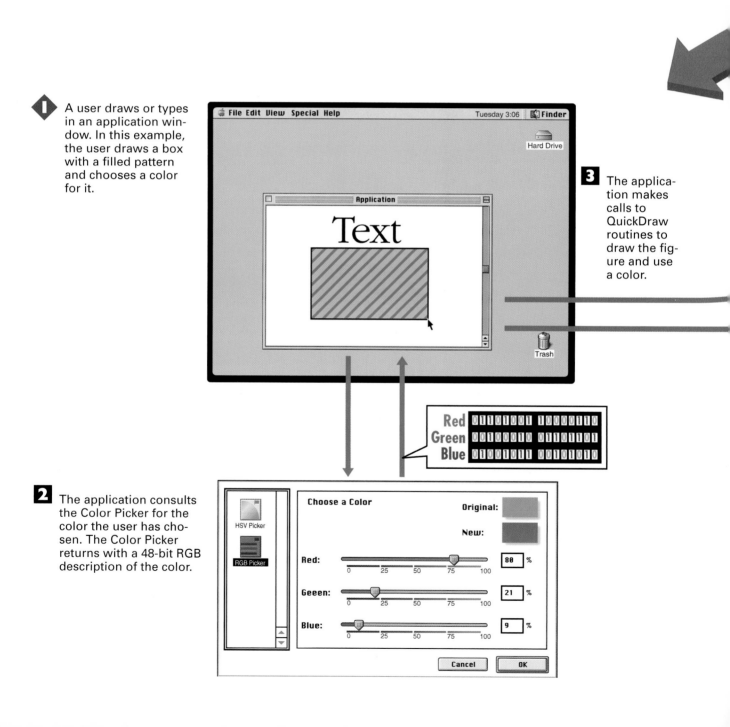

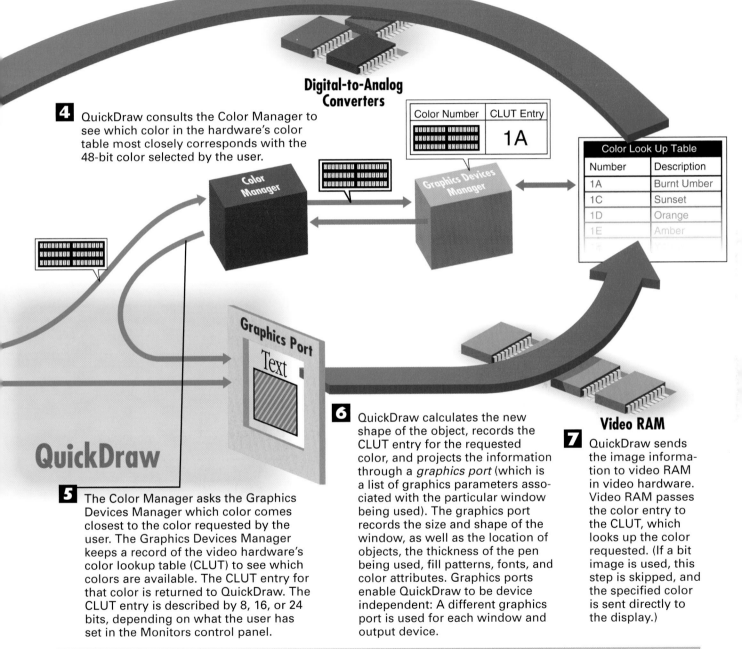

8 Digital-to-analog converters change the data from 8-, 16-, or 24-bit digital bits to continuously varying voltages and send the data to the monitor for the updating of the screen image.

Digital-to-Analog Converters

Color Number	CLUT Entry
	1A

4 QuickDraw consults the Color Manager to see which color in the hardware's color table most closely corresponds with the 48-bit color selected by the user.

Color Manager

Graphics Devices Manager

Color Look Up Table	
Number	Description
1A	Burnt Umber
1C	Sunset
1D	Orange
1E	Amber

Graphics Port

Text

QuickDraw

6 QuickDraw calculates the new shape of the object, records the CLUT entry for the requested color, and projects the information through a *graphics port* (which is a list of graphics parameters associated with the particular window being used). The graphics port records the size and shape of the window, as well as the location of objects, the thickness of the pen being used, fill patterns, fonts, and color attributes. Graphics ports enable QuickDraw to be device independent: A different graphics port is used for each window and output device.

Video RAM

7 QuickDraw sends the image information to video RAM in video hardware. Video RAM passes the color entry to the CLUT, which looks up the color requested. (If a bit image is used, this step is skipped, and the specified color is sent directly to the display.)

5 The Color Manager asks the Graphics Devices Manager which color comes closest to the color requested by the user. The Graphics Devices Manager keeps a record of the video hardware's color lookup table (CLUT) to see which colors are available. The CLUT entry for that color is returned to QuickDraw. The CLUT entry is described by 8, 16, or 24 bits, depending on what the user has set in the Monitors control panel.

MAC FACT

The original QuickDraw in the ROM of early Macs was designed for black-and-white display, but actually had the capability to display eight colors. Although the Macs themselves had no built-in way to connect to a color monitor, at least one company made an add-in card for the Mac SE that connected it to an eight-color monitor.

CHAPTER 23

How Aqua Works

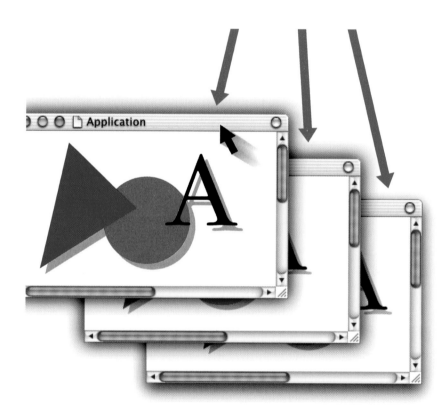

AQUA, the Mac OS X user interface, is the most striking advance in Mac look and feel since 1984. Aqua gives you translucent windows and dialog boxes, icons that can be any size (not just small and large), and windows that drag in their entirety instead of just outlines. Aqua also moves. Buttons pulsate, dialog boxes slide out from window titles, and minimized windows morph in and out of the Dock. Then there's what you don't see—jagged edges on text and graphics and strange drawing artifacts left onscreen when you close and move windows.

All these Aqua features indicate that Mac OS X does more graphics processing than does Mac OS 9. Yet, despite this, Mac OS X graphics are faster than in previous versions. Mac OS X graphics use the Altivec parallel processing unit in the PowerPC G4 processor of the Power Mac G4. But Mac OS X graphics are fast even when you run it on Macs with G3 processors, such as iMacs, iBooks, and PowerBooks.

Mac OS X integrates several old and new graphics technologies and offers them to all applications. The most important is Quartz, a new graphics system for 2D graphics, creating and managing windows, as well as printing. Elements are also included from the earlier QuickDraw (Chapter 22, "How QuickDraw Works"), industry-standard OpenGL for 3D graphics (Chapter 21, "How Multimedia Works"), as well as QuickTime for presenting video (Chapter 21). However, Quartz is the technology most responsible for producing the complex and fast Aqua interface.

One reason is that Quartz takes better advantage of the 2D graphics acceleration hardware in all modern Macs than does QuickDraw. Quartz also provides two modern software features. One is a new layer of control called a *windowing server*. The other is a new method of rendering 2D graphics based on PDF (portable document format).

The Quartz windowing server, called Core Graphics Services, provides a layer of coordination between what's going on in various application windows. The windowing server doesn't draw, or *render*, the graphics in the windows, but it ensures that the display is uniform in all the windows, and when you switch between windows. Core Graphics Services also performs *compositing*, which mixes multiple, separately rendered windows, allowing for translucency and antialiasing. By contrast, Mac OS 9 and earlier just switch between a window of one application and another and hope for the best.

Quartz also adds a new PDF-based method of rendering application windows, called Core Graphics Rendering. PDF offers several advantages, including good color management, continuous zooming, and font independence. You also can save a document as a PDF file in any application that uses Core Graphics Rendering.

PDF doesn't work with dots to begin with, but with objects that are then rendered into dots. This is often called *vector-based* drawing because of the type of mathematics used to describe the objects. PostScript printing (Chapter 31, "How PostScript Works") works this way. In fact, PDF is a superset of PostScript. The vector approach is yet another reason for the speed and quality of the graphics in Mac OS X.

Quartz: The Graphics Engine of Aqua

Application Commands

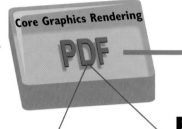

1 In Mac OS X's Quartz, Core Graphics Rendering is a set of code for *rendering* two-dimensional graphics—that is, taking commands from applications and turning them into dots to create the contents of a window. Core Graphics Rendering does this by first taking commands from software and turning them into a PDF-format image.

3 Core Graphics Rendering takes the PDF and creates a rasterized version of the window, turning the objects into dots (as a PostScript printer does). No jagged edges exist because the dots fade out at the edges. This is called *antialiasing*, another feature of the PDF-based graphics generation.

4 From its PDF version of the image, Quartz Core Graphics Rendering can create other types of output, including PDF files. (This is why OS X applications can Save As PDF files.) Other output includes print previews for applications, PostScript for laser printers, and rasterized print jobs for non-PostScript printers.

2 PDF is similar to PostScript, in that it describes text, shapes, lines, color, shading, transparency, and other graphical characteristics not as dots, but as objects or mathematical descriptions called *vectors*. (This is how a drawing program works, as opposed to a painting program that describes pixels.) As objects, they can be more easily and quickly rendered for any size window, as well as for morphing into the Dock.

5 Core Graphics Rendering also can understand some QuickDraw graphics commands and turn them into PDF. This gives software using QuickDraw code access to some of the output capabilities of Quartz, including PostScript and PDF.

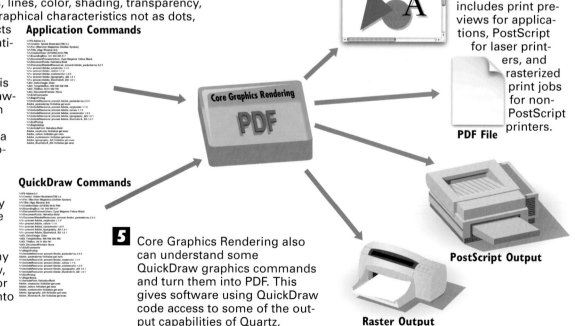

PDF File

PostScript Output

Raster Output

6 Core Graphics Rendering is just one type of image renderer applications can use. QuickDraw is used by applications ported OS X from OS 9. QuickTime renders real-time video, and OpenGL renders 3D graphics used in games. All the renderers pass the content of their windows to the Quartz Core Graphics Services, a *window server,* which manages the juxtaposition of multiple windows.

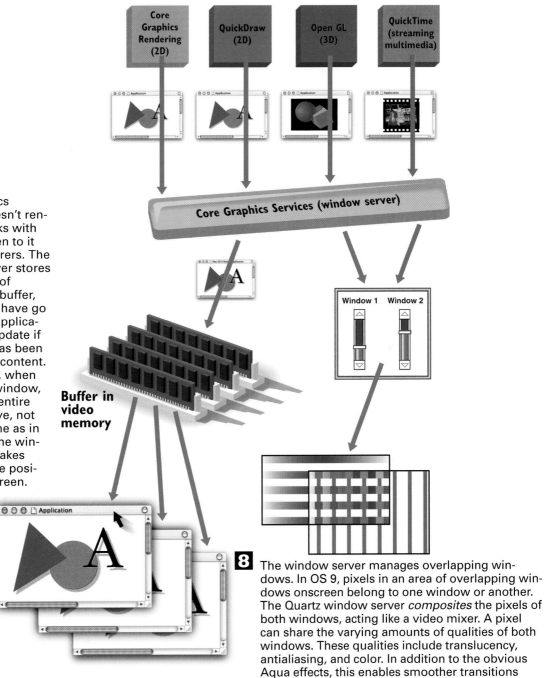

Core Graphics Services

7 Core Graphics Services doesn't render, but works with the dots given to it by the renderers. The window server stores the bitmaps of screens in a buffer, so it doesn't have go back to the application for an update if no change has been made to the content. For instance, when you drag a window, you see the entire window move, not just an outline as in Mac OS 9. The window server takes care of all the positioning onscreen.

Buffer in video memory

8 The window server manages overlapping windows. In OS 9, pixels in an area of overlapping windows onscreen belong to one window or another. The Quartz window server *composites* the pixels of both windows, acting like a video mixer. A pixel can share the varying amounts of qualities of both windows. These qualities include translucency, antialiasing, and color. In addition to the obvious Aqua effects, this enables smoother transitions when you switch between or resize windows.

CHAPTER

24

How a CRT Display Works

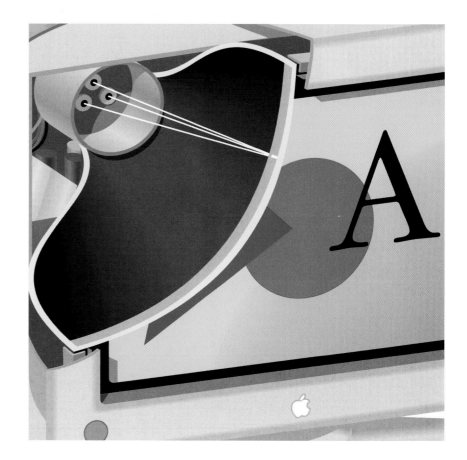

THE *cathode ray tube (CRT)* display in an iMac or a Power Mac's monitor is a producer of optical illusions. To the eye, a color screen appears as a steady image of solid colors, similar to a movie being projected on a screen. You might think you're looking at a photographic image of a basket of flowers, but the color monitor actually just displays tiny dots of red, green, and blue (in varying intensities). The colored dots are so close together that they blend in different color strengths, only seeming to produce all the colors of the rainbow.

You are also not looking at a steady image. A CRT display does not flash an image onscreen all at once, as does a movie projector. Instead, it draws one picture element (or *pixel*) at a time in lines across the screen, one line at a time. The lines of pixels are redrawn so rapidly that the screen appears to display a solid image. Apple displays redraw the screen 67–85 times per second or more. This number is the *hertz (Hz) rating* of the display. With displays that operate at below 60 hertz, your eye can actually detect the redrawing of the screen as flicker, which can lead to eyestrain and headaches.

The dots that make up the screen image originate in the QuickDraw routines of Mac OS 9.x and earlier or in Mac OS X's PDF display routines. The Mac's graphics hardware processes the data provided by these routines and turns it into a description of where the pixels should be. The display hardware then sends this information to the iMac's built-in monitor or a standalone monitor connected to a Power Mac.

CRT displays can produce images at several different pixel resolutions, which you can set in the Monitors control panel. When you increase the pixel resolution—such as from 640×480 pixels to 800×600 pixels—you will notice that icons and windows appear smaller onscreen. That's because your display packs more pixels in the same space, which means the pixels must be closer together.

Every display size has one pixel resolution that provides *WYSIWYG*—what you see is what you get (pronounced "wiz-ee-wig"). WYSIWYG occurs when one inch onscreen, such as displayed by an application's ruler, equals one inch on a ruler if you hold a ruler up to the display. The WYSIWYG resolution is the one that displays 72 pixels per inch, although this can vary by a few pixels.

For the iMac's 15-inch display, the WYSIWYG resolution is 800×600 pixels. For many 17-inch displays, you get 72 dots per inch at 1024×768 pixels. That's 786,432 pixels, all being redrawn some 75 times a second, which is enough to fool any eye.

Color CRT Display

This drawing depicts the outside of an Apple Studio Display, but also describes how an iMac display works. Any CRT display is controlled by the video circuitry on the Mac's logic board or on a separate video board in an expansion slot. Most of the monitor consists of a cathode-ray tube, the interior of which is a vacuum. Inside the tube, beams of electrons are projected against phosphors on the inside of the screen, which glow and produce the image.

Various types of signals come to the display through an internal or external 15-wire cable. Three of the signals control the levels of red, green, and blue arriving from the digital-to-analog converters on the Mac's video circuitry. The horizontal and vertical synchronization signals tell the monitor when to hit each pixel with what signal. Several ground signals also exist, which provide 0 volts as a reference voltage.

3 The electron beams are aimed at the screen, one pixel at a time. The beams start at the top-left corner of the screen and scan horizontally from left to right. The beams then shut off, aim at the left of the next line, and start shooting at the pixels from left to right. This continues until the beams reach the bottom right, when the beams shut off, return to the top left, and begin scanning again. A complete image is painted onscreen 67 to 85 times per second. This is called the *vertical scan rate*. At this rate, the eye is unable to detect the individual scans.

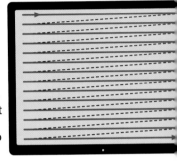

1 Three cathodes (negatively charged electron emitters) convert the signals for red, green, and blue into three beams of electrons.

2 Magnetic deflection coils, controlled by the synchronization signals, bend the electron beams horizontally and vertically, aiming them at the appropriate places onscreen. The three beams move in unison.

4 To help focus the electron beams on the spots at which they are aimed, and to separate one pixel from the next, the beams pass through some sort of grating. Some Mac monitors, including the Apple Studio Display, contain Sony Trinitron tubes, which use an aperture grill made of thin parallel wires (each about 195 microns thick). Other displays, such as that in the iMac, employ a shadow mask, a thin metal plate with holes in it. Aperture grill tubes tend to produce sharper and brighter images than monitors with shadow masks, although this isn't always the case. With either technology, the *dot pitch*, the distance between the holes or wires, is typically 0.2–0.3 millimeter. The closer the holes, the sharper the image.

Aperture Grill

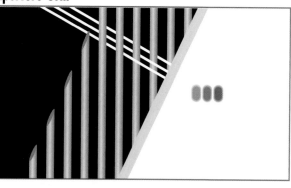

5 The electron beams each hit the phosphors that coat the inside of the cathode-ray tubes. One of the phosphors glows red when hit with electrons; another glows green; and a third glows blue. A pixel consists of one of each type of phosphor. After the beam moves on to the next pixel, the phosphors continue to glow until the beams strike them again on the next pass. The phosphors are so close to each other that they trick the eye into seeing the blended colors. The intensity of each beam determines how bright the phosphor will glow. White is produced when all three beams hit at maximum intensity, and black is produced when all three are shut off.

Shadow Mask

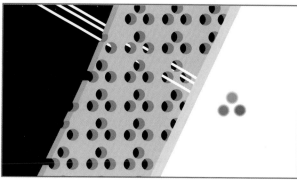

25

How Flat-Panel Displays Work

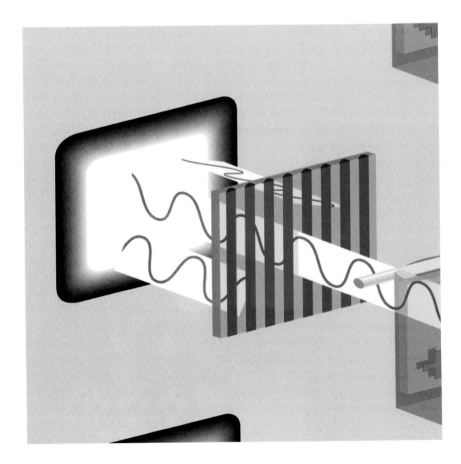

FIFTY years of televisions had produced cathode-ray tubes that were inexpensive and reliable by the time personal computers appeared in the 1980s. Using cathode-ray tubes as the personal computer's display technology was a natural. However, the appearance of notebook computers spurred the development of a new technology: compact and low-power flat-panel displays. PowerBooks and iBooks use flat-panel displays, but prices have dropped enough to support a market for desktop flat-panel displays, such as Apple's Cinema Display and Studio Displays, as well as displays from other vendors.

Flat-panel displays are still more expensive than traditional CRT-based monitors, but have some advantages: They are brighter, sharper, and more linear, and often offer better contrast. They also have no distortion at the edges and corners of the screen, as is often found in CRT monitors.

Flat-panel displays bear little resemblance to CRT displays found on desktop Macs. On a flat-panel screen, each pixel square is easy to identify with the naked eye. Unlike CRT pixels, flat-panel pixels are fixed in the display. This means flat-panel screens don't display in multiple resolutions. Instead, PowerBook, iBook, and desktop flat-panels offer simulated alternative resolutions, which is why they look a bit fuzzier when not at the home (or actual) pixel resolution.

Flat-panels use the liquid crystal display (LCD) technology first popularized in digital watches in the 1970s. Each pixel of a flat-panel display is filled with transparent material called *liquid crystal*, an odd substance that becomes opaque when an electric charge is applied to it.

LCD screens don't draw images one pixel at a time like the CRT displays do; instead they light the entire screen at once by shining light through the liquid crystal–filled pixel. Color LCDs use three rays of light that converge on each pixel. Each ray travels through either a red, green, or blue filter. The display varies the electric charge applied to the liquid crystal to produce several levels of translucence, which in turn appear as several layers of colors. The type of LCD screen used in today's flat-panel displays is called *thin film transistor active matrix technology*.

Active Matrix LCD Display

Flat-panel displays use two rather odd properties of physics—the polarization of light (a phenomenon used in sunglasses to partially block out light) and the interaction of light with liquid crystal, a liquid material that shows some properties of solid crystals.

1 The backlighting panel produces white light at the back of the display. Light consists of vibrating electro-magnetic waves. White light produces many light waves of every color vibrating in every different direction.

2 The light passes through a polarizing filter—a material with embedded crystals—which acts like a grating, allowing only light vibrating in one direction to pass.

3 Thin wires (column and row electrodes) deliver the graphics signals to thin-film transistors: three for each pixel to produce color. The transistor puts out several levels of current, which will eventually represent different levels of color or gray.

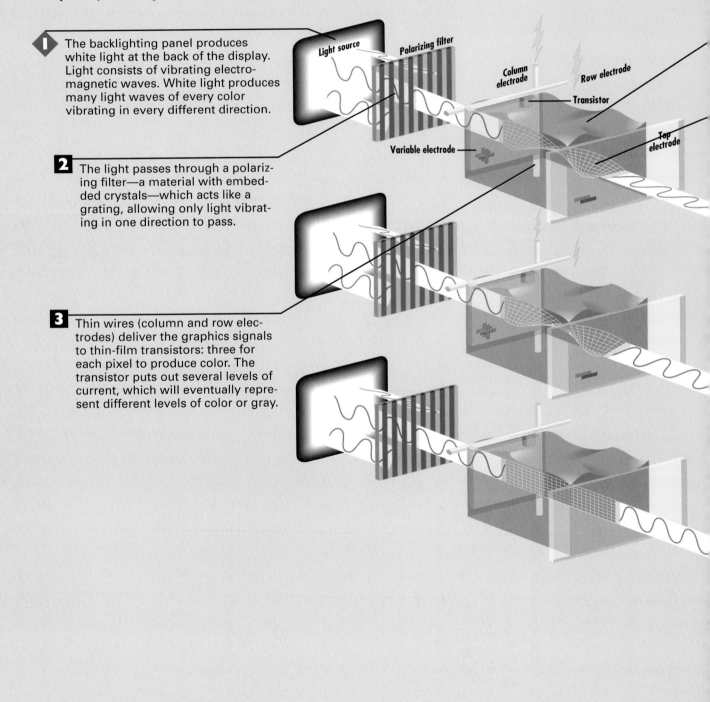

Light source

Polarizing filter

Column electrode

Row electrode

Transistor

Variable electrode

Top electrode

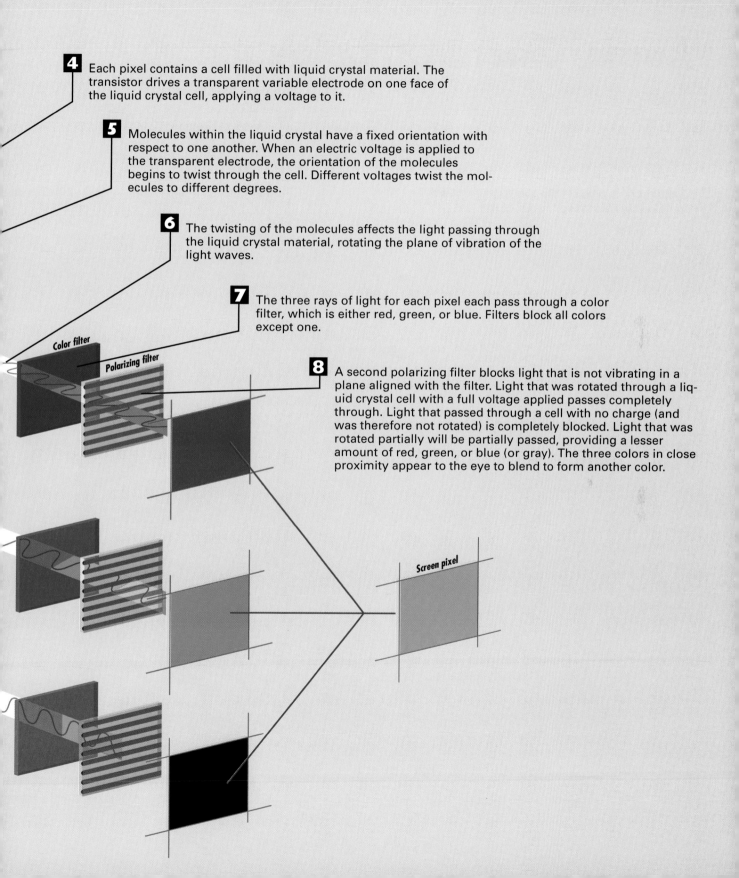

4 Each pixel contains a cell filled with liquid crystal material. The transistor drives a transparent variable electrode on one face of the liquid crystal cell, applying a voltage to it.

5 Molecules within the liquid crystal have a fixed orientation with respect to one another. When an electric voltage is applied to the transparent electrode, the orientation of the molecules begins to twist through the cell. Different voltages twist the molecules to different degrees.

6 The twisting of the molecules affects the light passing through the liquid crystal material, rotating the plane of vibration of the light waves.

7 The three rays of light for each pixel each pass through a color filter, which is either red, green, or blue. Filters block all colors except one.

8 A second polarizing filter blocks light that is not vibrating in a plane aligned with the filter. Light that was rotated through a liquid crystal cell with a full voltage applied passes completely through. Light that passed through a cell with no charge (and was therefore not rotated) is completely blocked. Light that was rotated partially will be partially passed, providing a lesser amount of red, green, or blue (or gray). The three colors in close proximity appear to the eye to blend to form another color.

Color filter

Polarizing filter

Screen pixel

Apple Cinema Display

Digital interface

As in the PowerBook and iBook displays, the signal remains digital from the graphics board to the display. Because ordinary graphics boards produce analogy output, the Cinema Display requires a special digital output found in the Power Mac G4's graphics card called *Digital Visual Interface*. This eliminates distortion and flicker.

TMDS transmitter and receiver

To transmit the digital graphics data over a cable without degradation, the Digital Visual Interface hardware uses a technique called *transition minimized differential signaling (TMDS)*. The Digital Visual Interface hardware in the Mac contains a TMDS transmitter, and the display contains a TMDS receiver. Half of the 24 wires are used for TMDS signals, which produces a stream of 1s and 0s centered on a threshold voltage. Voltages received above the threshold are 1s; those below it are 0s.

Two-port USB hubs

A tiny USB hub sits inside the back of the display, providing two ports for a keyboard, a mouse, or other devices. The USB cable is bundled in with the video cable coming out of the display and breaks out again on the Mac side of the cable.

Power button

Pressing it can turn on both the display and the Power Mac G4. It is similar to the power button on the keyboard and uses USB to transmit its signal.

Pixel resolution

The native resolution is 1600×1024 pixels. The wide screen is the reason for the name Cinema Display—because it can display full-screen movies without letter boxing (the black bands at the top and bottom of a screen). This width also enables you to display more than two full-sized pages.

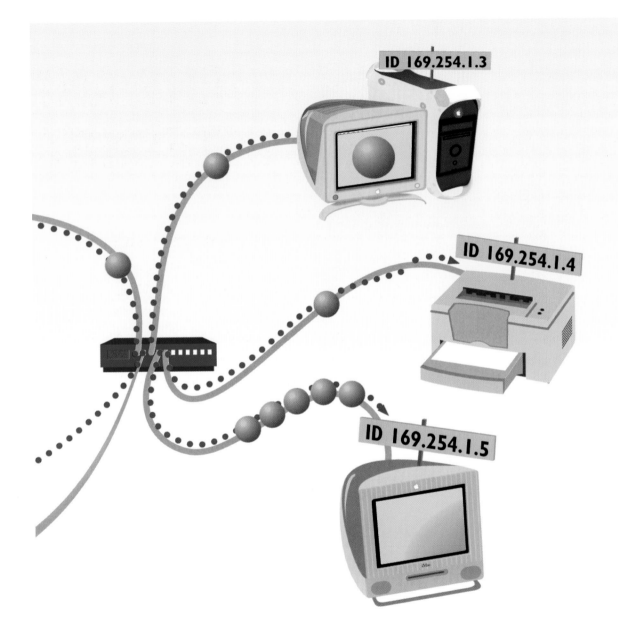

P A R T

7

NETWORKS AND THE INTERNET

Chapter 26: How Mac OS Networks

178

Chapter 27: How Networks Work

182

Chapter 28: How Wireless Networks Work

192

Chapter 29: How Internet Connections Work

196

TEN years ago, only computer geeks cared about networks. Today, people buy home computers for the sole reason of gaining access to the Internet. In fact, people are even setting up computer networks in their homes. Unfortunately, getting a handle on just what the Internet or a local network *is* often lands you back into the realm of the geeks.

You could think of a network in terms of the type of cable connecting computers. However, you don't even need wires anymore with products such as Apple's AirPort. So, you might describe a network as the hardware circuits generating signals to run over the cable. It's also useful to look at a network in terms of its *protocols*—the computer language that enables different devices to understand one another. When it comes down to it, a network is a system containing all these things, as well as computers, printers, servers, and other devices acting together to improve the usefulness of all the devices.

Networks bring to your Mac the benefits of shared resources. For instance, you can visit a Web site that is available to people all over the planet. You also can use networks locally to share the office printer. Other resources include electronic mail and file servers that enable you to send messages and files to people when they aren't at their desks, and electronic calendars that enable you to set up meetings and appointments with people you haven't seen for weeks.

These and other network resources, called *network services*, consist of software running on users' Macs and PCs or on dedicated computers called *servers*. Servers can be Macs, PCs, or UNIX computers in the next room or the next state. You use some services, such as email, directly. Other services sit behind the scenes, making the network function.

Locally, you don't always need server computers. When you directly access another user's Mac or a PC, this is called *peer-to-peer* networking. Mac OS comes with software that enables you to access both dedicated servers and peer-to-peer network devices. It also enables other users to access your Mac on a peer-to-peer basis.

Running underneath all the file, email, and other network services are the mechanisms that move the bits between computers. These are the network protocols that make up the language that computers on a network use to speak to each other.

AppleTalk was the first networking protocol built into Macs and most network printers. In fact, AppleTalk began as a method of sharing laser printers among multiple Mac users. It soon grew into a system that enables the movement of files between computers and the running of third-party networking software.

AppleTalk is designed to be as easy to set up and use as the Mac. Everything you need to set up an AppleTalk network is built into the Mac: the hardware that transmits and receives the signals, the protocols that enable communications, and the software that enables you to print and share files. You use the Chooser utility to access printers and file servers. The Mac's file sharing feature enables other network users to access designated files and folders on your hard disk.

Similar to other network protocols, AppleTalk runs on Ethernet cabling or over a telephone connection. Older Macs could run it over LocalTalk, a slower type of hardware that moved data at 230.4Kbps. Some older Macs have 10Mbps Ethernet ports as well as LocalTalk. By contrast, the Ethernet ports in modern Macs moves data at 100Mbps and in the case of recent Power Macs, at 1,024 Mbps—a gigabit per second.

AppleTalk isn't the only network protocol that runs over Ethernet or a dial-up modem. Another is TCP/IP (Transmission Control Protocol/ Internet Protocol), the protocol used on the Internet. TCP/IP is also widely used on local networks, in business, and at universities. TCP/IP has some advantages. It's faster than AppleTalk and runs a lot of software. It's still not as easy to set up or use as AppleTalk, which is the main reason why AppleTalk still exists. Apple has been gradually making TCP/IP easier to use in Macs, and it could eventually replace AppleTalk.

Right now, your Mac OS system software comes with both TCP/IP and AppleTalk protocols, and your system can use both at the same time. For instance, you do this when you print a Web page to an AppleTalk laser printer. You also can use TCP/IP to log on to AppleShare IP and Windows 2000 file servers.

A third network protocol you might run into is IPX. Some Macs in business still run IPX on older Novell NetWare networks. In addition, some multiplayer games come with the IPX protocol, which you add to the Mac by installing a few files.

The Mac became a real multiprotocol machine with the arrival of Open Transport, which is Mac OS network system software that began shipping around the time of Mac OS 8. Open Transport removes the Mac networking focus from AppleTalk and gives Mac OS equivalent access to TCP/IP and IPX networks. Open Transport also better conforms to industry networking standards than previous Mac network software and is designed to let you plug in software to enable the Mac to access other network systems as well.

Mac OS X retains the upper portions of Open Transport software—the parts that interact with your network applications, such as email and your Web browser. Underneath, Mac OS X uses the rock-solid networking software of BSD UNIX. Networking in Mac OS X is faster and more stable than in previous versions of Mac OS.

Apple also sells a special version of Mac OS X called Mac OS X Server, which is basically a UNIX-like server with Web and email servers, a file server, and other features. Mac OS X Server actually first shipped almost two years before the user version of Mac OS X. When it first shipped, it didn't have the Aqua interface graphics engines. Its job is to be an invisible part of your local network and the Internet.

CHAPTER
26

How Mac OS Networks

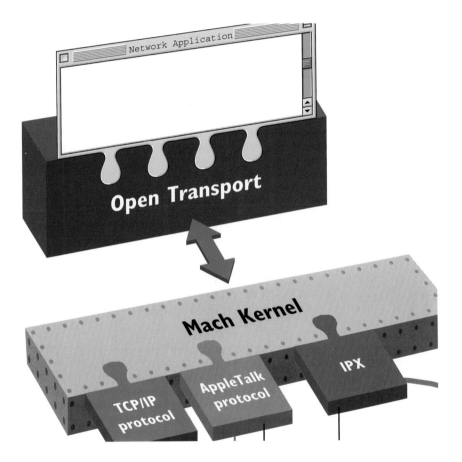

NETWORKING is as intrinsic a part of the Mac as any of the other input/output systems. As with the Mac's other data transport systems, the mechanics of networking are run by system software that takes its orders from your applications.

The network-enabling system software that connects network applications to networks is called Open Transport and was introduced in 1995. In Mac OS X, Open Transport still communicates with network applications such as email and Web browser software, but the lower-level core has been replaced by BSD UNIX networking.

Before Open Transport, AppleTalk was the Mac's native networking language. At its core was the AppleTalk Manager in ROM and AppleTalk protocol software in the System file and folder. The Mac spoke other network protocols, such as the Internet's TCP/IP and Novell's IPX, like a first-year student—slowly and with limited ability.

Open Transport enabled the Mac to speak non-AppleTalk network languages like a native, making networking faster. Open Transport's capability to speak multiple network languages fluently is called *transport independence*. Applications written to support Open Transport don't have to know anything about protocols. They can automatically use AppleTalk, TCP/IP, and IPX, as well as different types of links, including dial-up networks, Ethernet, and wireless.

Open Transport also enables an application to use multiple protocols at the same time. For instance, a Web browser can surf the Web over TCP/IP while printing to an AppleTalk network printer.

Open Transport also makes it easy to switch between various network setups. A PowerBook or iBook user can create and store Internet settings for several different locations and change them without having to restart the computer. And instead of loading all the network protocol software on-the-fly, Open Transport loads them as you need them, conserving RAM.

All this is also true of Open Transport in Mac OS X. However, the lower-level protocols and mechanisms are now controlled by the Mach kernel, which has BSD UNIX built into it. The kernel moves the data in and out of the Mac, and programmers build extensions to it called Network Kernel Extensions.

Why BSD UNIX? For one, the Internet and TCP/IP began as UNIX networking standards, and many servers on the Internet are still running UNIX or the Linux variant. BSD networking is more robust. It also gives Macs new server features, such as multihoming using IP aliasing—using multiple IP addresses with a single Ethernet card. This enables a Mac server to host multiple Web sites as if it were multiple servers.

Open Transport in Mac OS X also can keep better track of the system resources each network application is using. This helps overall efficiency.

Mac OS X focuses less on AppleTalk than before. You should still be able to access AppleTalk networks, but some AppleTalk programming techniques are no longer supported in Mac OS X. As time goes on, we will see TCP/IP become more sophisticated. Mac OS X's modular networking approach will enable new features to be easily added.

Network System Software

Mac OS 8.X and 9.X Open Transport

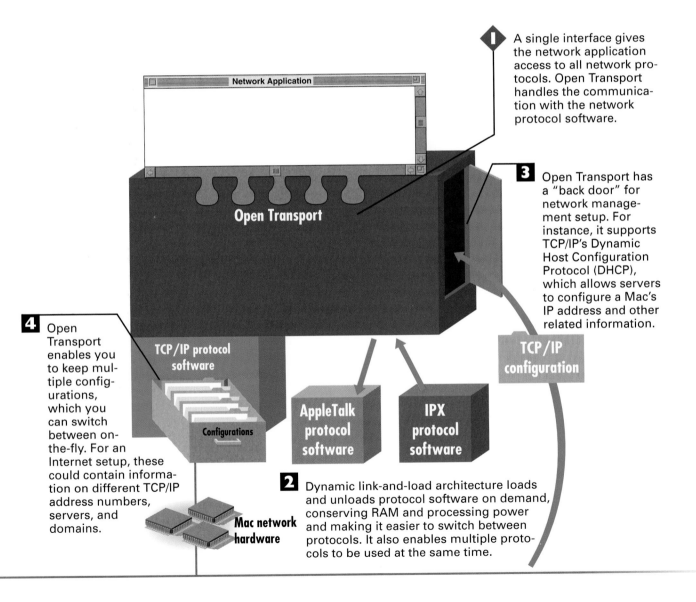

1 A single interface gives the network application access to all network protocols. Open Transport handles the communication with the network protocol software.

3 Open Transport has a "back door" for network management setup. For instance, it supports TCP/IP's Dynamic Host Configuration Protocol (DHCP), which allows servers to configure a Mac's IP address and other related information.

4 Open Transport enables you to keep multiple configurations, which you can switch between on-the-fly. For an Internet setup, these could contain information on different TCP/IP address numbers, servers, and domains.

2 Dynamic link-and-load architecture loads and unloads protocol software on demand, conserving RAM and processing power and making it easier to switch between protocols. It also enables multiple protocols to be used at the same time.

Network Application

Open Transport

TCP/IP protocol software

Configurations

AppleTalk protocol software

IPX protocol software

TCP/IP configuration

Mac network hardware

Mac OS X Network Kernel Extensions

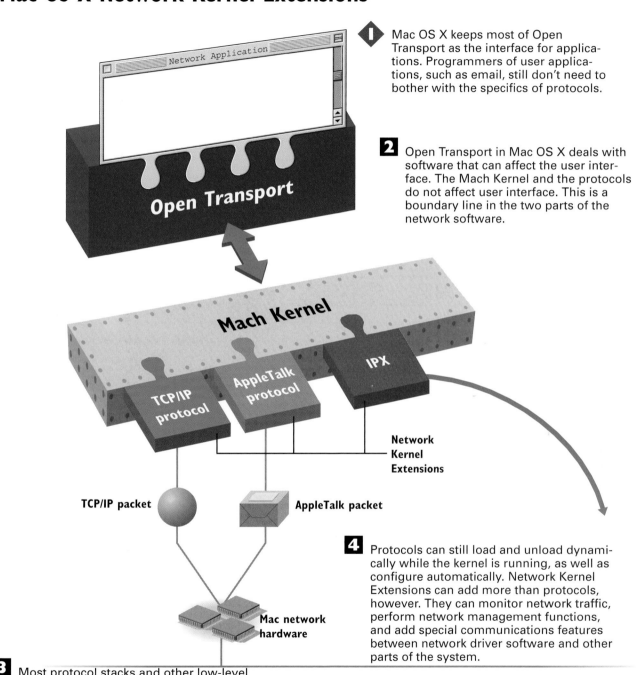

1 Mac OS X keeps most of Open Transport as the interface for applications. Programmers of user applications, such as email, still don't need to bother with the specifics of protocols.

2 Open Transport in Mac OS X deals with software that can affect the user interface. The Mach Kernel and the protocols do not affect user interface. This is a boundary line in the two parts of the network software.

Network Application

Open Transport

Mach Kernel

IPX

TCP/IP protocol

AppleTalk protocol

Network Kernel Extensions

TCP/IP packet

AppleTalk packet

Mac network hardware

4 Protocols can still load and unload dynamically while the kernel is running, as well as configure automatically. Network Kernel Extensions can add more than protocols, however. They can monitor network traffic, perform network management functions, and add special communications features between network driver software and other parts of the system.

3 Most protocol stacks and other low-level networking features of Mac OS X are written as Network Kernel Extensions, which add on to the networking infrastructure of the kernel. They enable the kernel to manage the movement of network data packets to and from the networking hardware.

27

How Networks Work

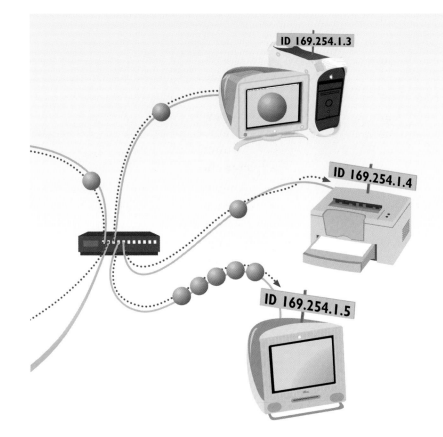

WIRES are wires and bits are bits. You can access a network over a modem or link a Mac and PC on the same Ethernet segment, but the wires and bits don't really care. If the networking software uses the same *protocols*—the network languages that computers speak—then the networking hardware is happy to pass along the data.

Network hardware starts with the transceiver chips in the interface hardware of computers, printers, and other network devices. The devices on a network segment must all use the same type of network interface hardware so that they'll all understand the signals being bounced through the wires. The different types of network interfaces, sometimes called *data links*, operate at different speeds and transmit data in different formats. *Ethernet*, the network interface built into every Mac, is the most common. You can add other network interface hardware, such as Apple's wireless AirPort or HomePNA, which sends signals through the in-wall telephone wires of your home. Earlier Macs also can use LocalTalk, the now-discontinued data link that runs only AppleTalk protocols.

The other pieces of network hardware that bring computers together include *hubs*, which boost the network signals traveling along the wires. *Bridges* and *routers* connect different network segments using different data links. Networks containing multiple segments are called *internetworks*. This is where the global Internet, the biggest network of networks, gets its name.

Most computer networks, whether they are running AppleTalk, TCP/IP, or both, transmit information in a similar manner. A computer broadcasts a message over the wires in the form of data bundles called *packets*, which contain the addresses of the intended recipients. All the computers on the network receive the packets, but only the intended recipients choose to read the message.

AppleTalk is still the easiest type of network to set up and use. A feature called *dynamic addressing* causes the Macs on the network to set their own addresses without your having to lift a finger. Browsing for AppleTalk file servers and printers is also easy because everything appears in the Chooser without any configuration.

However, TCP/IP is slowly catching up in terms of ease of use. Mac OS now has dynamic addressing for TCP/IP, although it's not as transparent as in AppleTalk. You can now browse for IP-based file servers and printers that are correctly set up. Despite its complexity, TCP/IP does have advantages over AppleTalk. One is that it's faster. And, as the protocol of the Internet, TCP/IP also has become the focus of local networking among network hardware and software manufacturers, including Apple and Microsoft.

Mac OS also includes user software, such as Web browsers and email software, which uses all these protocols and the networking hardware. But file-sharing software that enables you to pass files between Macs as well as PCs running software compatible with the Apple Filing Protocol (AFP) is also included. Networked hard disks and folders sitting on other computer servers all appear as desktop volumes—much like the hard disk in your Mac.

AppleTalk at Work

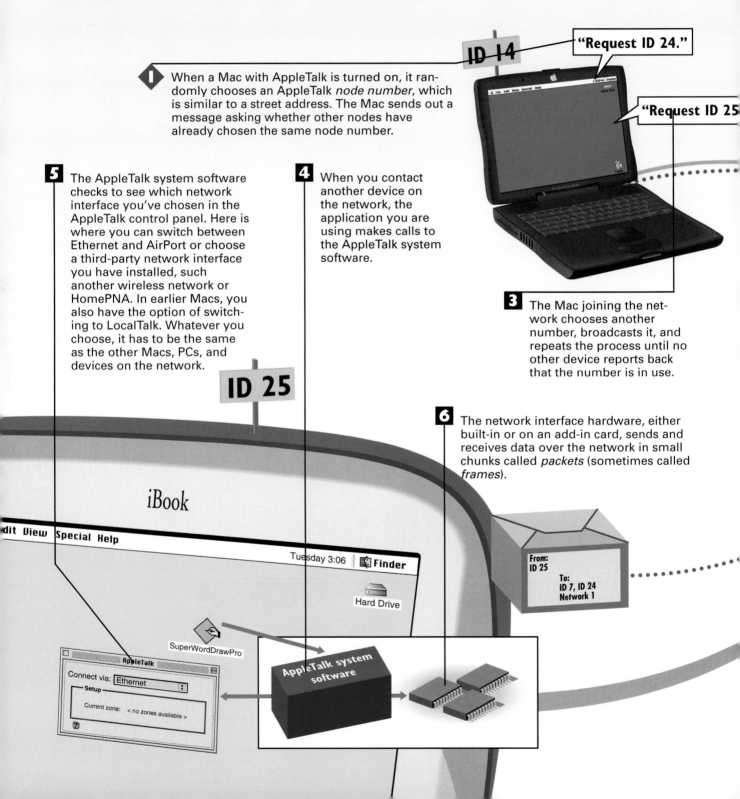

ID 14

"Request ID 24."

"Request ID 25"

1 When a Mac with AppleTalk is turned on, it randomly chooses an AppleTalk *node number*, which is similar to a street address. The Mac sends out a message asking whether other nodes have already chosen the same node number.

5 The AppleTalk system software checks to see which network interface you've chosen in the AppleTalk control panel. Here is where you can switch between Ethernet and AirPort or choose a third-party network interface you have installed, such another wireless network or HomePNA. In earlier Macs, you also have the option of switching to LocalTalk. Whatever you choose, it has to be the same as the other Macs, PCs, and devices on the network.

4 When you contact another device on the network, the application you are using makes calls to the AppleTalk system software.

3 The Mac joining the network chooses another number, broadcasts it, and repeats the process until no other device reports back that the number is in use.

ID 25

6 The network interface hardware, either built-in or on an add-in card, sends and receives data over the network in small chunks called *packets* (sometimes called *frames*).

iBook

dit View   Special Help

Tuesday 3:06   Finder

Hard Drive

SuperWordDrawPro

AppleTalk

Connect via: Ethernet

Setup

Current zone: < no zones available >

AppleTalk system software

From:
ID 25

To:
ID 7, ID 24
Network 1

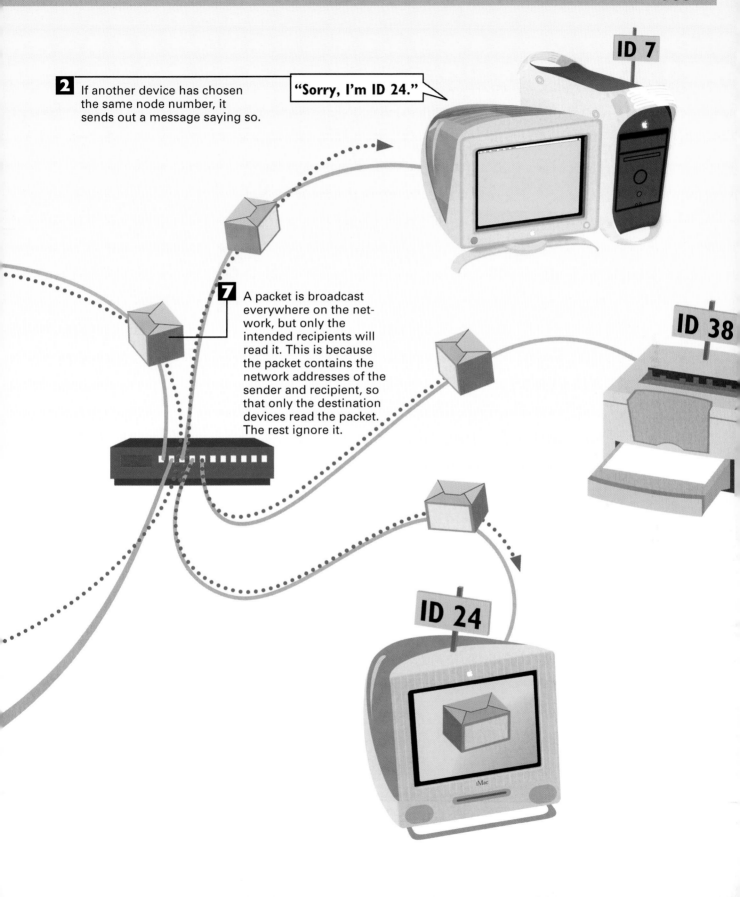

2 If another device has chosen the same node number, it sends out a message saying so.

"Sorry, I'm ID 24."

7 A packet is broadcast everywhere on the network, but only the intended recipients will read it. This is because the packet contains the network addresses of the sender and recipient, so that only the destination devices read the packet. The rest ignore it.

TCP/IP at Work

Whether you use TCP/IP to visit a Web site or transfer a file on your local network, your Mac uses the same basic methods of communication. Each computer identifies itself with an *IP address*, a number you can type in yourself or which your Mac can get from a server on the network. The IP address, combined with the subnet mask according to certain rules, also identifies the subnetwork in which the computer resides. This enables email messages to arrive on your computer from across the ocean or across the building.

"Is there DHCP server out there?"

"Request ID 169.254.1.1"

"Request ID 169.254.1.2"

I When a Mac's TCP/IP control panel is set to Use DHCP Server, the Mac sends out a call for a DHCP server. If a DHCP server exists on the network—or at your Internet service provider—the server sends the Mac an IP address. If no DHCP server responds, the Mac randomly chooses an IP address from a range of more than 65,000 numbers. The Mac sends out a message asking whether other nodes have already chosen the same IP address.

5 The TCP/IP system software checks to see whether an IP address exists for a domain name server listed in the TCP/IP control panel. This server could be on your local network or on the Internet. A domain name server keeps a list of IP addresses and their corresponding *universal resource locators*—URLs. This enables you to type a Web URL, such as *www.acme.com*, instead of the server's IP address. You might not need a domain name server if you are moving a file.

ID 169.254.1.1

3 The Mac joining the network chooses another IP address, broadcasts it, and repeats the process until no other device reports back that the number is in use.

4 When you make contact with another device on the network, the application you are using makes calls to the TCP/IP system software.

To: 169.254.1.5

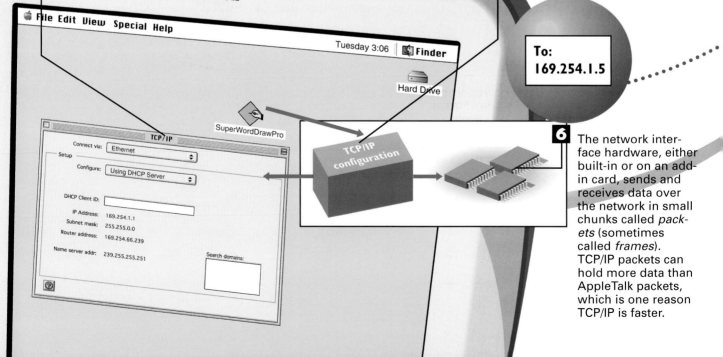

iBook

6 The network interface hardware, either built-in or on an add-in card, sends and receives data over the network in small chunks called *packets* (sometimes called *frames*). TCP/IP packets can hold more data than AppleTalk packets, which is one reason TCP/IP is faster.

ID 169.254.1.3

2 If another device has chosen the same IP address, it sends out a message saying so.

7 A packet is broadcast everywhere on the network, but only the intended recipients read it. This is because the packet contains the network addresses of the sender and recipient, so that only the destination devices read the packet. The rest ignore it.

ID 169.254.1.4

ID 169.254.1.5

8 TCP/IP has a feature called *streaming*, which is used to send large files and to download video to your Mac. With streaming, the computer sending data has to notify the receiving computer only once before sending a large number of packets. With AppleTalk, the sending and receiving computers exchange verification packets after every few data packets. This makes AppleTalk slower than TCP/IP.

Network Hardware

Networks require a few different devices to keep network traffic running. In larger networks (including the Internet), *routers* are used to move data between the originator and the destination. Routers read the address numbers for each network segment which is similar to a postal ZIP code. The network number enables the delivery of messages to the proper network segment. The network administrator must assign network address numbers to the routers. This is done separately for AppleTalk and TCP/IP.

1 Most Ethernet networks are set up in a star configuration with a hub at the center. The *hub* receives an incoming packet, boosts the signal, and rebroadcasts the packet to the other network devices. Ethernet hubs must be designed to run at 10Mbps 100Mbps, 1Gpbs, or all three. Hubs are protocol independent, running AppleTalk or TCP/IP or any other protocol.

2 Two or more hubs can be connected to expand a network. Often the hubs are stacked together in a utility closet.

5 A *network segment* is defined as the part of the network between routers or bridges. Two or more hubs linked together still constitute a single-network segment.

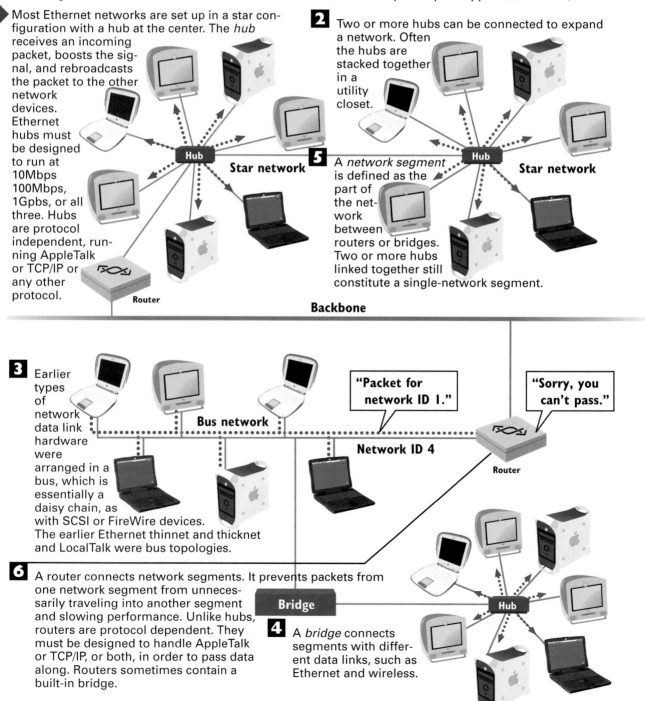

3 Earlier types of network data link hardware were arranged in a bus, which is essentially a daisy chain, as with SCSI or FireWire devices. The earlier Ethernet thinnet and thicknet and LocalTalk were bus topologies.

"Packet for network ID 1."

"Sorry, you can't pass."

Network ID 4

6 A router connects network segments. It prevents packets from one network segment from unnecessarily traveling into another segment and slowing performance. Unlike hubs, routers are protocol dependent. They must be designed to handle AppleTalk or TCP/IP, or both, in order to pass data along. Routers sometimes contain a built-in bridge.

4 A *bridge* connects segments with different data links, such as Ethernet and wireless.

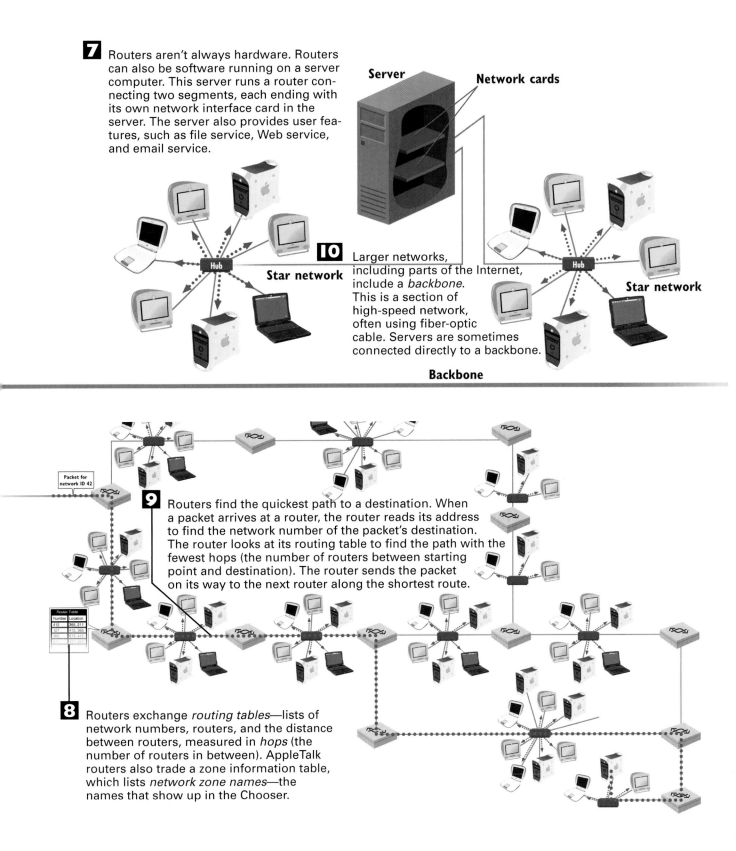

7 Routers aren't always hardware. Routers can also be software running on a server computer. This server runs a router connecting two segments, each ending with its own network interface card in the server. The server also provides user features, such as file service, Web service, and email service.

Server

Network cards

Star network

10 Larger networks, including parts of the Internet, include a *backbone*. This is a section of high-speed network, often using fiber-optic cable. Servers are sometimes connected directly to a backbone.

Star network

Backbone

Packet for network ID 42

9 Routers find the quickest path to a destination. When a packet arrives at a router, the router reads its address to find the network number of the packet's destination. The router looks at its routing table to find the path with the fewest hops (the number of routers between starting point and destination). The router sends the packet on its way to the next router along the shortest route.

Router Table

Number	Location
412	365, 211
107	412, 365
305	873, 412

8 Routers exchange *routing tables*—lists of network numbers, routers, and the distance between routers, measured in *hops* (the number of routers in between). AppleTalk routers also trade a zone information table, which lists *network zone names*—the names that show up in the Chooser.

Browsing AppleTalk with the Chooser

The Chooser in Mac OS 9 and earlier is an AppleTalk *network browser*. You use it to search for and log into file servers, shared folders on users' Macs, network printers, and other AppleTalk services. As an interface device, the Chooser has always been a bit of an oddball because it also lets you select and sometimes configure non-network devices, such as an inkjet printer, fax software, and sometimes TCP/IP services. It started as the Choose Printer command in 1985 as a method of selecting a printer. Apple finally did away with the Chooser in Mac OS X.

System Folder

Chooser

AppleShare   LaserWriter

Acme Printer

1 When you open the Chooser, it reads the network and printer device drivers, which are called Chooser *extensions* and are located in the Extensions folder in the System folder. A single extension exists—the AppleShare driver—for AppleShare-compatible file servers and shared folders. The data in the Chooser extension files tells the Chooser what to display when you click its icon.

AppleTalk Zones:

Art Department
Engineering
Marketing
Sales

2 If AppleTalk is active (turned on), the Chooser sends out packets requesting routers to send zone information packets. AppleTalk *zones* are logical groupings of network devices. Zones can contain all the devices in a network segment, or they can contain devices in different network segments that are related functionally. For instance, you could set up a zone consisting of the Macs of managers. Zones are created by the network manager when setting up AppleTalk routers.

"Art Department, Engineering, Marketing, Sales"

"Zones, please."

3 The Chooser reads any zone information packets it receives and displays a list of zones. If no zones or routers are detected, it does not display the zone field.

Router

Hub

5 The file servers that show up in the device field are any devices using the Apple Filing Protocol (AFP). This includes AppleShare file servers, Macs with file sharing turned on, and AFP-compatible servers running on PCs or UNIX machines. These servers are usually using AppleTalk, but sometimes AFP servers running on TCP/IP will be displayed here as long as AppleTalk is also running.

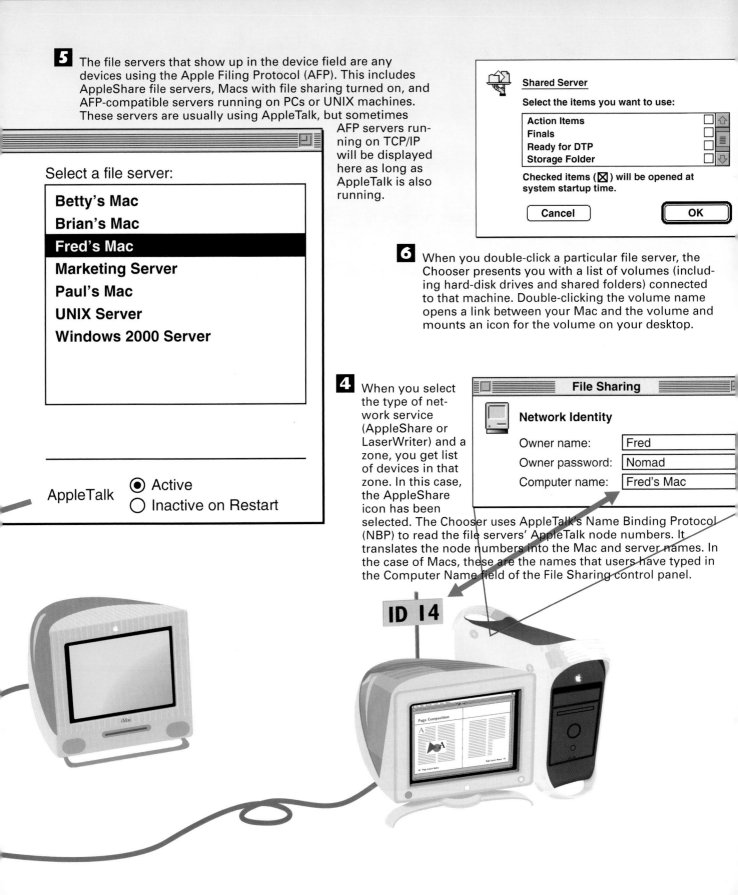

Select a file server:

Betty's Mac
Brian's Mac
Fred's Mac
Marketing Server
Paul's Mac
UNIX Server
Windows 2000 Server

AppleTalk ● Active
○ Inactive on Restart

Shared Server

Select the items you want to use:

Action Items ☐
Finals ☐
Ready for DTP ☐
Storage Folder ☐

Checked items (☒) will be opened at system startup time.

Cancel   OK

6 When you double-click a particular file server, the Chooser presents you with a list of volumes (including hard-disk drives and shared folders) connected to that machine. Double-clicking the volume name opens a link between your Mac and the volume and mounts an icon for the volume on your desktop.

4 When you select the type of network service (AppleShare or LaserWriter) and a zone, you get list of devices in that zone. In this case, the AppleShare icon has been selected. The Chooser uses AppleTalk's Name Binding Protocol (NBP) to read the file servers' AppleTalk node numbers. It translates the node numbers into the Mac and server names. In the case of Macs, these are the names that users have typed in the Computer Name field of the File Sharing control panel.

File Sharing

Network Identity

Owner name: Fred
Owner password: Nomad
Computer name: Fred's Mac

ID 14

CHAPTER

28

How Wireless Networks Work

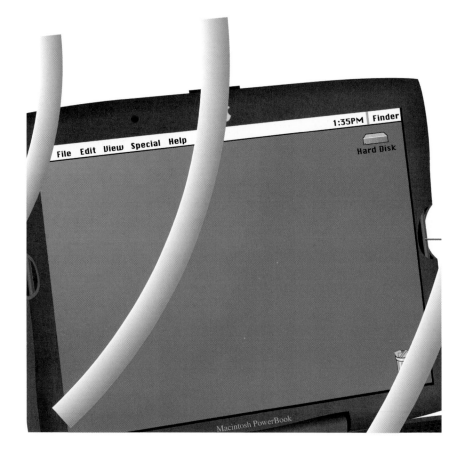

WIRELESS networking has some of the appeal of wireless telephones. It gives you the freedom to communicate with others without having to be where the wire is. (Fortunately, we don't see too many PowerBook users surfing the Net while driving.) But instead of sitting in your backyard talking to your broker, a wireless network lets you trade stock on the Internet.

Apple's wireless network technology, AirPort, debuted in the iBook in 1999. AirPort antennas are now built into every new Mac. Add an AirPort card, and your Mac is ready to join or start a wireless network. Add an AirPort Base Station, and you can connect everyone on the wireless network to the Internet. The Base Station also acts as "wireless hub," helping to boost signals and connect Macs spread out over a building.

Apple's AirPort was the first wireless network product to run at 11Mbps, the high end of wireless networking. This is about the same as the original 10BASE-T Ethernet, although still slower than Fast Ethernet. AirPort is very similar to Ethernet in the way it transmits network data, which means you can run the same networking software as you do on Ethernet. File sharing, Web browsers, email, and multiplayer games all work the same way they do on Ethernet.

AirPort uses an industry standard called IEEE 802.11 Direct Sequence Spread Spectrum (DSSS). It's a mouthful, but it enables AirPort-equipped Macs to communicate with computers running other IEEE 802.11 DSSS products. This includes earlier Macs that aren't AirPort enabled.

The IEEE 802.11 DSSS technology transmits data using high-frequency radio waves in the range of 2.4000–2.4835 gigahertz (GHz), or 2400MHz–2483.5MHz. By comparison, your favorite FM radio stations reside in the 88MHz–108MHz range. This means there's no chance that you'll accidentally pick up the "best of the oldies" on your PowerBook. The high frequency also means that you won't be broadcasting your private email messages to people across town—AirPort has a range of about 150 feet.

However, like your FM radio, AirPort sends signals through walls. To prevent iBook-equipped spies sitting outside your building from logging in, the IEEE 802.11 standard calls for the use of passwords. AirPort also uses encryption software to scramble all data sent over the air.

Additionally, DSSS is based on a technique developed during World War II for keeping radio transmissions secure. A spread spectrum transmission takes a narrow-band broadcast and spreads it out over a wider band. This is similar to taking your favorite FM radio station at 91.7MHz and spreading it out from 88.5MHz to 94.9MHz. However, it would be hard to pick up your station at any frequency because spreading out the same signal power over this wide band reduces the signal power at any one frequency. This makes the signal difficult to distinguish from noise—unless you have an AirPort-equipped Mac, of course, which decodes the wide-band signal back into a narrow band.

AirPort

1 AirPort uses radio signals, which can go through multiple walls, including the tiled wall of a bathroom. The spread-spectrum technique used in transmission is resistant to interference, and enables the 11Mbps data transfer rate. However, concrete walls reflect some of the signals, creating noise that degrades the signal.

2 The AirPort Base Station acts as a wireless hub, boosting signals received from each Mac. Because each Mac can be 150 feet away from the hub, two Macs can be positioned up to 300 feet from each other. Base Stations also can connect together wirelessly, extending the network farther. If you don't have a Base Station, Macs can communicate with each other directly.

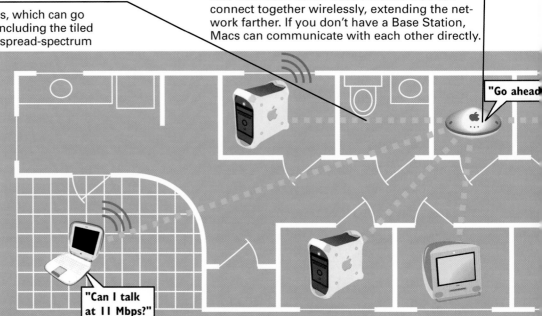

3 When a Mac first gets on an AirPort network, it tries to communicate at 11Mbps. If it can't (due to interference), it tries a rate of 5.5Mbps. Then, it tries 2Mbps, and then 1Mbps. If it can't make a connection at 1Mbps, the Mac tells you that AirPort is unable to connect. (This is similar to the way a modem negotiates speed over telephone lines, although AirPort is much faster.)

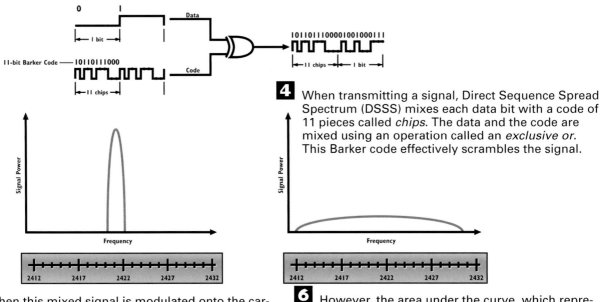

4 When transmitting a signal, Direct Sequence Spread Spectrum (DSSS) mixes each data bit with a code of 11 pieces called *chips*. The data and the code are mixed using an operation called an *exclusive or*. This Barker code effectively scrambles the signal.

5 When this mixed signal is modulated onto the carrier frequency of the radio broadcast, it has the effect of spreading out the broadcast frequency. It's as if one FM radio station could be picked up across the whole radio dial. This enables multiple users to transmit over the radio band at the same time.

6 However, the area under the curve, which represents the total signal power, remains constant after modulation. This means that the power of the signal at each frequency is much less than the original. This makes the signal more resistant to noise and interference and increases security.

8 The AirPort Base Station can connect a wireless network to an Ethernet network. It also can connect a wireless network to the Internet via its built-in modem or built-in Ethernet port. AirPort Base Station also contains Internet gateway software, including a Dynamic Host Configuration Protocol (DHCP) server to provide the Macs' IP addresses.

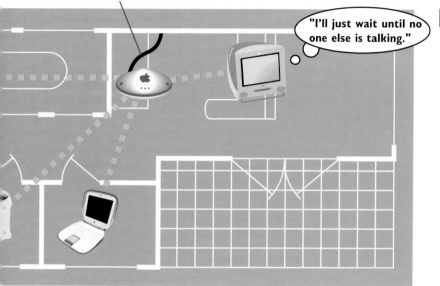

To Ethernet or Internet

"I'll just wait until no one else is talking."

7 AirPort breaks network data up into Ethernet-like packets. Ethernet sends out packets at any time. If an Ethernet Mac detects a *collision* of packets—another Mac has sent out a packet at the exact microsecond in time—then it resends the packet. In IEEE DSSS, no collisions occur. Instead, the Mac waits until no traffic exists to send a packet. This is called Carrier Sense, Multiple Access with Collision *Avoidance*. Ethernet uses a technique called Carrier Sense, Multiple Access with Collision *Detection*.

MAC FACT

AirPort and IEEE 802.11 are the most successful wireless networking technologies, but they weren't the first. Several technologies have existed that used infrared waves, which can't go through walls. The most recent was called IrDA, and was included on Macs as recently as the original iMac of 1998 and in several versions of the PowerBook G3.

9 Every iMac, iBook, Power Mac G4, and PowerBook now has two AirPort antennas built into it. A receiver feature called *diversity reception* compares the signals coming from each antenna and chooses the better one. This means you won't have to move the Mac around to get better reception.

Antenna

CHAPTER
29

How Internet Connections Work

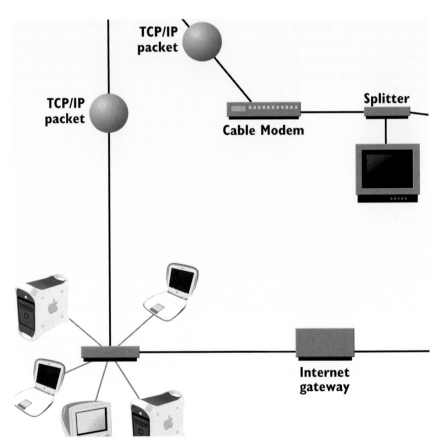

GETTING connected is the *raison d'être* of the Internet. You connect to a world of information and services and to your friends, family, and colleagues. Yet, getting connected is also the *method* of the Internet. Just about everything you do on the Internet is an act of reaching out and connecting to another computer somewhere.

If everything on the Internet were stored on one giant computer, it might be easy to see how you can get to a Web site simply by typing in its address (more technically, a universal resource locator, or URL). In reality, the Internet is millions of computers spread around the world. When you type in a URL, your Mac sends a message to one computer among the millions that holds the Web site.

At a basic level, the Internet is a lot like a local network. Your Mac sends and receives commands and data in the form of bundles of bits called *packets*. It uses TCP/IP (short for Transport Control Protocol/Internet Protocol) as the computer language used to create and exchange the packets. As on a local network, the TCP/IP packets on the Internet contain information as to where they are headed and where they came from. Devices throughout the Internet—including IP routers and various types of servers—read this information and forward the packets until they reach their destinations. Each device is processing millions of packets per second, and each packet travels along wires at the speed of light—186,000 miles per second.

Of course, the Internet doesn't seem all that fast when you're waiting for a complex Web page to load. The Internet speed (or lack of it) you experience depends on the type of connection your Mac has to your Internet service provider (ISP), the company that links you to the Internet. The slow speed of a modem dial-up connection has to do with the method of transmitting data. High-speed Internet connection methods, such as cable modem and digital subscriber lines (DSL), are more direct connections to the Internet that don't require a lot of the intermediate processing that a dial-up modem uses. A DSL link runs on the same telephone wire as a dial-up modem, but the connection is dozens of times faster.

Cable modem connections come over your cable TV wires. They're faster than DSL connections, but have the disadvantage of being shared with your neighbors. If everyone in the neighborhood were online at the same time, everyone's connection would be slower. A *DSL link* is a private connection from your building to the Internet. You can connect a local network of computers to a DSL line or other high-speed connection through the use of an *Internet gateway*. This can be a standalone box (including Apple's AirPort Base Station) or inexpensive software running on a computer.

Some Internet services, such as QuickTime streaming video, adjust to the speed of your Internet link. Instead of yielding slower video, slower connections provide smaller video at lower quality. Even a modem gets you connected to a live QuickTime movie broadcast.

Connecting to the Internet, Part I

1 An Internet connection starts with your software—Web browser, email, or some other program that sends a request to Open Transport, the Mac's TCP/IP protocol software. This turns commands and data into TCP/IP network packets.

Internet Application

5 Your modem converts digital PPP-TCP/IP signals into analog signals. A modem at the Internet provider converts the signals back to digital network form. Using a modem is the slowest but least expensive method of accessing the Internet.

Your Building

4 Remote access wraps outgoing TCP/IP packets in a PPP shell. The server at the other end unwraps them.

"Do you speak PPP?"

PPP packet

Modem

Open Transport

"Dial the modem."

PPP software

Digital signal

Analog signal

2 If you have a modem set up, Open Transport tells your PPP software, such as Remote Access in Mac OS 9, to dial the modem.

TCP/IP packet

TCP/IP packet

6 If you have a cable modem or DSL account, the TCP/IP packets travel out of your Mac's Ethernet port. From there, they go through a splitter box, which separates incoming TCP/IP packets from TV signals.

TCP/IP packet

Splitter

Cable Modem

8 A DSL account moves high-speed through telephone lines. You can use it with just your Mac or share it with a local network. If you do share it, you'll need an Internet gateway. This can be a standalone box or software running on a computer.

Splitter

Internet gateway

DSL Modem

Telephone

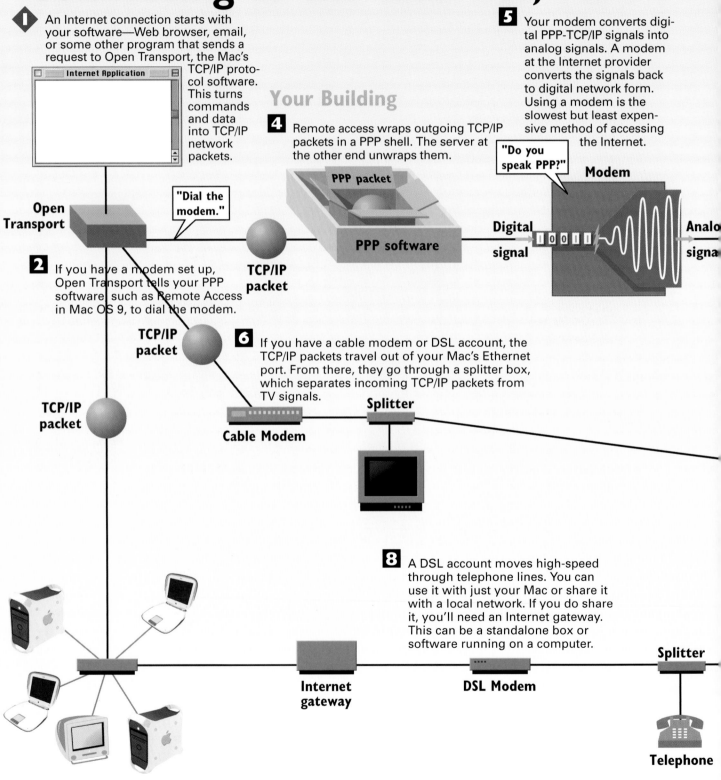

3 Your modem connects to a modem at your Internet service provider. The two linked modems first negotiate a communication speed. They then establish a *point-to-point-protocol* (PPP) session. Through the modems, your Mac sends the server your account name and password, and the server at the Internet service provider gives your Mac access to the Internet.

Internet Service Provider

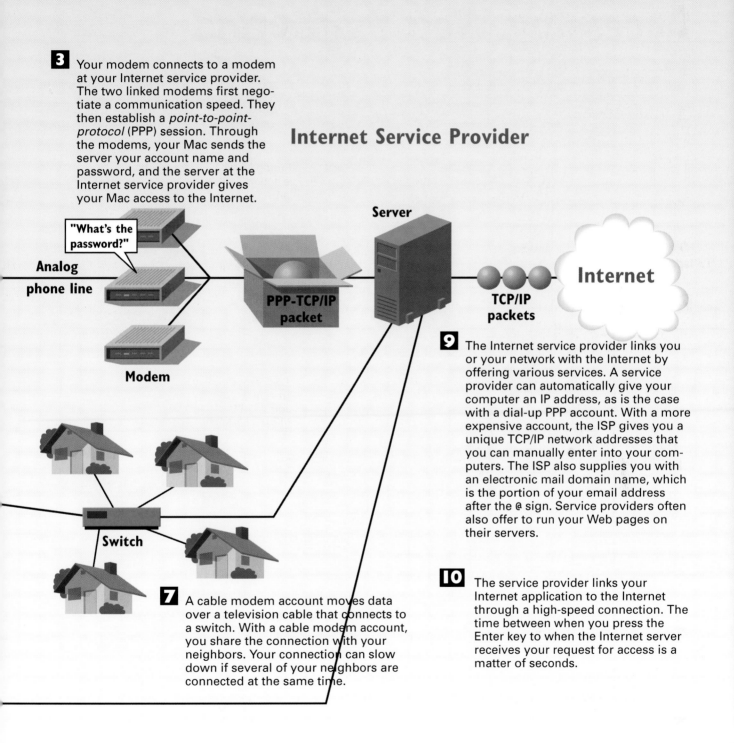

"What's the password?"

Analog phone line

Modem

PPP-TCP/IP packet

Server

TCP/IP packets

Internet

Switch

9 The Internet service provider links you or your network with the Internet by offering various services. A service provider can automatically give your computer an IP address, as is the case with a dial-up PPP account. With a more expensive account, the ISP gives you a unique TCP/IP network addresses that you can manually enter into your computers. The ISP also supplies you with an electronic mail domain name, which is the portion of your email address after the @ sign. Service providers often also offer to run your Web pages on their servers.

7 A cable modem account moves data over a television cable that connects to a switch. With a cable modem account, you share the connection with your neighbors. Your connection can slow down if several of your neighbors are connected at the same time.

10 The service provider links your Internet application to the Internet through a high-speed connection. The time between when you press the Enter key to when the Internet server receives your request for access is a matter of seconds.

Accessing Web Pages and Using Email

4 The Web browser sends a request for the Web page through the IP router listed in your TCP/IP control panel. It passes the request on to another router, which passes it on again. Each router consults lists of routers and reports of traffic to determine the quickest path to the final destination.

URL: http://www.acme.com/

IP Router

1 When you type a URL in a Web browser or click a hyperlink, your Mac contacts the domain name server listed in your TCP/IP control panel. It sends the *domain name* of the URL to the server, usually at your Internet service provider.

acme.com

Domain Name Server

105.21.69.254

3 If the domain name server finds a listing, it sends your browser the IP address for the computer running the Web site.

Domain	Address
aacar.com	213.159.10.82
acme.com	105.21.69.254
ajax.com	92.234.75.126
bliggy.com	145.65.228.26
bns.com	175.182.113.102

7 The SMTP server sends the domain name—this time, the part after the @ in the email address—to the domain name server. The domain name server returns an IP address for the mail server hosting the recipient's mail account.

bliggy.com

145.65.228.26

2 The domain name server keeps a database of Internet domain names and the IP addresses of the server computers running the Web sites. If the domain name server doesn't have your domain listed, it asks other domain name servers on the Internet.

Email Client

Send to: rob@bliggy.com

Dear Rob,
How ya been?

IP Router

6 When you send an email message, a request goes to your Internet service provider's *SMTP (simple mail transfer protocol) server*. The server acknowledges the request, and your Mac sends the email message to the SMTP server.

SMTP Server

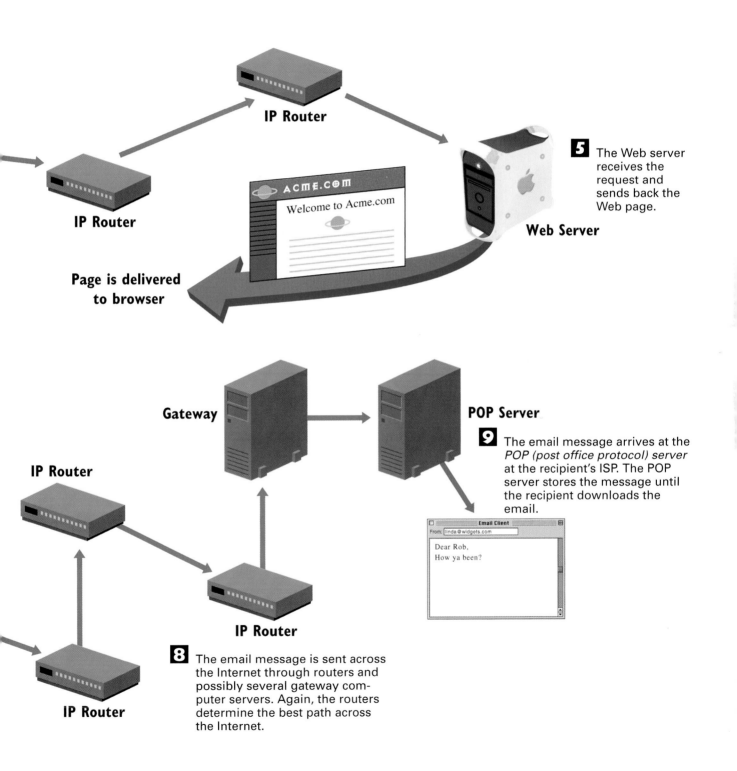

IP Router

IP Router

5 The Web server receives the request and sends back the Web page.

Web Server

Welcome to Acme.com

Page is delivered to browser

Gateway

POP Server

9 The email message arrives at the *POP (post office protocol) server* at the recipient's ISP. The POP server stores the message until the recipient downloads the email.

IP Router

IP Router

Email Client
From: linda@widgets.com

Dear Rob,
How ya been?

IP Router

8 The email message is sent across the Internet through routers and possibly several gateway computer servers. Again, the routers determine the best path across the Internet.

QuickTime Streaming Video

Streaming video and audio results when you receive a steady stream of data. Mac OS includes QuickTime software that can play online movies. QuickTime Streaming Server software hosts the movies. QuickTime can present two different types of streaming. *HTTP streaming* works by downloading an entire movie to your hard disk. You can start playing the movie while it's still downloading. *RTSP streaming* displays the data and discards it after you've seen it. RTSP streaming is useful for long movies. Streaming movies in real-time requires the use of protocols not used for other Internet activities.

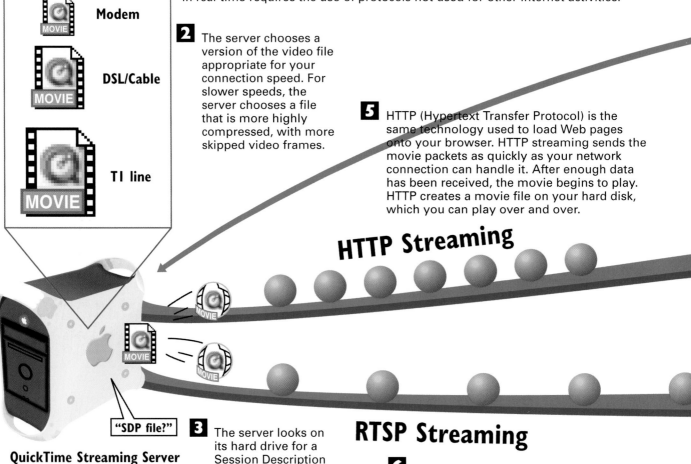

Modem

DSL/Cable

TI line

2 The server chooses a version of the video file appropriate for your connection speed. For slower speeds, the server chooses a file that is more highly compressed, with more skipped video frames.

5 HTTP (Hypertext Transfer Protocol) is the same technology used to load Web pages onto your browser. HTTP streaming sends the movie packets as quickly as your network connection can handle it. After enough data has been received, the movie begins to play. HTTP creates a movie file on your hard disk, which you can play over and over.

HTTP Streaming

"SDP file?"

QuickTime Streaming Server

RTSP Streaming

3 The server looks on its hard drive for a Session Description Protocol (SDP) file, which contains format and timing information about the broadcast.

4 The server begins to send the video to your computer, as well as others. (QuickTime Streaming Server can serve more than 2,000 streams at once.) The server uses the Real-Time Transport Protocol (RTP) to format the movie into network packets. The packets will be sent with either HTTP or RTSP.

6 RTSP (Real-Time Streaming Protocol) sends movie packets no more quickly than you need to view them, so that the data rate of the stream is smaller than the network speed. RTSP keeps your Mac in constant communication with the server running the movie. RTSP enables the user to pause or stop the stream, but does not create a file.

When you click a movie link or select a URL with QuickTime Player, your Web browser, or other QuickTime-aware software, your Mac sends a request to a computer running QuickTime Streaming Server. It also sends the server the speed of your connection, as set by the QuickTime Settings control panel.

8 With either type of video, the QuickTime software uses a CODEC (Compression-Decompression) method to decompress the movie and display it onscreen.

7 With RTSP streaming, your QuickTime software creates a cache in RAM to store 3–10 seconds of the movie data before it starts playing the movie. This is to make up for temporary interruptions in the Internet connection.

RAM

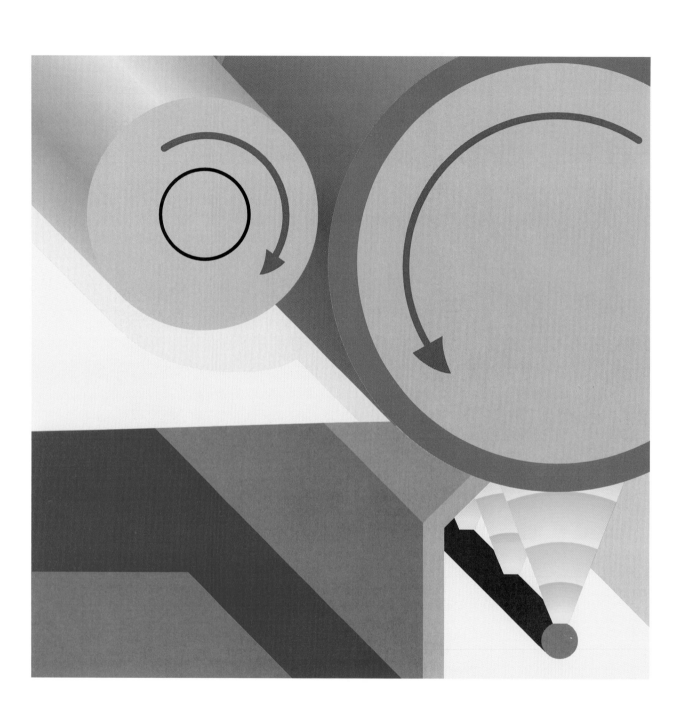

PART 8

PRINTING AND PUBLISHING

Chapter 30: How Printers Work
208

Chapter 31: How PostScript Works
214

Chapter 32: How Print Publishing Works
218

Chapter 33: How Web Publishing Works
226

THE *American Heritage Dictionary* defines the word *publish* as the act of preparing and issuing printed material for public distribution. In light of this definition, many of us are publishers in one way or another. The final result of our work on a Mac is often on paper, whether it's the 8 1/2×11-inch memo to be distributed among our co-workers or a four-color, illustrated brochure to be sent to clients. Other times, the final result of our work is electronic publishing, such as the posting of a Web page on the Internet. With the need to present our work in a manner that is informative and attractive, the phrase *publish or perish* doesn't just apply to college professors.

In 1984, Apple introduced two new pieces of hardware, the Macintosh and a printer. The ImageWriter I was the first Mac peripheral, preceding even the first hard-disk drive. This dot-matrix printer was noisy and slow, and it produced low-resolution printouts. Still, it and the new Macintosh computer had two big advantages—they made printing easy and they could print graphics as easily as text. The installation procedure consisted of plugging in a cable between the two devices. It also used a single software printer driver for all applications; you could select it once and then print anything from any program.

As convenient as the ImageWriter was, the introduction of the LaserWriter the following year was a much bigger advancement in printing technology, and it helped to start the desktop publishing revolution. The LaserWriter was one of the first laser printers for desktop computers. Laser printers use the same technology found in copy machines. The main difference is that while copy machines convert a paper image to an electronic form by scanning it, laser printers import the data already in digital form.

The LaserWriter was also the first network printer. Multiple Mac users could share one laser printer, and it put quality text and graphics printing in the hands of ordinary users. The LaserWriter was also the first printer to use the PostScript page description language. PostScript describes pages not as dots, but as a series of mathematical descriptions of shapes. PostScript made possible the scaling of type fonts to different sizes with acceptable results. Today, PostScript is heavily used by professional desktop printers to produce magazines, newspapers, and brochures.

Desktop publishing and graphics are what made the Mac a successful machine in the mid-1980s. Activities that were traditionally performed by a roomful of people and thousands of dollars of equipment could now be done at your desk. Page layout software replaced the scissors and glue used to design a page of a newsletter or magazine and made revisions quick and easy. Electronic files replaced expensive and time-consuming photographic techniques, and the ability to include graphics right in the document file replaced the use of expensive stripping equipment.

Today, the Mac's built-in graphics and printing technologies and ease of setup and use still make it a favorite among professional desktop publishers. The Mac is widely used by magazine and newspaper publishers, and it was used to create the graphics, text, and page layout of this book.

The advances in print publishing technology over the last decade have put more demands on hardware and software, particularly with the use of color. In 1992, Apple added support for color calibration to Mac OS in the form of ColorSync system software. ColorSync helps people get the same color output on different peripherals, so that what looks like burnt umber on one monitor doesn't look like traffic-cone orange on a color printer.

Electronic publishing was the second phase of the desktop publishing revolution in the 1990s. Many Mac publishing professionals have taken their skills over to the Internet, applying some of the same basic design principles to the newer medium. The tools for electronic publishing are almost as varied as those for print media. Key developers of desktop publishing and graphic software, including Adobe, offer powerful electronic publishing software. The features in today's popular Web page software often resemble the features in page layout programs.

However, some stark differences do exist between print and electronic publishing. Print publishing is high resolution, whereas electronic publishing is limited to the low resolutions of computer display. Print publishing often strives for the highest quality feasible, which can result in very large files. Electronic publishing strives for the smallest files feasible because readers must download them over slow modem connections.

Of course, printing on the Mac is not all high-end color production. The most popular printer in use today is the color inkjet printer, which is found mostly in homes and small offices. Inkjet printers are much simpler than laser printers, with fewer moving parts and fewer components. This makes them less expensive than laser printers. Over the past decade, inkjet costs have come way down, while the advancements in print head and ink technology have caused print quality to rise dramatically. We'll start our discussion of how desktop publishing and printing work with inkjet printers and the other printing workhorse, the laser printer.

CHAPTER

30

How Printers Work

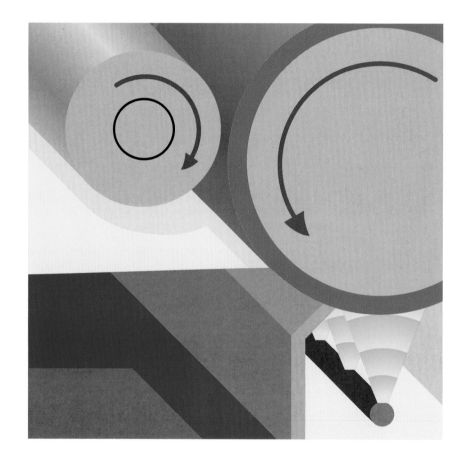

PRINTERS and Macs have gone hand-in-hand since the first Macs were paired with the ImageWriter dot-matrix printer. Since then, print quality has gone up while prices have come down. Dot matrix printers, which draw dots by striking the paper through an inked ribbon similar to a typewriter, are rare these days. Today, most printers used with Macs are either inkjet printers, which squirt tiny beads of ink at high speeds, or laser printers, which use a laser beam on an electrically charged drum.

Inkjet printers are popular because they're a great buy, offering low-cost color printing with some of the print quality of laser printers. Inkjet printers make great home printers because they're quiet, small in size, and typically lightweight.

Laser printers are ubiquitous office fixtures, as common as copy machines. Laser printers are more expensive than inkjet printers, but are faster and can produce better-quality pages. Laser printers are available to fit the high-volume printing needs of big organizations, as well as the more modest requirements of a small work-group and some individuals.

Printers of all types usually create an image by drawing dots on paper. Typical printers put down 600 dots per inch of paper, quite a bit more than a monitor's 72 dots per inch. Higher resolutions are commonly available.

Inkjet printers work the way their name implies, by squirting tiny jets of ink onto the paper. You usually can get better-quality printouts by using paper specifically designed to absorb the ink in the right proportions. Special photo-quality inks also can improve print quality.

Laser printers are similar in design to copy machines. For ink, they use a dry powdered toner, which is applied electrostatically to the paper and bonded by heat.

Both inkjet and laser printers come in color versions, although color is more common in inkjet printers. Color printers work the same way their black-and-white counterparts do, except they print each page four times—one time each in cyan, magenta, yellow, and black ink. These colors combine to form all the other colors you can see.

Color laser and inkjet printers represent the affordable end of color printing technology. Other types, such as wax-thermal and dye-sublimation printers, produce more realistic color images but cost more in hardware, ink, and paper. The most expensive printers can produce color images indistinguishable from photographic prints.

You can connect an inkjet to your Mac's USB port (or serial port in older Macs). In Mac OS 9 and earlier, use QuickDraw screen-drawing routines for printing to these types of printers. Mac OS X has a new printing technology.

Laser printers often use the PostScript page description language to print graphics and text. PostScript laser printers are often network printers, which enable you to share them over a network with other Macs. Network laser printers have Ethernet connectors built in, although older printers might have a LocalTalk connector (an older type of network). A simple LocalTalk-to-Ethernet converter enables you to print to an older Laser printer with a newer Mac.

Color Inkjet Printer

1 Unlike a PostScript laser printer, which does the processing of the page image itself, an inkjet printer uses software on the Mac that intercepts QuickDraw commands going to the screen. The Mac interprets the electronic description of the page and turns it into a set of dots to be printed. The printer driver software sends the location of the dots to the printer. The processed data for the first line of dots is sent through a ribbon cable to the ink-cartridge-and-nozzle assembly.

5 The cartridge-and-nozzle assembly moves slightly to the right. After a line is written, the paper advances slightly and the cartridge-and-nozzle assembly moves back to the other side to begin the next line of dots.

2 The print head contains four cartridges, one each for cyan, yellow, magenta, and black ink. Liquid ink is pumped into 50 chambers, each containing a heating element.

3 The heating element is switched on, and it heats the ink to its boiling point and vaporizes it.

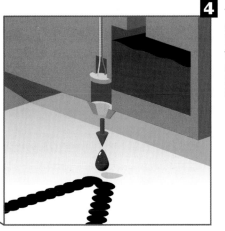

4 The increased pressure of the gaseous ink forces the ink through the tiny nozzle, squirting a dot of ink onto the paper at high velocity.

Laser Printer

1 Printing commands that come in through a network port are described by PostScript. In non-network printers, the commands are from QuickDraw. The signals describing the document to be printed are sent to RAM on the printer's logic board, where the printer's processor will *rasterize* the image—turn the description into a list of dots.

4 A laser beam is aimed at a rotating drum using a rotating polygonal mirror. The beam hits the drum one dot at a time. The laser is turned on where black dots will occur and is turned off where the page will remain white. Typically, a black area will have 600 dots in every inch.

Toner cartridge

Developing roller

Drum

RAM

ROM

3 The printer's processor converts the commands to light signals and motion control signals for the aiming of the light beam and the paper.

2 Some of the printing commands describe the fonts to be used in the document. Fonts are stored in the laser printer's ROM, in an external hard disk, or occasionally on a user's Mac. The requested fonts are loaded into the printer's RAM.

9 The toner is bonded to the paper by passing between two rollers heated to about 160 degrees centigrade.

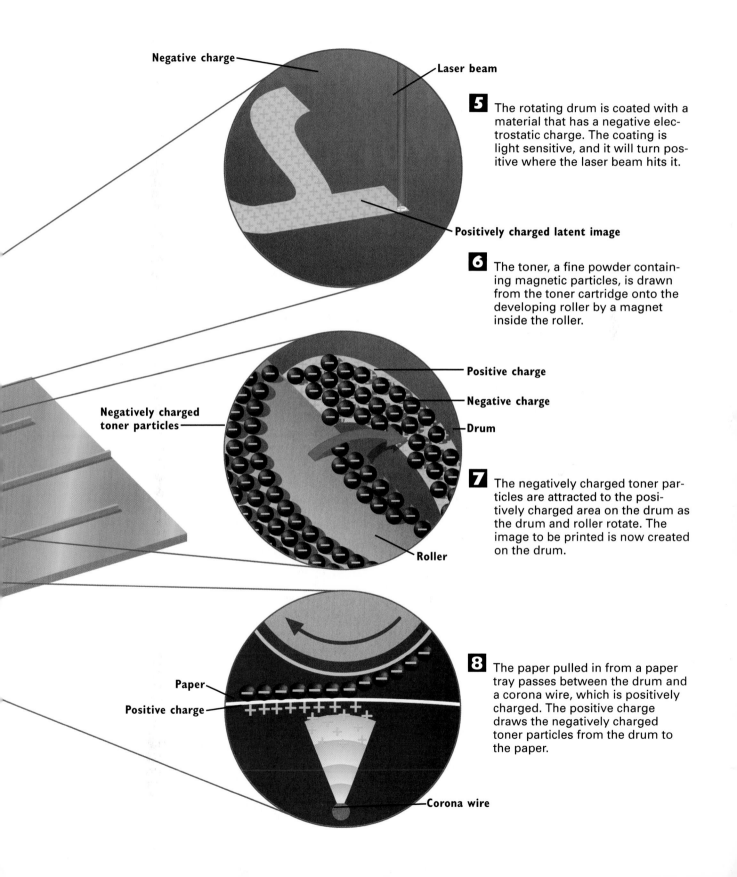

Negative charge

Laser beam

5 The rotating drum is coated with a material that has a negative electrostatic charge. The coating is light sensitive, and it will turn positive where the laser beam hits it.

Positively charged latent image

6 The toner, a fine powder containing magnetic particles, is drawn from the toner cartridge onto the developing roller by a magnet inside the roller.

Positive charge

Negative charge

Drum

Negatively charged toner particles

Roller

7 The negatively charged toner particles are attracted to the positively charged area on the drum as the drum and roller rotate. The image to be printed is now created on the drum.

Paper

Positive charge

8 The paper pulled in from a paper tray passes between the drum and a corona wire, which is positively charged. The positive charge draws the negatively charged toner particles from the drum to the paper.

Corona wire

CHAPTER 31

How PostScript Works

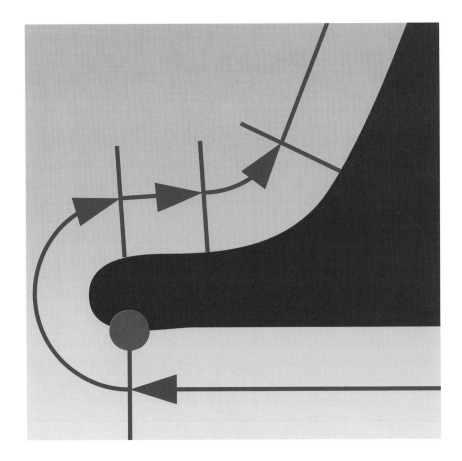

POSTSCRIPT printing has been a staple of high-quality and professional printing ever since 1985, when Apple included Adobe's technology in the LaserWriter, the first PostScript printer. Since then, PostScript has been a standard method of telling laser printers what to print. PostScript is now built into Mac OS X, where it is also used to draw images onscreen (as described in Chapter 23, "How Aqua Works") as well as print.

When you print a file, the Mac doesn't send the file itself to the printer. Instead, it sends a description of what's on the pages in a language the printer can understand. For printers connected to your Mac's USB port (or serial port in older Macs), the language is an extension of QuickDraw, the onscreen display software in Mac OS, or Hewlett-Packard's PCL (printer control language). These languages send the printer a *bitmap* representation, which is a dot-by-dot account of what's on the page. Most ink jet printers use this method.

Many laser printers do not receive bitmap print jobs from the computer. Instead, they use the PostScript page description language. Instead of describing each dot, PostScript describes everything in a document mathematically. PostScript specifies the text, fonts, style, shapes, fills, and colors used on the page. It is the printer that calculates where to put the dots on the paper, not the computer.

PostScript print jobs are actually small programs the printer executes. Because of this, PostScript printers are actually small computers themselves, containing their own processor, memory, and ROM. This hardware adds to the cost of the printer, which is why so many PostScript laser printers have networking ports built into them to enable groups of people to share them.

So, why use PostScript in printers if it costs more? The reason is quality. PostScript gives you more repeatable colors, better-quality grays and blacks, less visible dots, and smoother fonts.

PostScript draws text using *outline* fonts that describe each character by its shape. Outline fonts are usually stored in the printer. Most professional desktop publishers prefer to use PostScript Type 1 fonts, but PostScript printers can also use TrueType fonts, outline fonts that come with Mac OS, and the newer OpenType fonts.

You print to a PostScript printer with a PostScript driver, such as the LaserWriter driver found in the Chooser. You can use this (or any other PostScript driver) to print to any PostScript printer, regardless of manufacturer. That's because PostScript is printer independent—the mathematical method used to describe text and graphics is the same for every printer.

That being said, the PostScript printer language hasn't stood still since 1985. Since then, two major revisions have been made—PostScript Level 2 and PostScript Level 3. Each added new features for the printing and handling of specific printer features, such as paper trays. PostScript drivers are backward compatible, which means you can print to a PostScript Level 1 printer with a Level 2 driver. You can often print to a new version of PostScript using an older driver, but you won't get the features of the newer PostScript.

PostScript Printing and Outline Fonts

1 When you print a document to a PostScript printer, the application creates a *page description* (also called a print job), a small program the printer will run. The page description contains a set of print commands written in the PostScript page description language. These commands treat each page as a single graphic image, describing the lines, curves, circles, and squares, and more complex graphic objects made up of these elements. They also describe scanned images, such as photographs. The page description contains all the characters in the document and the names of the fonts and styles used. The commands describe where on the page to draw characters and graphics, as well as their sizes, colors, and other attributes.

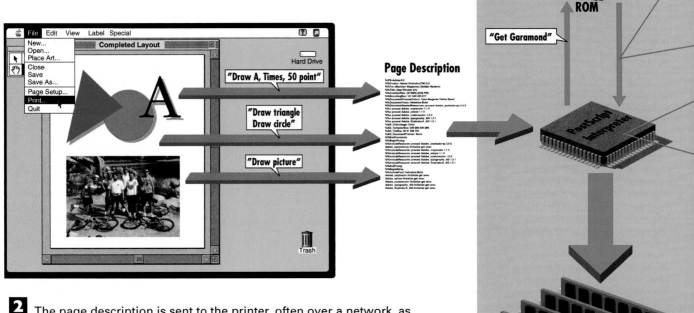

2 The page description is sent to the printer, often over a network, as PostScript code written in ASCII text. Because all PostScript printers understand PostScript code, you can print to any PostScript printer using the same LaserWriter print driver software.

3 The print job is processed by the *PostScript interpreter*, which is software in the printer that executes the commands and turns mathematical descriptions of shapes into dots placed on the paper. This process is called *raster image processing*. This is why PostScript interpreters are sometimes called *RIPs*.

4 The interpreter first creates an ideal image of the page in the printer's memory.

5 When a page description command asks for a font, the PostScript interpreter fetches the font stored in the printer's ROM, hard disk, or RAM if the font is downloaded from the Mac. PostScript can use several types of outline fonts. Each font is a set of mathematical descriptions of characters. Outline fonts are shapes, which are treated as graphic objects.

6 Outline fonts describe the outline of each character mathematically, which keeps the shape of the character the same at any size. *Bitmap* fonts, used to draw text onscreen, are not scalable, and the characters look different at each size.

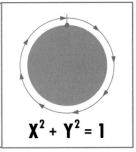

$$X^2 + Y^2 = 1$$

7 When the interpreter receives a command such as *draw a circle*, it creates the path of the shape's outline using a simple mathematical equation. The outlines of more complex shapes are described by many mathematical equations and geometric relationships. Page description commands tell the interpreter the thickness of the outline and the colors (for a color printer) of the fill pattern.

9 Color printers mix dots of cyan, magenta, yellow, and black in different proportions to make other colors. Some printers only approximate other colors by placing the four colored dots close to each other. This is called *dithering*. Black-and-white printers use dithering by using black-and-white dots in different amounts to appear as approximate shades of gray, which are called *halftones*. Newspaper publishers use dithering to produce grayscale and color photos.

8 With the document image re-created in the printer's RAM, the interpreter tells the printing mechanism to print dots of toner on the paper to fill in the outline. The number of dots per inch depends on the resolution and settings of the printer; the same page description code could produce 300 dots per inch on one printer and 1,200 on another. The resolution of the printout is completely independent of the computer display resolution.

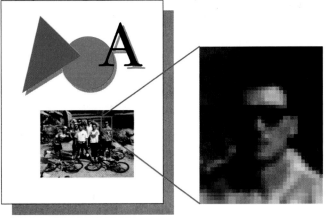

MAC FACT

Although applications create PostScript page descriptions automatically, PostScript is also a programming language that can be used to create special print effects not included in your applications—if you know the language. Many applications enable you to get a look at PostScript by creating a file containing all the PostScript code for a particular document. Usually, you create a file of PostScript code by clicking a button in the Print dialog box: Instead of sending a page description to a printer, the application saves it to your hard disk.

32

How Print Publishing Works

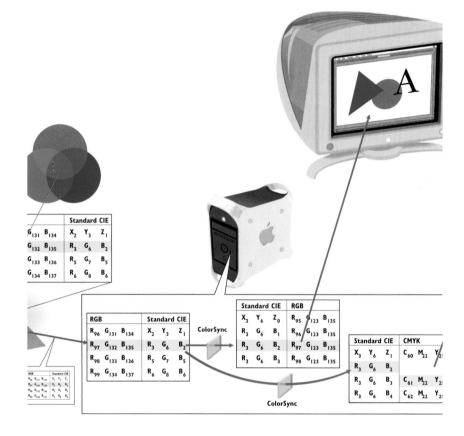

				Standard CIE		
G_{131}	B_{134}		X_2	Y_3	Z_1
G_{132}	B_{135}		R_3	G_6	B_2
G_{133}	B_{136}		R_5	G_7	B_5
G_{134}	B_{137}		R_6	G_8	B_6

RGB			Standard CIE		
R_{96} G_{131} B_{134}			X_2 Y_3 Z_1		
R_{97} G_{132} B_{135}			R_3 G_6 B_2		
R_{98} G_{133} B_{136}			R_5 G_7 B_5		
R_{99} G_{134} B_{137}			R_6 G_8 B_6		

ColorSync

Standard CIE			RGB		
X_3 Y_6 Z_0			R_{95} G_{123} B_{135}		
R_3 G_6 B_1			R_{96} G_{123} B_{135}		
R_3 G_6 B_2			R_{97} G_{123} B_{135}		
R_3 G_6 B_3			R_{98} G_{123} B_{135}		

Standard CIE			CMYK		
X_3 Y_6 Z_1			C_{60} M_{22} Y_{25}		
R_3 G_6 B_2					
R_3 G_6 B_3			C_{61} M_{22} Y_{25}		
R_3 G_6 B_4			C_{62} M_{22} Y_{25}		

ColorSync

DESKTOP publishing was born on the Macintosh. It was not something Apple invented, but instead grew out of a need to make publishing easier. The Mac supplied the first tools to produce a newsletter or brochure from your desk. These tools replaced the scissors and glue of page layout—formerly known as *paste up*—as well as the hundred-thousand-dollar machinery required for graphics. By reducing costs, making revisions easier, and making publications look better, the Mac put publishing in the hands of the individual, as well as streamlined the empires of the publishing industry.

In the professional publishing industry, the Mac is the favorite desktop publishing platform. Macs are used to produce newspapers and magazines all over the country. Even magazines covering PCs and Microsoft Windows use Macs in their production departments. The Mac's integrated design is still more versatile and easier to set up and learn than other platforms, and Macs still are better at PostScript output. Of course, desktop publishing isn't limited to book and magazine publishers. Your published work can be a color brochure, an 8-page newsletter, or an 8 1/2×11-inch sheet of paper.

At the heart of desktop print publishing is page layout software, which enables you to manipulate text and illustrations on a page. Page layout software has grown increasingly powerful, enabling detailed adjustments in the spacing of individual characters, as well as the placement and editing of illustrations. Today, you can choose from a wide selection of page layout programs, and you can even perform page layout in word processors.

Color is an important part of prepress production. In most service bureaus, Macs control the process of *color separation*, a production step before color printing. However, the color you see on a monitor is not usually the same as what prints, or what a scanner might capture. That's why part of the color desktop publishing procedure involves *color matching systems*. These systems calibrate computer devices to a device-independent color model, and use this standard to match the colors produced by various devices. The most common device-independent color model is the XYZ model created by the Commission Internationale de l'Éclairage (CIE) in 1931. The *CIE XYZ* color model is based purely on experimental data gathered from standard light sources, in contrast to mathematical color models such as RGB and CMYK.

The Mac's ColorSync software uses CIE XYZ to perform color matching and color compensation between scanners, monitors, digital cameras, printers, presses, and other color devices. It does this by using *color matching modules* (CMM), which convert images between colors' spaces (such as RGB and CMYK) while retaining the information in color profiles. You can add third-party CMMs as well. ColorSync is flexible and extensible and open to future innovations in color matching.

Desktop Publishing

4 The electronic files are sent to a Mac running a page layout program. The files can be sent over a local network or the Internet, or they can be transported on Zip disks or other removable media.

1 A writer creates the text of the document in a word processor. A full-featured word processor can be used as a page layout program for less complex documents.

2 Artists use drawing or painting software to create illustrations (such as the ones in this book) as well as decorative elements on a page.

3 A scanner electronically captures images of photographs or other art. Professionals often use a drum scanner. A flatbed scanner is used to capture images from books. A slide scanner can be used for capturing 35mm slide images.

Page Composition

A

A

43 Page Layout Basics

Page Layout Basics 43

5 Typically, a page designer creates the layout of the pages first. Sometimes page templates are stored on a server. The actual text is "poured" into the columns in the page layout software, and graphics are imported. Some sites use OPI network servers, which hold low-resolution versions of images for display on users' computers but insert a high-resolution version when the file is output for printing.

6 The pages are printed on a color or black-and-white printer. This could be a laser printer or a high-end, dye-sublimation color printer. In either case, this printout can be used either as the final output or as a page proof, which is used to check for errors before continuing with the process.

[Continued on next page.]

Desktop Publishing (continued)

Service Bureau

9 Color separation software on the Mac produces four electronic PostScript documents, each representing the amount of cyan, magenta, yellow, and black (or CMYK) that will go on the page.

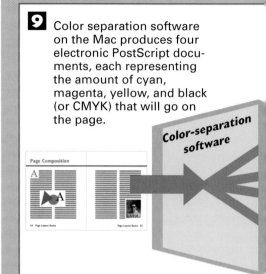

Color-separation software

Portable data storage

7 When printing on a printing press, the page layout file is sent to a service bureau over the Internet or on a removable cartridge by courier. At the service bureau, the page layout file is loaded onto a high-end Mac.

8 Images scanned on flatbed scanners are usually of lower resolution than required for professional print publishing. Production software on the Mac automatically strips out scanned images and replaces them with images that have been rescanned with a high-resolution drum scanner.

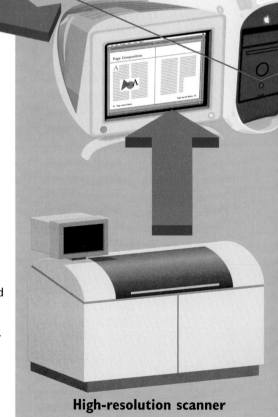

High-resolution scanner

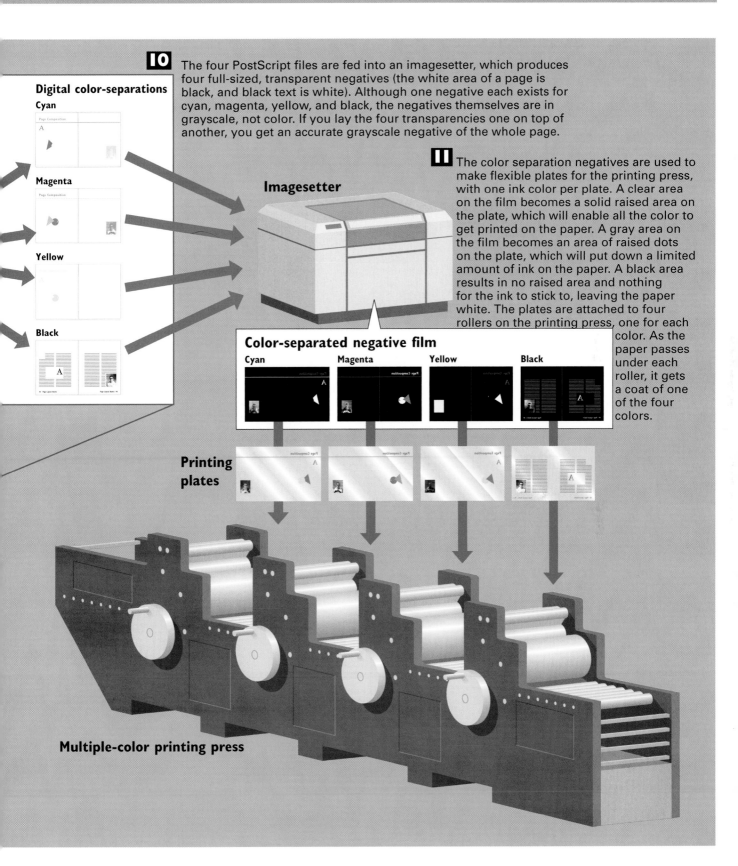

10 The four PostScript files are fed into an imagesetter, which produces four full-sized, transparent negatives (the white area of a page is black, and black text is white). Although one negative each exists for cyan, magenta, yellow, and black, the negatives themselves are in grayscale, not color. If you lay the four transparencies one on top of another, you get an accurate grayscale negative of the whole page.

11 The color separation negatives are used to make flexible plates for the printing press, with one ink color per plate. A clear area on the film becomes a solid raised area on the plate, which will enable all the color to get printed on the paper. A gray area on the film becomes an area of raised dots on the plate, which will put down a limited amount of ink on the paper. A black area results in no raised area and nothing for the ink to stick to, leaving the paper white. The plates are attached to four rollers on the printing press, one for each color. As the paper passes under each roller, it gets a coat of one of the four colors.

Digital color-separations

Cyan

Magenta

Yellow

Black

Imagesetter

Color-separated negative film

Cyan   Magenta   Yellow   Black

Printing plates

Multiple-color printing press

ColorSync Color Matching

ColorSync manages the matching of colors between scanners, monitors, and printers by comparing the description of a color by each system to a standard color model. It doesn't actually alter the electronic file being passed from scanner to printer. Scanners and monitors describe a color using three numbers that represent the amounts of red, green, and blue (or hue, saturation, and brightness) in the resulting color. Printers use four numbers that represent the amounts of cyan, magenta, yellow, and black ink used to create color. However, each device can create only a subset of the colors described in a standard color model.

1 Each color input or output device has a *color profile*, which is a table of the colors it can produce. A scanner profile describes each color in terms of RGB numbers and provides the best-fit equivalent in device-independent CIE XYZ numbers for each color. This is somewhat similar to an English-French dictionary that gives the English equivalents of French words. The profile can come with the device or can be created with a kit provided by the manufacturer or third party.

3 ColorSync receives the profile and manages an algebraic conversion of the scanner's RGB values by comparing each device's profile. The actual comparison can be performed by one of ColorSync's color matching modules (CMM) or by a CMM you add from another developer.

4 The first step of the conversion is to locate the image's colors listed in the profile as RGB values and then convert them to CIE XYZ values.

RGB			Standard CIE		
R_{96}	G_{131}	B_{134}	X_2	Y_3	Z_1
R_{97}	G_{132}	B_{135}	R_3	G_6	B_2
R_{98}	G_{133}	B_{136}	R_5	G_7	B_5
R_{99}	G_{134}	B_{137}	R_6	G_8	B_6

2 The scanner profile is sent to the Mac with the scanned image.

RGB			Standard CIE		
R_{96}	G_{131}	B_{134}	X_2	Y_3	Z_1
R_{97}	G_{132}	B_{135}	R_3	G_6	B_2
R_{98}	G_{133}	B_{136}	R_5	G_7	B_5
R_{99}	G_{134}	B_{137}	R_6	G_8	B_6

RGB			Standard CIE		
R_{96}	G_{131}	B_{134}	X_2	Y_3	Z_1
R_{97}	G_{132}	B_{135}	R_3	G_6	B_2
R_{98}	G_{133}	B_{136}	R_5	G_7	B_5
R_{99}	G_{134}	B_{137}	R_6	G_8	B_6

ColorSync

Standa...	
X_3	$Y...$
R_3	$G...$
R_3	$G...$
R_3	$G...$

5 ColorSync then uses the monitor profile to find the monitor's RGB values that best fit the CIE values. Corrections can be made at this time to compensate for any nonuniform display characteristics of the particular monitor.

6 When printing the original image, ColorSync compares the scanner profile with the printer profile, converting the scanner's RGB description of colors to the printer's CMYK (cyan, magenta, yellow, and black) numbers.

8 Printers use ink instead of light to create colors (scanners and monitors create colors using light). Unlike light, inks are *subtractive*, so that a superposition of all colors creates black. However, inks are not ideally subtractive in that a solid black is not produced. This is why a fourth ink, black, is added—to get better-quality black and dark colors. Because three colors can create any color and the fourth (black) ink adds another variable, multiple CMYK combinations exist that can create the *same* color. In addition, the type of paper used can alter color. For these and other reasons, printers are the most difficult devices to calibrate. In other words, creating an accurate color profile for printers is more difficult than doing so for other devices.

RGB		
R_{95}	G_{123}	B_{135}
R_{96}	G_{123}	B_{135}
R_{97}	G_{123}	B_{135}
R_{98}	G_{123}	B_{135}

Standard CIE			CMYK			
X_3	Y_6	Z_1	C_{60}	M_{22}	Y_{25}	K_{25}
R_3	G_6	B_2				
R_3	G_6	B_3	C_{61}	M_{22}	Y_{25}	K_{25}
R_3	G_6	B_4	C_{62}	M_{22}	Y_{25}	K_{25}

7 If ColorSync finds a color the printer can't reproduce (a color that is not in the printer's profile), it picks another that is close.

ync

CHAPTER

33

How Web Publishing Works

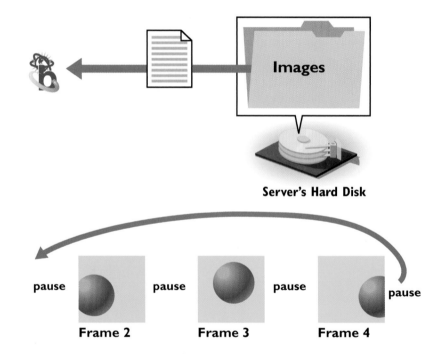

PUBLISHING on the World Wide Web in some ways resembles print output. Like a paper publication, a Web site must balance the graphic design concepts of space, color, and proportion to make it attractive yet easy to read. But the Web as a publication medium is fundamentally different from paper. The graphics are much lower in resolution and the sizes of files must be kept small. The Web offers multimedia—you can fill your Web pages with sound, video, and animation, as well as graphics and text. However, the biggest difference is the added dimension of user interactivity.

Interactivity requires the reader to play a role in the appearance and function of the page. Servers create brand-new Web pages just for you whenever you search a Web site or fill out an online form. Interactivity has created the e-commerce industry that continues to proliferate throughout the Internet.

The Web's first interactive concept is *hypertext*, an idea conceived in 1965 by computer futurist Ted Nelson. When you click a highlighted word or picture, the server sends you another portion of the document or a related document. The link can send you material from other Web servers without your having to know anything about them.

Behind the Web's interface is a programming language called the *Hypertext Markup Language (HTML)*. Web pages are written as text files containing HTML commands. These tell your Web browser how to format the text, what colors to use, and where to place the graphics, among other things.

In addition to HTML, Web publishers have many other tools to add interactivity to Web pages. Some of them, such as JavaScript, are add-ons to the HTML language. JavaScript isn't the same as Java, the program language created by Sun Microsystems. Rather, it's a specialty language that Web browsers understand. It is often used for creating interactive user interface features such as pop-up menus, buttons that change when you move your cursor, and alert windows that present special messages.

Other interactive technologies act outside HTML and the browser. A common tool is the *CGI (common gateway interface) script*, which runs on the server side. An HTML command on the Web page calls a CGI script running on a server, similar to how it links to another Web page. CGI scripts often contact database servers to find information requested by the user.

Many more technologies are used on Web pages, which we won't get the chance to highlight in this chapter. These include Java, a programming language that produces small programs called applets that can run on any computer. Also included is Dynamic HTML, a type of Web page that uses the concept of layers to produce interactive effects. Another technology, Flash, which is based on Macromedia's Director program, produces sophisticated animations.

Web pages also use several technologies already discussed in this book, including QuickTime video movies, 3D graphics, and high-quality sound. This fast-moving industry might produce even more new technologies for our Web pages a few years from now. For those, we'll have to wait for the fourth edition of *How the Mac Works*!

How a Web Page Works

1 A Web page is a text document consisting of commands written in the Hypertext Markup Language, or HTML. It also contains the text that the users will see on the Web page.

2 When a user types the URL for the page or clicks a hyperlink, the server holding the **Web server** Web page sends a copy to the user. The Web server can be a Mac, a PC, or a computer running a UNIX or Linux operating system.

3 The HTML commands tell the Web browser how to display the page. The browser displays the user text but hides the commands. The HTML commands specify the color of the page and the layout of the text, as well as other files to be used with the Web page. Before graphics are loaded, the browser displays a placeholder box with a generic graphics icon.

Web Browser

MacSite.com

ACME Printer Banner Ad

Macs get even better!!
Learn more about the latest Mac models in our Special Report.

New Software Washes Your Laundry
SoftWash version 2 gets whites whiter but has some conflicts with

4 Each graphic image on a Web page is stored as a separate file, typically as a GIF or JPEG file. The HTML code specifies the folder on the server in which the graphics reside.

Web browser

"Get graphics in the Images folder."

IMG SRC="Images/newimac.gif"

Images

MacSite.com

New super-fast printers available now!
ACME Printers 1-800-555-0000

| NAME | COMPANIES | SHOP | CONTACT US | SEARCH |

- HARDWARE
- SOFTWARE
- LATEST HITS
- TOP TEN
- ARCHIVES
- SITE MAP

Macs get even better!!
Learn more about the latest Mac models in our Special Report.

New Software Washes Your Laundry
SoftWash version 2 gets whites whiter but has some conflicts with

Server's Hard Disk

5 Each graphic file is loaded separately. Graphics can be images to display information, such as photographs and diagrams, or user interface features, such as buttons and lines. These files are held temporarily in your browser's cache folder.

6 HTML can link specific words and graphics to other Web pages anywhere on the Internet. When a user clicks a high-lighted word, the HTML code of the highlighted word invokes the Hypertext Transport Protocol (HTTP), which sends a uni-versal resource locator (URL) out onto the Internet. The *URL* is the address of a linked HTTP document. HTTP on the user's machine locates the correct server and opens a connection.

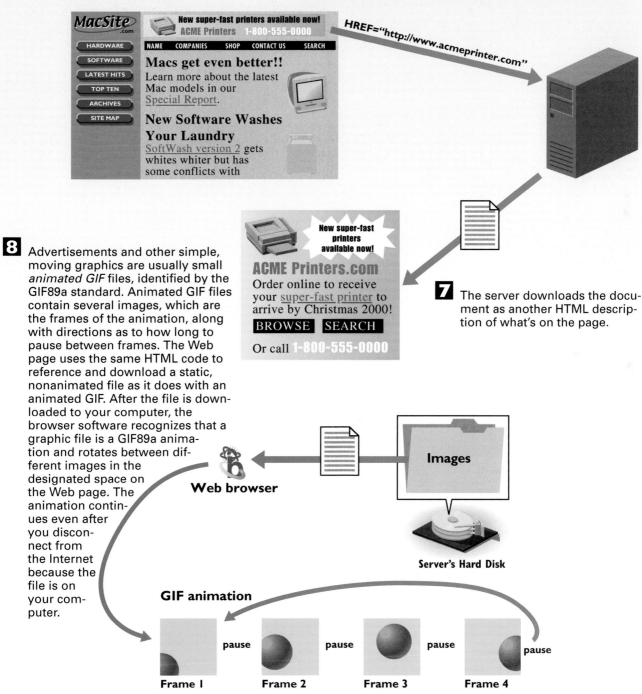

8 Advertisements and other simple, moving graphics are usually small *animated GIF* files, identified by the GIF89a standard. Animated GIF files contain several images, which are the frames of the animation, along with directions as to how long to pause between frames. The Web page uses the same HTML code to reference and download a static, nonanimated file as it does with an animated GIF. After the file is down-loaded to your computer, the browser software recognizes that a graphic file is a GIF89a anima-tion and rotates between dif-ferent images in the designated space on the Web page. The animation contin-ues even after you discon-nect from the Internet because the file is on your com-puter.

7 The server downloads the docu-ment as another HTML descrip-tion of what's on the page.

Web browser

Images

Server's Hard Disk

GIF animation

Frame 1   pause   Frame 2   pause   Frame 3   pause   Frame 4   pause

How a Web Page Works (continued)

9 A more interactive method of animating elements is to use JavaScript, a programming language modern browsers understand. JavaScript code is inserted directly on the HTML page. With JavaScript, you can change an image when a user positions the cursor over it. Both images are downloaded to the user at the same time.

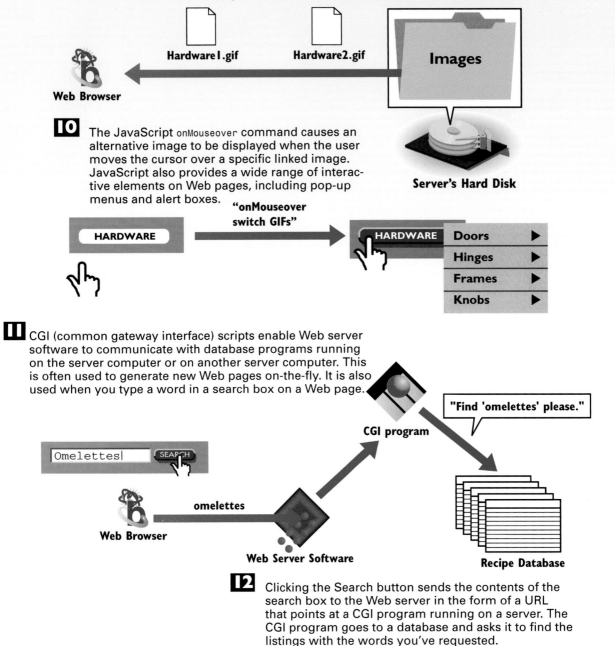

Hardware1.gif

Hardware2.gif

Images

Web Browser

10 The JavaScript onMouseover command causes an alternative image to be displayed when the user moves the cursor over a specific linked image. JavaScript also provides a wide range of interactive elements on Web pages, including pop-up menus and alert boxes.

Server's Hard Disk

"onMouseover switch GIFs"

HARDWARE

HARDWARE

Doors	▶
Hinges	▶
Frames	▶
Knobs	▶

11 CGI (common gateway interface) scripts enable Web server software to communicate with database programs running on the server computer or on another server computer. This is often used to generate new Web pages on-the-fly. It is also used when you type a word in a search box on a Web page.

CGI program

"Find 'omelettes' please."

Omelettes| SEARCH

omelettes

Web Browser

Web Server Software

Recipe Database

12 Clicking the Search button sends the contents of the search box to the Web server in the form of a URL that points at a CGI program running on a server. The CGI program goes to a database and asks it to find the listings with the words you've requested.

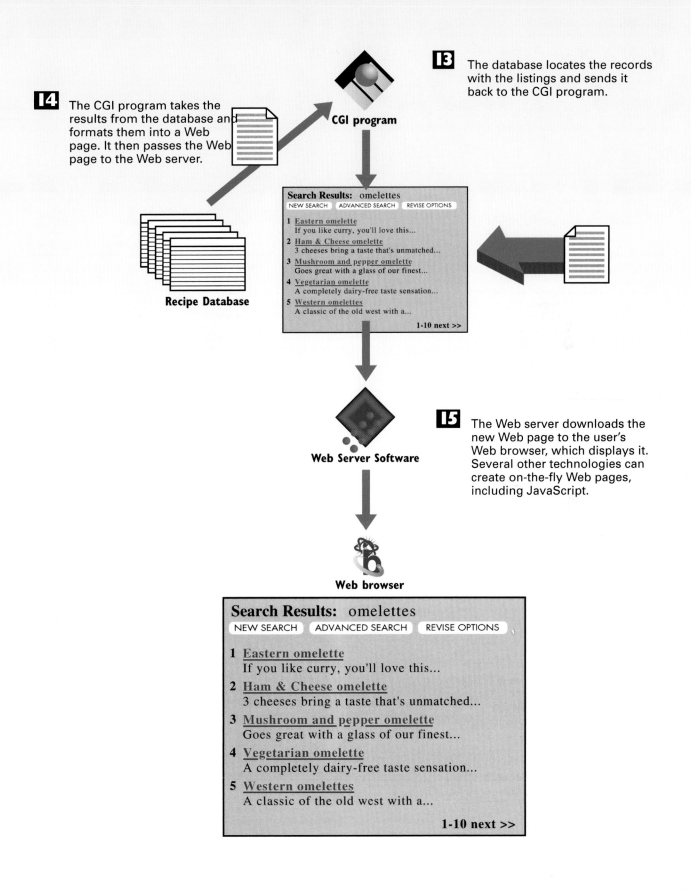

14 The CGI program takes the results from the database and formats them into a Web page. It then passes the Web page to the Web server.

CGI program

13 The database locates the records with the listings and sends it back to the CGI program.

Recipe Database

Search Results: omelettes

NEW SEARCH   ADVANCED SEARCH   REVISE OPTIONS

1 Eastern omelette
   If you like curry, you'll love this...
2 Ham & Cheese omelette
   3 cheeses bring a taste that's unmatched...
3 Mushroom and pepper omelette
   Goes great with a glass of our finest...
4 Vegetarian omelette
   A completely dairy-free taste sensation...
5 Western omelettes
   A classic of the old west with a...

1-10 next >>

Web Server Software

15 The Web server downloads the new Web page to the user's Web browser, which displays it. Several other technologies can create on-the-fly Web pages, including JavaScript.

Web browser

Search Results: omelettes

NEW SEARCH   ADVANCED SEARCH   REVISE OPTIONS

1 **Eastern omelette**
   If you like curry, you'll love this...
2 **Ham & Cheese omelette**
   3 cheeses bring a taste that's unmatched...
3 **Mushroom and pepper omelette**
   Goes great with a glass of our finest...
4 **Vegetarian omelette**
   A completely dairy-free taste sensation...
5 **Western omelettes**
   A classic of the old west with a...

1-10 next >>

Index

Symbols

2D images (OpenGL), 146
3D graphics
  multimedia, 139
  OpenGL
    2D images, 146
    double buffering, 147
    geometric primitives, 146
    rasterization, 147
    texture bitmaps, 146

A

A/D (analog-to-digital) converter, 142
A5 World, 63
accelerated graphics port slots. *See* AGP slots
accessing
  disks, speeding process of, 73-77
  RAM, speeding process of, 73-77
  Web pages, 200-201
ADB (Apple Desktop Bus), 109
adding
  memory, iMacs, 6
  new features, extension files, 32-33
  ports, FireWire, 114-115
  USB ports, 111
addresses
  IP, 186-187
    assigning, 199
  memory, 67
  RAM, 61-63
addressing, dynamic, 183
Adobe Photoshop, AltiVec, 54
AFP (Apple Filing Protocol), 183, 191
  servers, 191
AGP slots (accelerated graphics port slots), 127-133
  Power Mac G4, 11
  speed of, 127-133
AIFF (audio interchange file format), 140
AirPort, 183-184. *See also* wireless, networks
  antennas, 195
    iBooks, 15
    PowerBook G3, 14
  card slots, 193
    iBooks, 15
    iMacs, 7
    PowerBook G3, 14
    Power Mac G4, 10
  frequency, 193-194
  security, 193
  transmitting signal, 194
AirPort Base Station. *See* Base Station

Alias Manager, 40
  aliases, 37
    creating, 40
  records, 40
aliasing, IP, 179
allocating RAM, Mac OS 9.x, 61-63
AltiVec, 59
  Adobe Photoshop, 54
  technology, 54
amorphous state (CD-RW), 101
analog
  processing chips, creating sound, 141
  signals, converting, 198
  video, converting to digital, 142
animated graphics, Web pages, 229-230
antennas, AirPort, 195
  iBooks, 15
  PowerBook G3, 14
antialiasing (PDF-based graphics), 162-163
aperture grill tubes, 167
Apple Cinema Display, 172
  Digital Visual Interface, 172
  pixel resolution, 173
  power button, 173
  turning on/off, 173
  USB
    cables, 172
    hubs, 172
Apple Desktop Bus (ADB), 109
Apple Filing Protocol. *See* AFP
Apple Pro Mouse, 117-120
Apple Sound Chip, 140-141
AppleShare
  driver, 190
  icon, 191
AppleTalk, 179, 183
  browsing, chooser, 190-191
  dynamic addressing, 183
  node numbers, 184-185
  packets, 184
    broadcasting, 185
  system software, 184
  zones, 190
application heap, 63-65
application stack, 63-64
applications
  jump table, 63
  Mac OSX, running, 35
  memory partitions, 61-67
  system
    Mac OS, 27
    quitting, 28
  using virtual memory, 70-71
Aqua, 161-163
assigning IP addresses, 199
asynchronous transfers (data), 115
  Serial Bus Protocol-2, 115
Attributes file, 43

audio
  CDs, iMacs, 6
  streaming, 202-203
audio interchange file format (AIFF), 140

B

backbones (networks), 189
backside caches, 55, 59, 73-77. *See also* RAM cache
Barker code, 194
Base Station, 193-194
  connecting wireless networks
    to Ethernet networks, 195
    to Internet, 195
bases, 49-51
batteries
  iBooks, 15
  PowerBook G3, 14
Berkeley Standard Distribution (BSD) UNIX operating system, 35
binary
  notation, 49
  numbers, 49-50
bit image, QuickDraw, 158-159
bitmaps, 215
  fonts, 217
  volume, 95
bits, 49
  bits per pixel, 153-155
blocks, 92
  boot blocks, 93
  contiguous, 93
  noncontiguous, 95
  sectors, 92
  size, 92
  volume information, 93
boundaries, sectors, 94
bridges, 183, 188
brightness, 224
broadcasting packets
  AppleTalk, 185
  TCP/IP, 187
browsing, AppleTalk Chooser, 190-191
BSD (Berkeley Standard Distribution), 35
  UNIX, networking advantages, 179
  user IDs, Mac OS X, 35
built-in speakers
  playing sound, 141
  iMacs, 6
bundle folders, 43
burning CDs, 101
buses
  AGP (accelerated graphics port), 127-133
  PC CardBus, 127-129

PCI (peripheral component interface), 127-131
SCSI, 123
buttons, Search, 230
bytes, 49

C

cable modems, 197-199
cables
 FireWire, 115
 SCSI, 124
 USB, 111
  Apple Cinema Display, 172
caches, 55. *See also* L1 caches, L2 caches
 backside, 55-59, 73. *See also* RAM cache
 disk, 73-77
 L1, 55-56
 L2, 55-57
 RAM cache, 73-75. *See also* backside caches
 write, 94
caching, 73-77
capabilities, QuickTime Player, 138-139
capacitance
 capacitance-sensing, trackpads, 121
 keyboards, 118-119
CardBus cards
 comparisons with PC Cards, 128-129
 functions, 128-129
CardBus slots, 127-129
 PowerBooks, 134-135
cards
 AirPort, 193
 SCSI, 124
Carrier Sense
 Multiple Access with Collision Avoidance, 195
 Multiple Access with Collision Detection, 195
cartridge-and-nozzle assembly (printers), 210
cartridges, magnetic removable, 97-103
catalog trees, 93
cathode ray tube. *See* CRT
cathodes, 166
CD-ROM
 computer startup, 23-25
 disks, pits, 98-99
 drives, iBooks, 15
 optical storage, 97-99
CD-ROM/DVD-ROM drives, iMacs, 6
CD-RW (CD read/write), 97
 phase change, 101
 pits, 101

reading data, 101
storage, 101
CDs
 audio, optical storage, 97-99
 burning, 101
CGI(common gateway interface), 227-230
chains
 daisy, 114-115
 FireWire, 114-115
check boxes, Save and Shutdown, 79
chips (code), 194
Chooser
 browsing AppleTalk, 190-191
 extensions, 190
CIE XYZ
 color model, 219
 values, converting from RGB values, 224
Cinema Display. *See* Apple Cinema Display
circuit boards, keyboard functions, 118-119
Classic environment, 67
 crashes, 67
clock cycles, processors
 instructions, 53
 measuring, 53
CLUT (color lookup table), 159
 graphics port, 159
CMMs(color matching modules), 219, 224
CMYK (cyan, magenta, yellow, and black), 156-157, 219, 222
code
 Barker, 194
 chips, 194
 PostScript, creating, 217
CODECs (compression/decompression algorithms), 137, 203
 QuickTime Player, 145
 video, 143
collectors, 49, 51
collisions of packets, 195
color
 color matching modules. *See* CMMs
 CRT displays, 166-167
 hue/saturation/brightness, 224
 LCD screens, 169-171
 matching, 219, 224-225. *See also* CMMs
 models
  CIE XYZ, 219
  CMYK, 156-157, 219
  HLS, 156-157
  RGB, 156-158, 219
  RGB values, converting to CIE XYZ values, 224
 printers, 209, 217
  inkjet printing, 210-211

profiles, 224
separation, 219
 color separation negatives, 222-223
 space (RGB), 156-157
color lookup table. *See* CLUT
Color Manager (QuickDraw), 159
color matching modules. *See* CMMs
Color Picker (QuickDraw), 156-158
ColorSync, 219, 225
 color matching, 224-225
commands
 entering, devices, 117-121
 File menu, Make Alias, 40
 Special menu, Empty Trash, 41
 write, 94
common gateway interface. *See* CGI
communicating devices, FireWire, 115
Component Manager (QuickTime), 144
composite video, 142
compressing data, digital video, 142-143
compression/decompression algorithms. *See* CODECs
computer crashes, 65
configuring IP addresses, 180
connecting to
 ports, 111
 wireless networks
  Ethernet networks, 195
  Internet, 195-199
connections
 FireWire, 113-115
 Internet, 197-198
  speed, 197
constant linear velocity, 99
contiguous blocks, 93
control boxes, Memory, 79
control panels
 Memory, setting RAM disk size, 80
 QuickTime Settings, 202
controllers
 SCSI, 124
 USB, 110-111
converting
 analog signals, 198
 digital signals, 198
 RGB values to CIE XYZ values, 224
 video, analog to digital, 142
coordinate plane (QuickDraw), 154-155
Core Graphics Rendering, 161-163
 OpenGL, 163
 QuickDraw, 163
 QuickTime, 163
Core Graphics Services, Quartz, 161-163
Core Services, 34

crashes (computers), 65
    Classic environment, 67
creating
    aliases, 40
    illustrations, 220
    partitions, hard disk drives, 93
    PostScript code, 217
    RAM disks, 80
creator codes, 38
CRT (cathode ray tube) displays, 165
    color, 166
        producing color, 167
    controlling, 166
    producing images, 166
crystalline state (CD-RW), 101
Cube (Power Mac G4 cube), 9
currents, 51
    trickle, 51

D

D/A (digital-to-analog), 141
daisy chaining, 113-115
    networks, 188
data
    area, 93
    asynchronous transfers, 115
        Serial Bus Protocol-2, 115
    isynchronous transfers, 115
    links, 183. See also networks,
        interfaces
    reading
        CD-RW, 101
        DVD-RAM, 102-103
        hard disk drives, 95
        Zip drives, 100
    saving, RAM disk, 79
    sending/receiving, 29
    writing to hard disk drives, 89,
        94-95
Data+ wires, 111
Data- wires, 111
defragmenting disks, 95
deleting files, 41
demultiplex (transceivers), 131-133
design
    iBooks, 13-15
    iMacs, 4
    Power Macs, 9
    PowerBooks, 13-15
desktop, 37
    files, 37
        RAM disk, 80-81
    icons, size, 42
    publishing, 219-220
        printing pages, 221-223
    rebuilding, 39
Device manager, 29
devices
    asynchronous transfers, 115
        Serial Bus Protocol-2, 115

entering commands, 117-121
FireWire, plugging in, 114-115
isynchronous transfers, 115
keyboards, 117-119
mouse, 117-120
peripheral, 117-121
SCSI, handshakes, 125
trackpads, 117, 121
DHCP (Dynamic Host
    Configuration Protocol), 180
    servers, 186
diaphragm, speakers, 141
digital
    audio, viewing, 142
    signals, converting, 198
    video, converted from analog, 142
digital subscriber lines. See DSL
digital versatile disk. See DVD
Digital Visual Interface, 172
    TMDS (transition minimized
        differential signaling), 172
digital-to-analog converters
    (QuickDraw), 159
digitizing multimedia sound, 137-140
DIMMs (dual inline memory
    modules), 61
direct memory access mode
    (DMA), 135
direct pixel (QuickDraw), 158-159
Direct Sequence Spread Spectrum
    (DSSS), 193-194
directories, extents, 93
disk cache, 73-77
disks
    accessing, 73-77
    defragmenting, 95
    DVD-RAM, 102-103
        read-only information,
            102-103
        zones, 102-103
    floppy, 87-89
        ejecting, 87-89
        inserting, 88-89
        storage, 88-89
    fragmented, 95
    RAM, 79
        creating, 80
        Desktop file, 80-81
        optimizing performance, 81
        saving data, 79
        seek time, 79
        setting size, 80
    space, wasted, 92
    virtual, 79
Dispatch unit, 58-59
displaying
    icons, Finder, 42-43
    zone fields, 190
displays
    Apple Cinema Display, 172
        Digital Visual Interface, 172
        pixel resolution, 173

power button, 173
turning on/off, 173
USB cables, 172
USB hubs, 172
CRT, 165
    color, 166-167
    controlling, 166
    producing images, 166
flat panels, 169. See also LCD
    screens
    advantages, 169
    pixels, 169
    resolutions, 169
Hz (hertz) rating, 165
iBooks, 15
PowerBook G3, 14
dithering, 217
diversity reception, 195
DMA (direct memory access), 135
domain name servers, 186, 200
door locks, Power Mac G4, 11
doors, Power Mac G4, 11
dot matrix printers, 209
dot pitch, 167
double buffering (OpenGL), 147
downloading Web pages, 231
DRAM (dynamic random-access
    memory). See RAM
drawing programs. See QuickDraw
Drive Setup utility, 91
driver software, 110-111
drivers
    AppleShare, 190
    PostScript, 215
drives
    CD-ROM/DVD-ROM, iMacs, 6
    DVD, PowerBook G3, 14
    DVD-RAM, Power Mac G4, 10
    DVD-ROM, Power Mac G4, 10
    floppy disk, 87-89
        disk storage, 88-89
        external USB, 87
        internal, 87
    hard
        iBooks, 15
        Power Mac G4, 10
        PowerBook G3, 14
    hard disk, 91, 94
        formatting, 91. See also hard
            disk drives, formatting
        reading data from, 95
        speed, 91
        writing data to, 94-95
    heads, 88-89
    icons, 42-43
    IDE ATA, Power Macs, 9-10
    removable, 97-103
        optical, 97-103
    SCSI, Power Macs, 9-10
    slot loading, iMacs, 6
    Zip, Power Mac G4, 10

drum scanners, 220-222
DSL (digital subscriber lines),
    197-199
DSSS(Direct Sequence Spread
    Spectrum), 193-194
dual inline memory modules
    (DIMMs), 61
DV models
    CD-ROM/DVD-ROM drives, 6
    video format, 142
DVD (digital versatile disk), 97-99
    iMacs, 4
        CD-ROM/DVD-ROM, 6
    PowerBook G3, 14
    video, MPEG2 compression
        format, 142
DVD-RAM
    disks, 102-103
        read-only information,
            102-103
        zones, 102-103
    drives, Power Mac G4, 10
    optical storage, 97-99
    phase change, 103
    pits, 103
    reading data, 102-103
    storage, 102-103
DVD-ROM
    drives, Power Mac G4, 10
    optical storage, 97-99
    pits, 98-99
    playing movies, 97
DVD-ROM/CD-ROM drives,
    iMacs, 6
DVD-video, optical storage, 97-99
dye sublimation printers, 209
dynamic addressing, 183
Dynamic Host Configuration
    Protocol. See DHCP
Dynamic HTML, 227
dynamic link-and-load
    architecture, 180
dynamic random-access memory
    (DRAM). See RAM

E

ejecting floppy disks, 87-89
    manually, 89
electron beams, 166
    focusing, 167
email, sending/receiving, 200-201
emitters, 49-51
Empty Trash command (Special
    menu), 41
emptying Trash, 41
entering commands, devices,
    117-121
erasing data, crystalline state, 101

Ethernet
    networks, 183-184
        connecting wireless networks
            to, 195
        star configuration, 188
    port, iMacs, 7
exclusive or (DSSS), 194
execution units, 54-58
    floating-point calculations, 54
    integer units, 54
    vector processing unit, 54-59
expansion bays
    PowerBook G3, 14
    Power Mac G4, 10
expansion cards, 127-135
    AGP, 129-133
    history of, 129
    PCI, 129
        ROM, 130-131
expansion ports, history of, 129
expansion slots, 127-135
    AGP slots, 127-128
    capabilities with, 127-135
    computer startup, 22-25
    expansion cards, 127-135
    history of, 129
    PCI, 132-133
        slots, 127-128
    Power Mac G4, PCI, 11
Extended Desktop mode
    (QuickDraw), 154
extension files
    adding new features, 32-33
    Mac OS, 32-33
extensions
    Chooser, 190
    Network Kernel Extensions, 179
        advantages, 181
Extensions folder, 32-33, 190
extents directory, 93
external USB floppy disk drives, 87

F

features, adding, extension files,
    32-33
field distortion sensing
    (trackpads), 121
fields, zone, displaying, 190
File manager, 29
File menu commands, Make
    Alias, 40
files
    aliases, 37
        creating, 40
    Attributes, 43
    creator codes, 38
    deleting, 41
    Desktop, 37
        RAM disk, 80-81

extension
    adding new features, 32-33
    Mac OS, 32-33
GIF, 228-229
INIT, 33
JPEG, 228
opening in Finder, 38-39
saving, 29
SDP (Session Description
    Protocol), 202
type codes, 43
filters, polarization, 170-171
Finder, 37, 42
    files
        deleting, 41
        opening, 38-39
    icons, displaying, 42-43
    launching, 37
    window, 42
FireWire, 113-115
    cables, 115
    card, 113
    comparisons
        with SCSI drives, 113
        with USB, 113
    connections, 113-115
    daisy chaining, 113-115
    devices
        communicating, 115
        plugging in, 114-115
    FireWire Family Services, 114-115
    peer-to-peer communication
        basis, 113
    ports, 114-115
        iMacs, 4-7
        Power Macs G4, 9-11
        Power Macs G3, 9-10
        video viewing, 142
    speed, 113-115
    synchronous transport, 114-115
Flash, 227
flat panel displays, 169. See also LCD
    screens
    advantages, 169
    pixels, 169
    resolution, 169
flatbed scanners, 220-222
floating-point
    calculations, 54
    units, 59
floppy disk drives, 87-89
    disk storage, 88-89
    ejecting, 87-89
        manually, 89
    external USB, 87
    inserting, 88-89
    internal, 87
    storage, 88-89
focusing, electron beams, 167

folders
  bundle, 43
  Extensions, 190
  System, 81
fonts
  bitmap, 217
  OpenType, 215
  outline, 215-217
  TrueType, 215
formatting hard disk drives, 91
  logical formatting, 92
  partitions, 93
  physical formatting, 92
fragmented disks, 95
frames, 184. *See also* packets
frequency, AirPort, 193-194
functionality
  iBooks, 13-15
    AirPort antenna, 15
    AirPort card slot, 15
    battery, 15
    built-in speakers, 15
    CD-ROM drive, 15
    display, 15
    fold-out handles, 15
    hard drives, 15
    keyboards, 15
    logic boards, 15
    modems, 15
    RAM, 15
    trackpad, 15
  iMacs, 4
    AirPort card slots, 7
    built-in stereo speakers, 6
    CD-ROM/DVD-ROM
      drives, 6
    hard-disk drives, 6
    Input/Ouput ports, 7
    logic boards, 7
    power supply, 7
    processors, 7
    RAM, 6
    ROM, 7
    video display tubes, 6
  Power Macs, 9-11
    AGP slots, 11
    AirPort slot, 10
    door locks, 11
    doors, 11
    DVD-RAM drives, 10
    DVD-ROM drives, 10
    expansion bays, 10
    graphic cards, 11
    handles, 10
    hard drives, 10
    Input/Ouput ports, 11
    internal FireWire port, 11
    modem cards, 10
    optional SCSI cards, 11

    PCI expansion slots, 11
    power supply, 10
    processors, 11
    RAM, 11
    Zip drives, 10
  PowerBooks, 13-15
    AirPort antenna, 14
    AirPort card slot, 14
    battery, 14
    built-in microphones, 14
    built-in speakers, 14
    display, 14
    DVD drives, 14
    expansion bay, 14
    hard drives, 14
    keyboards, 14
    logic boards, 14
    modems, 14
    PC card slots, 14
    RAM, 14
    trackpad, 14
functions (devices)
  CardBus cards, 128-129
  keyboards, 117-119
  mouse, 120
  PC cards, 128-129
  trackpad, 121

G

G3 processor, 53
  execution units, 54-57
  floating-point calculations, 54
  integer units, 54
G4 AltiVec vector, 54
G4 Cube, 9
G4 processor, 53
  execution units, 54, 58-59
  floating-point calculations, 54
  integer units, 54
  vector processing unit, 54
generating Web pages, on-the-fly, 230
generations, PowerPC processors,
    53-55
geometric primitives, 146
GIF files, 228-229
gigaflop, 54
graphic cards, Power Mac G4, 11
graphics
  address remapping table
    (UniNorth IC chip), 133
  Mac OS X, Aqua, 161-163
  port (QuickDraw), 159
  PDF-based, 162-163
  Quartz, 153
    technology, 35
  QuickDraw, 153-155
  Web pages, 228
    animated, 229-230

H

halftones, 217
handles
  iBooks, fold-out, 15
  Power Mac G4, 10
handshaking (data transfer), 131
  handshakes, 125
hard disk drives, 91-94
  computer startup, 22-25
  formatting, 91
    logical formatting, 92
    partitions, 93
    physical formatting, 92
  iBooks, 15
  IDE ATA, Power Macs, 9-10
  iMacs, 6
  mechanisms, 91
  Power Mac G4, 10
  PowerBook G3, 14
  reading data from, 95
  SCSI, Power Macs, 9-10
  speed, 91
  writing data to, 94-95
hardware
  multimedia, 137-141
  networks, 183, 188-189
Harmon-Hardon iSub subwoofer, 6
heads, 91
  actuators, 94
  head crashes, 91
heap (application), 63-65
hertz. *See* Hz
HFS (Hierarchical File System), 91
  HFS Extended, 91
  HFS Plus, 91
high memory, RAM, 61-67
HLS (hue, lightness, and saturation),
    156-157
HomePNA, 183-184
hops, 189
hot-pluggable, 109
HTML (Hypertext Markup
    Language), 227-229
HTTP (Hypertext Transfer
    Protocol), 202, 229
  streaming, 202
hubs, 109, 183, 188
  powered, 111
  USB, Apple Cinema Display, 172
  wireless, 193-194
hues, 224
hyper-desktop (QuickDraw), 157
hyperlinks, 228
hypertext, 227
Hypertext Markup Language
    (HTML), 227
Hypertext Transfer Protocol. *See*
    HTTP
Hz (hertz), 165
  rating, 165

I

i.Link (Sony), 115
iBooks
    AirPort antenna, 15
    AirPort card slot, 15
    battery, 15
    built-in speakers, 15
    CD-ROM drive, 15
    design, 13-15
    display, 15
    fold-out handles, 15
    functionality, 13-15
    hard drives, 15
    keyboards, 15
    logic boards, 15
    modems, 15
    RAM, 15
    trackpad, 15, 117
icons
    AppleShare, 191
    desktop size, 42
    displaying, Finder, 42-43
    drive, 42-43
    Network, 42
    RAM disk, 80
    Trash, 41
IDE ATA hard drive, Power Macs,
    9-10
IDs, user, 35
IEEE 1394 High Performance Serial
    Bus, 113-115
IEEE 802.11 DSSS(Direct Sequence
    Spread Spectrum).See DSSS
illustrations, creating, 220
iMacs, 4
    AirPort card slots, 7
    built-in stereo speakers, 6
    CD-ROM/DVD-ROM drives, 6
    design, 4
    DV Special Edition, 4
    DVD drives, 4
        CD-ROM/DVD-ROM, 6
    functionality, 4
    hard disk drives, 6
    Input/Output ports, 7
    logic boards, 7
    Odyssey sound system, 6
    power supply, 7
    processors, 7
    RAM, 6
    ROM, 7
    video display tubes, 6
Image Compression Manager,
    144-145
images
    producing, 166
    rasterizing, 212, 216
    scanning, flatbed scanners, 222
    sharpening, 167
iMovie software (Apple), 4

INIT files, 33
inkjet printers, 209-210
    color printing, 210-211
inks, subtractive, 225
Input/Ouput ports, 7
    iMacs, 7
    Power Mac G4, 11
inserting floppy disks, 88-89
instructions, clock cycles
    (processors), 53
integer units, 54
interfaces, network, 184. See also data
    links
internal
    FireWire port, Power Mac G4, 11
    floppy disk drives, 87
Internet, 197
    connections, 197-198
        speed, 197
    connecting to, 198-199
    connecting wireless networks
        to, 195
    gateways, 197
Internet service providers. See ISPs
internetworks, 183
interrupt priority (Mac OS USB
    Manager), 111
invisible partitions, 93
IP addresses, 186-187
    assigning, 199
    configuring, 180
IP aliasing, 179
ISPs (Internet service providers),
    assigning IP addresses,
    197-199
isynchronous transfers (data), 115

J

Java, 227
JavaScript, 230-231
Jaz drives, 97
JPEG (Joint Photographic Experts
    Group), 137
    files, 228
jump table applications, 63

K-L

kernels, Mach, 179, 181
keyboards, 117-119
    capacitance, 118-119
    functions, 117-119
        circuit boards, 118-119
    iBooks, 15
    PowerBook G3, 14
    Qwerty standard, 117
    USB
        controller, 118
        manager, 118
        transceiver, 119

L1 caches (Level 1 caches), 55-56
L2 caches (Level 2 caches), 55-57
laser printers, 209, 212-213
launching Finder, 37
LCD (liquid crystal display) screens.
        See also flat panel displays
    color, 169
    producing color, 170-171
Level 1 caches (L1 caches), 55-56
Level 2 caches (L2 caches), 55-57
light, white, 170
liquid crystal display. See LCD
load and store execution units, 57
Load/Store units, 57
loading protocols, 181
LocalTalk, 183
logic boards
    iBooks, 15
    iMacs, 7
    PowerBook G3, 14
logical formatting, hard disk drives, 92
low memory, RAM, 61-67
lower sled (floppy disk drives), 88-89

M

Mac OS
    3D graphics, OpenGL, 139
    extension files, 32-33
    FireWire Family Services, 114-115
    managers, 27
    QuickTime Player, 137-140
        capabilities, 138-139
        Component Manager, 144
        copy/paste movies from
            applications, 138-139
        Movie format, 138-139
        Movie Toolbox, 144
        PC sound files, 138-139
        SimpleText, 138-139
        VR (virtual reality) feature,
            138-139
        Windows AVI format,
            138-139
    ROM file, 28
        Macintosh Toolbox, 28
    system
        applications, 27
        folder, 27
        resources, 27
        software, 27
Mac OS 9.x, 27. See also Mac OS
    computer startup, 23-25
    preemptive multitasking, 67
    RAM, allocating, 61-63
    startup
        resources, 30
        system files, 30
    system resources, 31

virtual memory, 69
launching applications, 70-71
launching applications with, 70-71
Mac OS X. *See also* Mac OS
applications, running, 35
Aqua, 161-163
BSD, enabling UNIX to run, 35
computer startup, 23-25
graphics, speed, 161-163
managers, 34
memory partitions, 66-67
protected memory, 61, 66-67
Quartz, 153, 161-163
virtual memory, 69
Mach kernel, 27, 179-181
preemptive multitasking, 27, 34
Macintosh Toolbox, Mac OS Rom file, 28
magnetic
deflection coils, 166
removable cartridges, 97-103
Make Alias command (File menu), 40
managers
Device, 29
File, 29
Mac OS, 27, 34
Macintosh Toolbox, Mac OS, 28
Memory, 29
Menu, 28
Process, 28
Resource, 28-31
Window, 28
manual eject plate (floppy disk drives), 89
manually ejecting floppy disks, 89
matching colors, 224-225
measuring clock cycles (processors), 53
media, 137-142
memory, 61-67. *See also* RAM
adding, iMacs, 6
addresses, 67
application requests, processing, 74-77
managing Mach kernel, 34
partitions
applications, 61-67
using virtual memory, 70-71
protected, 61-62
Mac OS X, 66-67 ·
virtual, 69, 79
launching applications with, 70-71
Memory control box, 79
Memory control panel, setting RAM disk size, 80
memory management units (MMUs), 56-57

Memory manager, 29
application heap, 65
RAM, 63
Menu Manager, 28
microphones, PowerBook G3, 14
microprocessors. *See* processors
MIDI files, 137
MMUs (memory management units), 56-57
virtual memory, 69-71
modem cards, Power Mac G4, 10
modems, 197
cable, 197-199
iBooks, 15
PowerBook G3, 14
monitor profile, 225
monitors, startup screen (QuickDraw), 155
Monitors control panel (QuickDraw), 154-155
Motion Picture Experts Group (MPEG), 137
mouse, 117
functions, 120
optical, 117-120
USB controller, 120
Movie format (QuickTime Player), 138-139
Movie Toolbox (QuickTime), 144
movies, playing online, 202-203
MP3 files, 137-140
MPEG (Motion Picture Experts Group), 137
MPEG2, data compression, 142
MultiFinder, 41
multihoming, 179
multimedia, 137-142
hardware, 137-141
software, 137-141
decompressing sound, 143
decompressing video, 137
sound, 140
translating DV video format, 142
video, 142
sound, 137-139
digitizing, 137-140
mixing multiple sound channels, 140
speakers, 141
storage, 140
synthesizers, 140
system alerts, 140
storage methods, 137-141
video, viewing from sources, 142
multiplex (transceivers), 131-133
multitasking, preemptive
Mac OS 9.x, 67
Mach kernel, 34

N

n-type silicon, 49-51
Name Binding Protocol (NBP), 191
names, domain, 200
navigating Web pages, 229
NBP (Name Binding Protocol), 191
networks
backbones, 189
browsers, Chooser, 190-191
configurations, switching between, 180
daisy chains, 188
hardware, 183, 188-189
interfaces, choosing, 183-184. *See also* data, links
protocol software, 180-181
segments, 188
star configuration, 188
wireless, 193. *See also* AirPort
connecting to Ethernet networks, 195
connecting to Internet, 195
zone names, 189
Network icon, 42
Network Kernel Extensions, 179
advantages, 181
networking, 179
BSD UNIX, advantages, 179
Open Transport, 180-181
advantages, 179
multiple configurations, 180
node numbers, 184-185
noncontiguous blocks, 95
notation, binary, 49
notebooks. See PowerBooks; iMacs
npn transistors, 49-51
numbers, binary, 49-50

O

Odyssey sound system, iMacs, 6
online movies, playing, 202-203
Open Transport, 179-181, 198
advantages, 179
multiple network configurations, 180
OpenGL (3D graphics), 139
2D images, 146
double buffering, 147
geometric primitives, 146
rasterization, 147
texture bitmaps, 146
opening files in Finder, 38-39
OpenType fonts, 215
OPI servers, 221
optical mouse, 117-120
optical removable cartridges, 97-103
optimizing performance, RAM disk, 81
OS 9. *See* Mac OS 9.x
OS X. *See* Mac OS X
outline fonts, 215-217

P

p-type silicon, 49-51
packets, 183-184. *See also* frames
  AppleTalk, 184
    broadcasting, 185
    collisions, 195
    TCP/IP, 186, 197
      broadcasting, 187
      wrapping/upwrapping, 198
page description languages,
      PostScript, 209, 216. *See also*
      print jobs
partitions
  creating hard disk drives, 93
  invisible, 93
  maps, 93
  memory
    applications, 61-67
    using virtual memory, 70-71
paste up, 219
PC
  cards
    comparisons with CardBus
      cards, 128-129
    functions, 128-129
    slots, PowerBook G3, 14
  sound files (QuickTime Player),
      138-139
PCI (peripheral component
      interface slots)
  cards
    RAM, 130-131
    ROM, 130-131
  expansion slots, Power Mac G4,
      11, 127-133
  speed of, 127-131
  transceivers, 131
PCI-to-PCI bridge chip, 131
PCMCIA (Personal Computer
      Memory Card International
      Association), 128
PDF (portable document format),
      161-163
  PDF-based graphics, 162-163
performance, optimizing, RAM disk,
      81
peripheral component interface
      slots. *See* PCI slots
peripheral devices, 117-121
Personal Computer Memory Card
      International Association
      (PCMCIA), 128
phase change
  CD-RW, 101
  DVD-RAM, 103
phosphors, 167
physical formatting, hard disk
      drives, 92
pipelining, 128

pits
  CD-ROM disks, 98-99
  CD-RW, 101
  DVD-RAM, 103
  DVD-ROM disks, 98-99
pixels, 165
  compositing, Quartz window
      server, 163
  flat panel displays, 169
  phosphors, 167
  resolution, 165
    Apple Cinema Display, 173
    flat panel displays, 169
    QuickDraw, 153-155
    setting, 165
platters, 91
  tracks, 92
playing online movies, 202-203
plugging in devices, FireWire,
      114-115
point-to-point protocol. *See* PPP
points (resolution), 153-155
polarization filters, 170-171
POP (post office protocol), 201
portable document format. *See* PDF
ports
  adding, 111
  computer startup, 22-25
  connecting, 111
  Ethernet, iMacs, 7
  FireWire, 114-115
    iMacs, 4, 6-7
    Power Mac G3, 9
    Power Mac G4, 9-11
  Input/Ouput, 7
    Power Mac G4, 11
  USB, iMacs, 4, 7
post office protocol (POP), 201
PostScript, 162-163, 212-215
  code, creating, 217
  drivers, 215
  interpreters, 216. *See also* RIPs
  Level 2, 215
  Level 3, 215
  page description language, 209
  printers, 215-217
power button, Apple Cinema
      Display, 173
power control circuitry, computer
      startup, 22-25
Power G3 processor, MMUs, 56-57
Power Mac G4
  AGP bus controller
      slots, 11
      UniNorth chip, 132-133
  AirPort slot, 10
  door locks, 11
  doors, 11
  DVD-RAM drive, 10
  DVD-ROM drive, 10
  expansion bays, 10

graphic cards, 11
handles, 10
hard drive, 10
Input/Ouput ports, 11
internal FireWire port, 11
modem cards, 10
optional SCSI cards, 11
PCI
  AGP slots, 127-133
  bus controller, UniNorth
      chip, 131
  expansion slots, 11
power supply, 10
processors, 11
RAM, 11
Zip drive, 10
Power Macs
  AGP cards, 132-133
    unplugging cards, 129
  design, 9
  expansion slots, 127-128
  functionality, 9-11
  PCI cards, 130
    unplugging cards, 129-131
  PCI slots, 127-131
  Power Mac G4
    AGP slots, 11
    AirPort slot, 10
    door locks, 11
    doors, 11
    DVD-RAM drive, 10
    DVD-ROM drive, 10
    expansion bays, 10
    graphic cards, 11
    handles, 10
    hard drive, 10
    Input/Output ports, 11
    internal FireWire port, 11
    modem cards, 10
    optional SCSI cards, 11
    PCI expansion slots, 11
    power supply, 10
    processors, 11
    RAM, 11
    Zip drive, 10
Power Mac G4 cube, 9
power supply
  iMacs, 7
  Power Mac G4, 10
PowerBook G3
  AirPort antenna, 14
  AirPort card slot, 14
  battery, 14
  built-in microphones, 14
  built-in speakers, 14
  display, 14
  DVD drive, 14
  expansion bay, 14
  hard drives, 14
  keyboards, 14
  logic boards, 14

modems, 14
PC card slots, 14
RAM, 14
trackpad, 14
PowerBooks
    CardBus slots, 127-129, 134-135
    design, 13-15
    expansion slots, 127-128
    functionality, 13-15
    PowerBook G3
        AirPort antenna, 14
        AirPort card slot, 14
        battery, 14
        built-in microphones, 14
        built-in speakers, 14
        display, 14
        DVD drive, 14
        expansion bay, 14
        hard drives, 14
        keyboards, 14
        logic boards, 14
        modems, 14
        PC card slots, 14
        RAM, 14
        trackpad, 14
    trackpad, 117
powered hubs, 111
PowerPC
    processors, generations of, 53-55
        PowerPC 7400 processor, 53
        PowerPC 750 processor, 53
PowerPC G3
    backside caches, 57
    L1 caches, 56
    L2 caches, 57
    microprocessor, 56-57
    processor, 53-55. See also G3
        processor
    iMacs, 7
PowerPC G4
    backside caches, 57
    L2 caches, 57
    microprocessor, 58
        backside caches, 59
        floating-point unit, 59
    processor, 53-55. See also G4
        processor
PPP (point-to-point protocol), 199
    sessions, establishing, 199
    shells, 198
    software, 198
preemptive multitasking, 27
    Mac OS 9.x, 67
    Mach kernel, 34
print jobs, 216. See also page
        description languages
    color printers, inkjet, 210-211
    desktop publishing, 221-223
    laser printers, 212-213
printers, 209
    cartridge-and-nozzle
        assembly, 210

color, 209, 217
dot matrix, 209
dye sublimation, 209
inkjet, 209-210
    printing color, 210-211
laser, 209, 212-213
PostScript, 215-217
resolution, 209, 217
toner, 209
wax thermal, 209
priority, interrupt, 111
processing application requests,
        74-77
processors, 53-55
    caching, 73-77
    clock cycles
        instructions, 53
        measuring, 53
    computer startup, 22-25
    iMacs, PowerPC G3, 7
    MMUs, virtual memory, 69-71
    Power Mac G4, 11
    PowerPC, generations of, 53-55
    PowerPC 7400, 53
    PowerPC 750, 53
    PowerPC G3, 53-55. See also G3
        processor
    PowerPC G4, 53-55. See also G4
        processor
        backside caches, 59
        floating-point unit, 59
    mouse, 120RAM, 61-67
    speed, 53-54
        backside caches, 55
    virtual memory, 69
        launching applications with,
            70-71
producing
    color
        CRT displays, 167
        LCD screens, 170-171
    images, 166
profiles
    color, 224
    monitor, 225
    scanner, 224
protected memory, 61-62
    Mac OS X, 66-67
protocol dependent/independent, 188
protocols, 183
    loading/unloading, 181
    NBP (Name Binding
        Protocol), 191
    stacks, 181. See also Network
        Kernel extensions
    switching between, 180
publishing
    desktop, 219-220
        printing pages, 221-223
    Web, 227-230

Q

Quartz (graphics engine), 35, 153
    Core Graphics Rendering,
        161-163
    Core Graphics Services, 161-163
    Mac OS X, 161-163
    rendering 2D graphics, 161-163
    window server, 163
    windowing server, 161
QuickDraw, 28, 153-155, 212
    bit image, 158-159
    CLUT, 159
        graphics port, 159
    Color Manager, 159
    Color Picker, 156-158
    coordinate plane, 154-155
    digital-to-analog converters, 159
    direct pixel, 158-159
    Extended Desktop mode, 154
    hyper-desktop, 157
    monitors, startup screen, 155
    Monitors control panel, 154-155
    resolution, pixels, 153-155
    RGB color model, 156-158
    speed, 153-155
QuickDraw screen-drawing
        routines, 209
QuickTime Player, 137-140, 202
    capabilities, 138-139
    Component Manager, 144
    copy/paste movies from
        applications, 138-139
    Movie format, 138-139
    Movie Toolbox, 144
    PC sound files, 138-139
    SimpleText, 138-139
    VR (virtual reality) feature,
        138-139
    Windows AVI format, 138-139
QuickTime Settings control
        panel, 202
QuickTime Streaming Server
        software, 202
quitting system applications, 28
Qwerty standard (keyboards), 117

R

RAM (random-access memory),
        61-67. See also memory
    accessing, 73-77
    addresses, 61-63
    application heap, 63-65
    application stack, 63-64
    computer crashes, 65
    computer startup, 21-25
    high memory, 61-67
    iBooks, 15
    iMacs, 6
    low memory, 61-67
    Mac OS 9.x, allocating, 61-63

PCI cards, 130-131
Power Mac G4, 11
PowerBook G3, 14
virtual memory, 69
launching applications with, 70-71
RAM cache, 73-75. *See also* backside caches
RAM disk. *See also* virtual disk
creating, 80
data, saving, 79
Desktop file, 80-81
icon, 80
optimizing performance, 81
seek time, 79
size, setting, 80
raster image processors, 212, 216. *See* RIPs
rasterization, 147
read-only information, DVD-RAM disks, 102-103
read/write heads (floppy disk drives), 88-89, 98
reading
data, 89
CD-RW, 101
DVD-RAM, 102-103
hard disk drives, 95
Zip drives, 100
Real Time Streaming Protocol. *See* RTSP
Real-Time Transport Protocol. *See* RTP
rebuilding, Desktop, 39
receivers, TMDS, 172
receiving
data, 29
email, 200-201
removable DVD drives, PowerBook G3, 14
REQs (request signals), 125
resolution, 165
Apple Cinema Display, 173
flat panel displays, 169
pixels (QuickDraw), 153-155
points, 153-155
printers, 209, 217
setting, 165
WYSIWYG (what-you-see-is-what-you-get), 165
resource files, searching (Resource Manager), 31
Resource managers, 28-31
resources, system
Mac OS, 27
Mac OS 9.x, 30-31
revolutions per minute (rpm), 91
RGB (red, green, and blue) color model, 156-158, 219
color space, 156-157
QuickDraw, 156-158

values, converting to CIE XYZ values, 224
RIPs (raster image processors), 216. *See also* PostScript, interpreters
ROM
chip, computer startup, 21-25
file, Mac OS, 28
Macintosh Toolbox, 28
iMacs, 7
PCI cards, 130-131
routers, 183, 188-189
hops, 189
tables, 189
routines, screen-drawing (QuickDraw), 209
rpm (revolutions per minute), 91
RTP (Real-Time Transport Protocol), 202
RTSP(Real Time Streaming Protocol), 202
running Mac OSX applications, 35

S

s-video, 142
saturation, 224
Save and Shutdown check box, 79
saving
data, RAM disk, 79
files, 29
scanner profiles, 224
scanners
drum, 220-222
flatbed, 220-222
slide, 220
scanning images, flatbed scanners, 222
screen-drawing routines (QuickDraw), 209
screens (LCD), 169. *See also* flat panel displays
color, 169
producing color, 170-171
SCSI (small computer system interface), 123
advantages/disadvantages, 123
bus, 123
cables, 124
cards, 124
Power Mac G4, 11
chains, 123-124
controller, 124
devices, handshakes, 125
drives, compared with FireWire, 113
hard drive, Power Macs, 9-10
software, 124
transactions, 124-125
SCSI Manager software, 124
SDP (Session Description Protocol) files, 202

SDRAM, iMacs, 6
Search button, 230
sectors, 92
boundaries, 94
security, AirPort, 193
seek time, 79
SELs (select signals), 125
sending
data, 29
email, 200-201
Serial Bus Protocol-2, 115
servers
AFP (Apple Filing Protocol), 191
DHCP, 186
domain names, 186, 200
OPI, 221
POP, 201
SMTP (simple mail transfer protocol), 200
Web, 231
service bureaus, printing pages (desktop publishing), 222
Session Description Protocol (SDP) files, 202
setting
pixel resolution, 165
size, RAM disk, 80
shadow masks, 167
sharpening images, 167
shells (PPP), 198
signals
AirPort, transmitting, 194
analog, converting, 198
digital, converting, 198
TMDS, threshold voltages, 172
silicon, 49
n-type, 49-51
p-type, 49-51
SIMD (single instruction-multiple data), 53-54
simple mail transfer protocol (SMTP) server, 200
SimpleText, 138-139
single instruction-multiple data (SIMD), 53-54
size
blocks, 92
desktop icons, 42
RAM disk, setting, 80
slide scanners, 220
slot loading drives, 98
iMacs, 6
slots
CardBus, 134-135
PCI, 127-131
small computer system interface. *See* SCSI
SMTP (simple mail transfer protocol) server, 200
SO-DIMMs (small outline dual inline memory modules), 61